The
Psych
101
series

James C. Kaufman, PhD, Series Editor

Director, Learning Research Institute
California State University at San Bernardino

Gorkan Ahmetoglu, PhD, is an occupational psychologist and visiting lecturer at the University of London's Goldsmiths, City, and Heythrop Colleges. He is an expert in psychometrics, personnel selection, and organizational training and development. His core areas of research include personality psychology, entrepreneurship, and consumer psychology. Gorkan's pioneering research on entrepreneurship is funded by the Economic and Social Research Council, and he has published numerous research articles in important scientific journals. Gorkan has also made several media appearances and frequently acts as a governmental, media, and organizational adviser. His clients include HSBC, BBC, Channel 4, Google, Ford, Tesco, Sainsbury's, Mars, The Edrington Group, the Office of Fair Trading, the British Brand Groups, The Grocer, *Marketing* magazine, KPMG, and Harvard's Entrepreneurial Finance Lab, with which he is now an associate.

Tomas Chamorro-Premuzic, PhD, is an international authority in personality profiling and psychometric testing. He is currently professor of business psychology at University College London (UCL) and visiting professor at New York University, and has previously taught at the London School of Economics. Tomas has published six books and over 100 scientific papers, making him one of the most prolific social scientists of his generation. His work has received awards from the American Psychological Association and the International Society for the Study of Individual Differences, for which he is now director. Tomas is also the director of the MSc program in industrial-organizational and business psychology at UCL and has previously codirected the MSc program in occupational psychology at University of London's Goldsmiths. Over the past two decades, Tomas has provided consultancy services to a wide range of organizations, in both the private and public sectors. His clients have included the following: JP Morgan, HSBC, the JLT group, Prudential, Unilever, Reckitt Benckiser, the British army, the BBC, Hogan Assessment Systems, and Harvard's Entrepreneurial Finance Lab. Tomas frequently appears in the media to offer psychological expertise to a wide audience. His broadcasting career includes more than 200 media appearances and over 70 TV appearances for the BBC, CNN, and Sky News. Tomas is also a regular keynote speaker for the Institute of Economic Affairs.

Personality

101

Gorkan Ahmetoglu, PhD
Tomas Chamorro-Premuzic, PhD

SPRINGER PUBLISHING COMPANY
NEW YORK

Springer Publishing Company, LLC
11 West 42nd Street
New York, NY 10036
www.springerpub.com

Acquisitions Editor: Nancy S. Hale
Composition: Newgen Imaging

ISBN: 978-0-8261-0784-8
E-book ISBN: 978-0-8261-0785-5

12 13 14/ 5 4 3 2 1

The author and the publisher of this Work have made every effort to use sources believed to be reliable to provide information that is accurate and compatible with the standards generally accepted at the time of publication. The author and publisher shall not be liable for any special, consequential, or exemplary damages resulting, in whole or in part, from the readers' use of, or reliance on, the information contained in this book. The publisher has no responsibility for the persistence or accuracy of URLs for external or third-party Internet websites referred to in this publication and does not guarantee that any content on such websites is, or will remain, accurate or appropriate.

Library of Congress Cataloging-in-Publication Data
Ahmetoglu, Gorkan.
  Personality 101 / Gorkan Ahmetoglu, Tomas Chamorro-Premuzic.
     p. cm.
  Includes bibliographical references and index.
  ISBN 978-0-8261-0784-8–ISBN 978-0-8261-0785-5 (ebk)
  1. Personality. I. Chamorro-Premuzic, Tomas. II. Title. III. Title: Personality one hundred one. IV. Title: Personality one hundred and one.
  BF698.A335 2013
  155.2–dc23

                                                                    2012025999

Contents

Preface

eople's interest in understanding people is universal. Students choose to study psychology because they want to know more about who they are, and why they behave the way they do. Personality psychology answers these questions because it concerns the nature of human nature. It tells us how a person will act in different situations and why. It also tells us what a person is likely to do in the future. Finally, personality reveals whether and to what degree people change.

While many personality books have been written, there are no concise books that address this topic from a scientific but jargon-free way. Most books on personality fall into one of two categories: academic textbooks or pop-psychology books. The former are usually too complex for a lay audience and too long to read. The latter fail to discuss recent scientific findings about the nature of personality. This book attempts to bridge both categories.

Indeed, *Personality 101* has been written in an attempt to make cutting-edge research in personality accessible to a wide audience in a compact book. It is a book that tells the story about the differences and similarities between people, and the causes and consequences of these differences. This story is based on more than a century of research and thousands of scientific studies. It encompasses state-of-the-art investigations and the most widely accepted theories and facts in the field. It reveals to the reader the current state of affairs in personality psychology and the anticipated future directions of this field.

Finally, we hope to challenge some of our readers' preconceptions about people. Personality is often the subject of people's conversations—it is used to describe friends, partners, and work colleagues—but lay beliefs about personality are often in stark contrast with the research evidence. Whatever your purpose for reading this book, we hope that it will make you a bit more knowledgeable in this area and encourage you to read more about it. To this end, we have included an extensive bibliography.

Creativity 101
James C. Kaufman, PhD

Genius 101
Dean Keith Simonton, PhD

IQ Testing 101
Alan S. Kaufman, PhD

Leadership 101
Michael D. Mumford, PhD

Psycholinguistics 101
H. Wind Cowles, PhD

Anxiety 101
Moshe Zeidner, PhD
Gerald Matthews, PhD

Humor 101
Mitch Earleywine, PhD

Obesity 101
Lauren M. Rossen, MS
Eric A. Rossen, PhD

Emotional Intelligence 101
Gerald Matthews, PhD
Moshe Zeidner, PhD
Richard D. Roberts, PhD

Personality 101
Gorkan Ahmetoglu, PhD
Tomas Chamorro-Premuzic, PhD

Intelligence 101
Jonathan Plucker, PhD
Amber Esping, PhD

Personality

101

What Is Personality and Where Does It Come From?

What is personality and why should we study it? What can we learn about human nature by studying personality? These questions are fundamental to anyone interested in this subject, and especially those who are not. Robert Hogan, the personality psychologist, defined personality as the area of psychology that is concerned with "the nature of human nature" (Hogan, 2007, p. 1). In that sense, we could say that personality is one of the most essential fields of inquiry in psychology. In line with this, a great amount of theoretical and empirical work has been done in this area and the study of personality is now one of the broadest research areas in psychology, with links to neuroscience and clinical, educational, and work psychology (to mention only a few). In this section, we provide some background on the historical as well as current "big" theories of personality, that is, the major paradigms that have dominated the field for the past century (Chapter 1). We also discuss where personality comes from and how it develops throughout the course of life (Chapter 2). Finally, we look at how psychologists have measured and are currently measuring personality and how accurate this assessment is (Chapter 3).

What Is Personality And Why Be Interested?

Our attempt to understand personality is driven by two main goals: (a) We are interested in predicting behavior, specifically, what different people are likely to do and (b) we are interested in explaining why people do the things they do (as opposed to something else) and why different people act in different ways. In its broadest sense, "personality" is a generic answer to both questions. People do what they do because of certain singularities or characteristics of their psychological profile (if you want, you could replace "personality" by these two words), and their profiles are only accurate to the extent that they enable us to predict what they will do. In that sense, our attempts to understand and conceptualize theories of personality mirror our desire to understand ourselves and others around us. Indeed, personality is essential to explaining who we are and how others see us, how we relate to others within different environments, and why our idea of others (who they are) remains pretty much unchanged throughout time. Thus, personality is highly consequential: You may think of it as a dominant force underlying the dynamics of social behavior and affecting the laws of history (Hogan & Chamorro-Premuzic, 2011). Personality is a core determinant of individual differences in everyday behaviors; it affects our educational and occupational success, our health and longevity, our marital status and relationship satisfaction, and even our eating and sleeping preferences (see Chapter 4). Understanding one's own and others' personality is therefore important because it enables us to make sense of the world in which we live, as well as to predict the behavior and actions of others.

Individual differences in personality have been of great interest to scholars since the time of Aristotle and Plato. There are many views of personality, and many ways in which it can be conceptualized and even measured. Typically, personality psychologists have studied normal behavior or the patterns of thought and emotionality that are found in 90% of the population. However, a great deal of what we know about normal personality has derived from our understanding of abnormal or clinical behaviors (e.g., depression, schizophrenia, and anxiety disorders). The last section in this chapter discusses the difference between what psychologists broadly refer to as "normal" and what they regard as abnormal or clinical/mental illness. Most of this book will focus on the normal behavior and attempt to illustrate how most people differ from each other. If you are interested in mental disorders, you should probably consult specific books on the subject, such as *Abnormal Psychology* (Kring, Davison, Neale, & Johnson, 2007), *Anxiety 101* (Zeidner & Matthews, 2010), and *Obesity 101* (Rossen & Rossen, 2011).

GRAND THEORIES OF PERSONALITY

The Psychodynamic Approach to Personality and Freud

If one looks for an Elvis among personality psychologists, Freud (1856–1939) would be the one. There has, in fact, been nobody as influential as Freud in the history of psychology: He is the most widely cited psychologist of all times (Haggbloom et al., 2002) and one of the most widely cited social scientists (if not the most). He is the first psychologist most people can name anywhere in the world, and, in some cases, the only one; he is responsible for popularizing the view that personality psychologists can read the secrets in other people's minds, giving psychology a somewhat unscientific and obscure status among other sciences. Although Freud's influence on the modern science of personality is beyond dispute, the fact that his method for treating psychological disorders has long been discredited by the scientific community of clinical psychologists and psychiatrists has made Freud an unpopular and often neglected figure in personality research. For instance, our U.K. and U.S. students would major in psychology without ever reading anything about Freud if we didn't force them to do so (because our colleagues would never even recommend that they read Freud). You can surely criticize Elvis too, but would you teach the history of rock 'n' roll without mentioning him?

So what is Freud's main legacy? For starters, his psychoanalytic theory is one of the most comprehensive theories of human behavior, as far reaching as Darwin's evolutionary theory. While Darwin based his theory on his observations of other species and nature, Freud's theory of the mind was the result of his clinical observations (of people with rather obscure mental disorders). Freud saw himself as an archeologist of the mind and was never shy to draw from metaphysics, poetry, and literature when it came to explaining why people think the way they think and act the way they act. Second, Freud's preference for complexity meant he provided one of the most cryptic and intriguing accounts of human nature; yet he still managed to make it relatively clear to most readers, and, moreover, tap into somewhat far-fetched but still believable explanations of behavior. As Oscar Wilde said, "I can believe anything so long as it is unbelievable" (Wilde, 2003). Freud is responsible for making most other psychological theories, and personality is no exception, seem rather dull. His intriguing account of human behavior is rather like a mysterious sci-fi novel where nothing is what it seems; and who wants to watch reality TV after a great sci-fi film? Finally, Freud talked about some of the most important themes of human life: ambition, sex, and power. Oddly, most psychologists appear to have forgotten that these things rule the world, especially "positive psychology."

Freud's comprehensive theory of personality has many distinct components making it difficult to integrate into a unitary model, especially in the short space of this book. Nevertheless, it is generally useful to divide these components into three models. The most important feature of the first model is the unconsciousness. Freud argued that our real motives and desires are unconscious or hidden from conscious awareness; we think we do things because of x, but, in fact, it is y or z that is driving us. So, one of the goals of psychoanalysis is to uncover the real motives underlying our behavior, via therapy, in a way that is not too traumatic (because, as psychoanalysis argues, there is a psychological benefit in repressing those unpleasant real motives). This makes Freud's personality theory very different from modern theories: To Freud, the you that you know is hardly worth knowing because you made it up (Hogan & Chamorro-Premuzic, 2011). Today, most personality research focuses on self-reports and takes these statements as more or less valid indicators of your personality, but these are just conscious fabrications masking real unconscious motives for Freud.

Freud's second model suggests that the self can be thought of in terms of three mental structures, namely the id, the ego, and the superego. The id is closely linked to instinctual drives that are beneath our conscious awareness and irrational. It is like a wild animal or rock-'n'-roll child inside us pushing us to do naughty things ("naughty" because civilization aims to suppress them). The superego, on the other hand, is the internalized moral conscience and the reason why, unless you are a psychopath, you feel guilty when you do the things that you enjoy but most societies condemn, albeit hypocritically at times. Finally, the ego is our conscious state and the agent that "negotiates" between the pleasure-seeking impulses of the id and the moral constraints of the superego. The ego is thus in permanent or "dynamic" (this is where psychodynamic comes from) struggle to manage the pleasure-seeking id, and obey the voice of societal rules and restrictions posed by the superego.

According to Freud, adult personality reflects the id, ego, and superego struggles in childhood. It is what emerges from those never-ending conflicts or from how you deal with the conflicting forces governing your mind. For instance, if the superego dominates in childhood, the person may become rule-bound, conservative, and rigid as an adult; if the superego is too weak, the person may become a psychopath and suffer disorders of moral conduct, and so forth. The only issue with Freud is that he was focusing too much on clinical symptoms, which he saw as a physical or somatic attempt to deal with these inner churns. For example, a woman who is unable to come to terms with her sexual fantasies (for religious or moral reasons) may feel anxious when in the presence of attractive men, even though she may be unaware of the causes of her anxieties, and so forth. One of Freud's genius ideas was to treat many normal behaviors as symptoms, highlighting various manifestations of psychopathology in everyday life (this is the title of a famous book he wrote). This is why slips of the tongue became Freudian slips and where dreams become the "royal road to the unconscious" (Freud, 1900, p. 613).

Personality also reflects an individual's sexual development—Freud also uses the term "sexuality" to refer to pleasurable childish experiences rather than just adult or genital sexuality. Events and reactions to somewhat universal stages of psychosexual development interact to determine one's adult character. More specifically, Freud believed that most humans go through four critical psychosexual stages in their lives: oral, anal, phallic, and genital. Most stages involve biological changes. The first physical stage, the oral stage, involves the biological predisposition to suck (an innate reflex). The anal stage involves control of muscles including excretion. The phallic stage focuses on the genitalia as the erogenous zone. And the genital stage involves the biological surge of sexual energy in puberty. All these stages are also followed by psychological developments. For instance, each physical change also changes parents' behavior toward the child, particularly in terms of what they allow, prohibit, or demand. Physical changes mean that a child is first nursed and then weaned. It means that it is diapered and then toilet-trained. When passing through each of these stages, the child's former ways of getting pleasure are supplanted. This causes frustration and conflict.

According to Freud, conflicts in these stages during childhood have substantial impact on people's personalities. For instance, an important conflict during the anal stage involves toilet training, with struggles over the parent's demand that the child control its defecation according to rules. These conflicts, if not resolved correctly, can lead to various reactions, such as the child inhibiting rather than relaxing its bowels. This pattern then becomes general in adulthood, such as becoming compulsively clean or orderly; hence, the term "anal" is used to refer to obsessional personalities (perfectionists, or people with a cleaning fetish). On the whole then, personality may, according to Freud, be organized around the themes of the id, ego, and superego and conflicts during the stages of psychosexual development.

Despite its popularity and intriguing nature, however, the psychodynamic theory has been widely criticized by mainstream psychologists, especially since the 1950s. This partly reflects the ambitious, bold, and all-encompassing nature of the theory, combined with its reliance on tautological and nonfalsifiable claims. Some theoretical criticisms have focused on the limited scope of the sexual drive theory to explain human motivation. Others involve the unreliability of the inferences drawn from psychoanalytic theory. A final criticism relates to the fact that even when it is tested, the theory has often met very little empirical evidence in its support. For instance, studies that have examined the effect of various events in the psychosexual stages on later personality find no evidence to support the claim that differences in feeding or toilet training in childhood have any long-term effects on personality (Beloff, 1957). Moreover, Freud's view was that almost everybody in the world is neurotic (that was the best case scenario for him) and he ignored important individual differences in emotional adjustment, as well as other major personality traits. In many ways, the phenomena he was trying to explain are unrepresentative of human behavior, even when some of his explanations applied also to more universal human behaviors.

So, Freud's legacy is sort of mixed. Psychodynamic theory has received very little backing from personality psychologists, as well as mainstream psychologists, in general. Despite its theoretical and empirical limitations, however, the theory has had an important impact on the field and should therefore not be ignored. Indeed, it would be erroneous to brush aside psychoanalytic theory as a group of crazy ideas about human nature, not the least because it concerns a wider "chunk" of human nature than most current personality theories. While many of Freud's specific observations have failed to receive experimental support, the more generic concepts he put forward have mostly stood the test of time, and their influence beyond the academic community is unrivaled by other psychological concepts. There is, for example, much evidence for the existence of unconscious mental processes, as well as conflicts between these processes and conscious cognition (Chamorro-Premuzic, 2011). Perhaps the major problem here is that the number of Freud's critics far exceeds the number of his readers, not least because of the huge volume of Freud's work. We hope that this very brief overview of his personality theory may have encouraged some of you to pay more attention to his work or, at least, refrain from criticizing him until you do!

Behaviorism

During the mid-20th century, behaviorism emerged as a dominant paradigm for understanding human behavior, including personality. Indeed, this paradigm would dominate the entire field of psychology for several decades. As the name suggests, behaviorism is an attempt to reduce most psychological explanations to our understanding of observable behavioral events. As such, it is pretty much the opposite of psychoanalysis or psychodynamic theory, which concerns itself with unobservable mental constructs. In fact, some behaviorists went as far as to avoid any discussion of nonobservable entities, such as the mind or thought, hoping that this strategy would make psychology a science as robust as the natural sciences (biology, chemistry, etc.). Behaviorism's answer to the Freudian id, ego, and superego is sheer observable behavior, such as a dog salivating or a child running away from a rat. In its most radical form, behaviorism postulated that in order to become a proper science, psychology needed to focus entirely on observable behavior. This is when the science of the mind became the science of behavior.

Early pioneers of behaviorism were E. L. Thorndike (1874–1949) and John Watson (1878–1958). However, the major developments in this field are often credited to B. F. Skinner (1904–1990). Indeed, while Freud may be the most famous of all psychologists, some argue that Skinner was the one who made the greatest contribution to the discipline (Korn, Davis, & Davis, 1991), at least in the United States. He is also the second or third most famous psychologist of all time (after Freud and Bandura, or just before him).

Before we discuss the behavioristic view of personality, it is important to illustrate two important facts: First, behaviorism is as much a philosophy of science or "epistemology" as a specific theory in this field. Second, it was not intended to be a theory of personality per se, but rather a theory of human (and animal) behavior. However due to space limitations here, we will focus only on the salient behaviorist arguments and their implications for personality theory.

The first aim of behaviorists such as Watson and Skinner was to make psychology a "respectable" science, exempt from the troubles of metaphysical or pseudoscientific concepts (i.e., anything that cannot be physically sensed or empirically examined). This can only be done, they argued, by studying what we can observe, and nothing else. Thus, environmental stimuli and observable effects became the main targets of psychological studies for behaviorists. Referring to inner "mental states" is neither useful nor necessary. As Skinner (1971) famously put it,

> We can follow the path taken by physics and biology by turning directly to the relation between behavior and the environment and neglecting supposed mediating states of mind. Physics did not advance by looking more closely at the jubilance of a falling body, or biology by looking at the nature of vital spirits, and we do not need to try to discover what personalities, states of mind, feelings, traits of character, plans, purposes, intentions, or the other prerequisites of autonomous man really are in order to get on with a scientific analysis of behavior. (p. 15)

Thus, according to behaviorists, we should stop asking "what is it about this person that makes him or her act the way they do," and start asking "what in the environment has made this person act the way they do." In this way, they shifted the source of behavior from the mind, and the person, to the environment: something we can physically observe. The environment can be the here and now—such as the temperature affecting what clothes you wear. However, more often it refers to past experiences that have led to learning (the conditioned behavior). In classical conditioning, a dog automatically salivates on the sound of a doorbell because it has "learned" (been conditioned) to associate the doorbell with the arrival of food. In operant conditioning, learning occurs through rewards and punishments. Behavior that was rewarded is more likely to occur in the future, and behavior that was punished is less likely to occur. If you were rewarded for being outspoken in social occasions in the past, you will be more likely to be outspoken during these occasions in the future. If you weren't rewarded, or were punished for being outspoken in social occasions in the past, then you are less likely to be outspoken during these occasions in the future.

Thus, according to behaviorists, all current behavior is a function of the present environment, and of the patterns of reinforcements in the person's past. Personality would then simply constitute the sum of all learned associations, though strictly speaking behaviorists wouldn't use the word personality as it refers to mental structures (such as the id, ego, and superego or traits) that govern behavior. Skinner argued that such constant or stable structures are illusionary; if the environment changes, so will behavior. If behavior can potentially change depending on the environment, there is no room (or need) for any "inner" structures to influence this outcome.

We should note that Skinner did not deny the existence of inner states such as thoughts and feelings. However, he argued that even these were the consequence of the person's life history, that is, the environment he or she has encountered. Thus, individual differences in what appears to be, or what we call, personality are simply individual differences in people's life histories.

Skinner's theory of human behavior—often referred to as radical behaviorism—soon expanded into a philosophical and political system. This line of behaviorism proposed that "everything important in psychology...can be investigated in essence through the continued experimental and theoretical analysis of the determiners of rat behavior at a choice point in a maze" (Tolman, 1938, p. 34). Research based on behaviorist principles had great successes in achieving precise experimental control. Behaviorism's commitment to the scientific method has left a great mark on psychology as a discipline. Its learning principles have also had a highly important impact in several applied settings, such as in clinical and organizational contexts.

Despite its important legacy, however, the constrained behaviorist approach to explaining human behavior was eventually found to be unsustainable. Critics pointed out that behaviorism cannot account for learning that occurs in the absence of reinforcements simply through observation. Neither is it possible, they proposed, to predict future behavior without referring to inner states, such as expectancies, beliefs, and feelings. As Hempel (1966) noted, "in order to characterize behavioral patterns, propensities, or capacities, we need not only a suitable behavioristic vocabulary, but psychological terms as well" (p. 110). Thus, often it is one's belief about potential reinforcements, not the reinforcements themselves, that determine behavior.

These so-called moderate behaviorist approaches resurrected unobservable variables, such as memories, emotions, and perceptions, in personality to expand the theoretical and explanatory scope of behaviorism. Somewhat ironically, behaviorism, the discipline that aimed to abolish inner mental states from psychological analysis, therefore led the way to the paradigm of cognitive psychology and social cognitive theory, which put the study of unobservable, internal, mental constructs at center stage. The social cognitive theory of personality was largely based on this paradigm.

Social Cognitive Theory

Although the *social cognitive theory* of personality has its origins in the radical behaviorist tradition, it emerged in clear opposition to it. Psychologists endorsing this approach share the behaviorist view that learning has a key part in personality formation. However, they depart from behavioristic views in their focus on mental representations (unobservable constructs), such as motivation, personal agency, and self-efficacy. Indeed, these concepts are the key themes in social cognitive theory, which therefore contrasts with behaviorists' position about the environment as the sole or primary determinant of behavior. Rather, social cognitive theorists argue that, unlike animals, human beings have unique cognitive capacities and that the study of nonhuman species will provide only limited information about human nature. As humans, we can reflect on our past, interpret the present, plan and anticipate the future, and, ultimately, *decide* how to behave. These are all different "cognitive processes," and ignoring them would mean throwing away the most important issues about human behavior. In effect, the social cognitive paradigm put psychology back in its original path of investigating "the mind," even if behavior still remained an important observable variable in psychological studies. Importantly, the *agentic* causes of behavior shifted from the environment to "inside the person" or the human mind. This was an important paradigmatic shift in the history of psychology—and personality was no exception.

The great German philosopher Friedrich Hegel (1770–1831) believed that the evolution of ideas (and theories) occurs in cycles, where a new theory emerges in refutation of a previous theory, until a third theory can integrate both—this is what philosophers usually refer to as *dialectics*. Thus, we could say that social cognitive theory synthesizes elements of both psychodynamics (with its focus on mental representations or cognitions, albeit conscious rather than unconscious ones) and behaviorism (with its focus on experience and learning as the main causes of the cognitions that drive human behaviors). Therefore, we could think of social cognitive theory as a compromise between both previous paradigms, paying attention to both internal and external factors. As Albert Bandura (1925–the present), the leading figure and in some ways founder of the social cognitive movement, describes it, causality is a two-way street, where individuals are affected by the environment and experience, but their experiences and environments are also shaped by them (e.g., their minds, thoughts, and needs; Bandura, 1986).

This reciprocal determinism can be illustrated by many everyday life examples. For instance, imagine that you find yourself in a party where you only know one person. You want to make a good impression and don't want to look awkward; so you smile, make jokes, and try to interact with other guests. In this scenario, how do we decide what is the cause of your behavior? We could say that it is the environment, as other guests led you to behave in a specific way. So, you behave in a way that is adaptive and somehow required by the environment. On the other hand, we could say that you *interpreted* the situation in this way. That's right, *you* believed that you needed to make a good impression and *you* believed that behaving differently would be awkward. These interpretations are features of your personality. What's more, your behavior of smiling and particular way of interacting with others has affected the people you interact with. They smile back, share their stories and introduce you to others. Finally, and as a consequence of this, your successful interactions alter your mood and confidence, that is, your belief about your ability to interact with others in social events. The belief may well be based on experience, but that experience was also preceded by an initial self-belief (which may have come from previous experiences!). This "catch-22" or chicken-and-egg approach to causality illustrates the complexity of understanding human personality according to social cognitive theory. But what we need to emphasize is that Bandura and colleagues did a lot to rescue personality and psychology from the empty realm of behaviorism, where people were seen as mindless beings who are alive to respond to changes in the environment (just like fish or squirrels).

So, how do social cognitive theorists describe the structure of personality? In essence, they contend that key cognitions or beliefs are acquired over the course of an individual's life and entail different ways of seeing the world, thinking about it, and interacting with it. While many such structural concepts exist, four are particularly noteworthy.

The first concerns *competencies and skills*, things that a person can actually do, like the ability to climb a mountain or cheer up a heartbroken friend (these two are obviously unrelated). The second is *expectancies*, that is, beliefs about the likely consequences of actions, the likely actions of other people, the likelihood of succeeding in a particular task, and so on. If you believe that you are capable of passing an exam, and that revising will increase the likelihood that you will pass, you are more likely to revise, which would improve your performance on the exam. Conversely, if you think you will fail, even if you study, you will probably avoid studying and, in turn, fail. This is where Bandura claims that beliefs are self-fulfilling (as Henry Ford said, whether you think you can do it or not, you are right). The third process concerns *subjective values*, how much a person desires or dreads an outcome that he or she believes the behavior will produce. Thus, if in addition to your expectations about passing the exam you also strongly *value* academic success, you are more likely to revise for it. This is why we pay people for doing things they are perfectly able to do, because they don't really care (for most people, this is the meaning of "work" or a job). The final concept concerns *goals*, that is, mental representations of the goals that our actions pursue. Goals are what enable us to regulate and direct our behavior. They contribute to our capacity to exert control over our lives. If you set difficult but achievable goals and you make these goals specific, your behavior will be more persistent and more directed than if you set easy and vague goals (Latham, Ganegoda, & Locke, 2011).

According to social cognitive theory, these are some key cognitive processes along which personalities can vary. But how does this differ from other structural theories, such as psychodynamic and trait theory (see sections The Psychodynamic Approach to Personality and Freud and The Trait Approach)? According to social cognitive theorists, it does so in two important ways. First, unlike other personality theories, which suggest broad or "context-free" structures, these cognitive processes are proposed to be highly situation-specific. For instance, one important expectancy construct is *perceived self-efficacy* (Bandura, 1977), a person's belief concerning his or her ability to perform the behaviors needed to achieve desired outcomes. Unlike other broad constructs (e.g., psychodynamic motives or personality "traits"), people may differ substantially in their self-efficacy perceptions across different situations. For instance, you may have a low sense of self-efficacy for getting a high grade on the math exam but a high sense of self-efficacy for getting a date on the weekend.

The second important distinction between trait or motivational structures and cognitive processes is *flexibility*, that is, the capacity to change. As mentioned above, according to social cognitive theorists, most cognitive processes are acquired through learning. In true behaviorist fashion, they acknowledge that many behaviors are learned through classical and operant conditioning. However, they contrast with behaviorism in that they believe the majority of learning occurs through social interaction and observation of the social world, what they call "modeling," even in the absence of reinforcements. You may be familiar with Bandura's famous study on the Bobo dolls (Bandura, Ross, & Ross, 1961) (if not, you can look it up on YouTube). The reason this study was so influential is that it highlighted that learning can occur without conditioning or reenforcement such that children who simply observe an adult hit an inflatable doll somehow "learned" to play with guns and hit other (noninflatable) children. Bandura's studies could not be explained by behaviorism, because something else was clearly happening inside the mind of the kids for them to modify their behavior without conditioning or specific instructions to do so.

Furthermore, unlike other theories that see personality as fixed, social cognitivists assert that people can and do change throughout their life span. People who are lacking in skill or belief can engage in new interactions and new observations of the world and thereby acquire new skills, beliefs, and ways of seeing things. Your confidence in your ability to get a date on the weekend will be higher if you had recently got a date. If you get another date, it will be even higher the next time you are out. Thus, people not only vary in their competencies and beliefs from one domain to another, they also have the capacity to change their skill and beliefs in any given domain. As we will see in the next section (and more in the next chapter), however, this view of a flexible and context dependent personality is not shared by all. Indeed, the degree to which personality changes from situation to situation and over time has been the topic of numerous heated debates and decades of research. We examine some of these debates and research in detail in the next section.

DISPOSITIONAL APPROACHES TO PERSONALITY

The Trait Approach

In the previous section, we reviewed some of the major theories of personality. Each of these theories has informed our understanding about the nature of personality. Psychodynamic theory has enlightened us about unconscious motivational processes, behaviorism about the role of the environment, and the social cognitive theory about the role of cognitions, in shaping our behavior and, thus, personalities. Despite their unquestionable legacy, it would not be unreasonable to suggest that the theories rather scarcely reflect the way most people would refer to, or view, personality today. If you, for example, asked a person to describe their best friend's character, you would probably not expect a response stating that their best friend has strong repressed sexual impulses of which they are unaware, or that they start cheering and moving rapidly to the sound of *Winds of Change*, or that their mere belief that they can win a marathon will make them win it.

In contrast, most people simply describe others by listing some adjectives, such as kind, talkative, cheerful, and reliable— this is the common sense or layperson's approach to psychological profiling, and dispositional approaches are not much more complex than that (except for the use of advanced statistics to demonstrate that the correct choice of adjectives has been made). Indeed, people commonly describe others and themselves by using words that reflect specific personal attributes. In dating sites, for instance, people describe their physical attributes, such as tall, blonde, female, and so on, but also commonly include words that reflect personality attributes, such as friendly, loving, and kind (in addition to socioeconomic and material attributes, of course, such as homeowner, rich, etc.). What they look for in a potential partner will similarly include not only attributes of a person's physicality but also personality (e.g., looking for a tall, dark male, and someone who is outgoing, talkative, ambitious, etc.). Thus, people seem to view such attributes, or what psychologists refer to as traits, as central to personality.

Likewise, many psychologists believe that traits are an essential aspect of personality. Importantly, they believe that traits are also the most appropriate unit of analysis in the study of personality. This may seem obvious; however, note that, in contrast to this, the theories reviewed in the previous sections rarely make reference to the notion of traits. Indeed, some of the concepts proposed in these theories actually contradict this notion. Consequently, the trait theory of personality and the trait approach is considered a separate research field in its own right.

What Is a Trait?

What exactly is a trait? Simply put, a trait is a consistent pattern in the way a person behaves, thinks, or feels. If you describe someone as "nice," you have already made the assumption of consistency. Consistency has two elements: (a) consistency across situations and (b) consistency over a period of time. So when you refer to someone as "nice," you don't usually mean that they are nice only in specific circumstances, say, in parties, or that they were nice to you yesterday; you usually think of them as being nice in general (e.g., in parties, when alone, with friends and family, etc.) and having been so over a significant period of time (i.e., weeks, months, or years). Of course, they may not always be equally nice, but when they are not, you would probably think there are justified reasons for their behavior, as the person is usually nice. As we all know, even the nicest person may become frustrated or argumentative if somebody insulted him or her, or his or her loved ones. So, describing someone with certain traits means that they are more likely than the average person to behave in those trait-like ways most of the time.

Psychologists usually refer to this "consistency approach" as the dispositional view of personality. This reflects the fact that people seem predisposed to acting in these consistent ways. Thus, in contrast to theories that argue that people are primarily influenced by previous life experiences and the environment they are currently in, dispositional theories suggest that people's personalities remain stable across time and space. Accordingly, trait theories advocate that despite all the changes people experience throughout their lives, there seems to be some consistency in their characters. A person may change several schools, make new friends, move to a different city or even country, marry, divorce, and so on and yet people will still be able to tell who he or she really is, and they will be able to tell when the person is acting uncharacteristically. Thus, this consistency found in a person's personality lays the foundations to the trait theory.

The Trait Universe

Two other essential aspects of the trait approach are description and classification. That is, traits allow us to describe how individuals differ from one another, and thus classify them accordingly. For instance, how would you describe the difference between two of your best friends in terms of their personality? As in dating sites, you would most probably use different trait words. For instance, you might say that Sanchez is ambitious, determined, and hardworking, whereas Jack is laid-back, fun-loving, and careless. You could also use the same words to describe both. You might say that Jack is not as ambitious, determined, and hardworking as Sanchez, or that Sanchez is not very fun-loving, and generally, very careful. By using various trait terms, therefore, you are able to describe your friends, as well as differentiate between them. Being able to differentiate between people's personalities (e.g., who is trustworthy or untrustworthy, kind or aggressive, argumentative or agreeable) is, needless to say, essential for the decisions we make and thus our functioning. Such "classifications" allow us to predict people's behavior and to alter our own accordingly.

Indeed, classification is an essential first step in any scientific endeavor. Chemistry has its periodic table of elements, zoology has its taxonomy of biological species, and physics has its classification of elementary particles. These are classification systems, or taxonomies, that researchers use to differentiate between the units under study. For instance, biologists recognize that creatures differ in a multitude of ways—in their size, color, in the absence or the presence of a skeleton, and so on—and need to differentiate between these creatures and classify them based of a specified taxonomy. Psychological traits have a similar function; they allow us to differentiate one person from another.

However, one important question here is how many trait terms do we need in order to be able differentiate between people? How many trait terms would you need in order to fully describe your friends—or at least to give us a good idea of what they are like (say so that we could predict their behavior)? How many traits do we need to ascribe to Jack and Sanchez to be able to differentiate between them? Do we need 2? 10? 50? 100? As you can probably imagine, one could use an incredibly large number of trait terms. And according to some psychologists, it is necessary to do so because every individual will have a unique set of traits; no two people can be described by the same traits. This view, known as the ideographic view of personality, may initially sound intuitive, but is it really so? Consider for a moment how many trait terms you use to describe a person (probably only a few). Beyond practical reasons, could it be that only a few trait terms are needed because they can in essence give us enough information about the person? That is, might it be that a few trait terms already are capturing most of the information that many of the other trait terms could provide?

Consider this scenario: If you describe someone as very kind, would saying that he is also friendly add much to our understanding of what this person is like? There is clearly a conceptual distinction between being kind and friendly, but we also know that people who are one are also usually the other. We would be hard pressed to find a person who is very kind but not friendly. Accordingly, we would probably take it for granted that if the person is very kind they are likely also to be friendly, and not really feel the need to use the term "friendly" to describe or understand the person further. Perhaps, we would neither need to use trait terms such as generous, altruistic, aggressive, or offensive. We would probably take it for granted that if a person is very kind they would also likely to be generous and altruistic, and not aggressive or offensive. The reason for this is simple: We know intuitively that some traits and the behaviors they represent generally go together—they co-occur. A person who likes going to parties and meeting people is generally also talkative. A person who is methodical with planning and organizing usually doesn't like being late to class or meetings. This may sound straightforward, but it is an important piece of information. Why? The fact that certain behaviors (traits) go together may in itself suggest that these behaviors are all indicative of some more fundamental, or "basic," traits.

To make this clear, consider a person who has long legs, long arms, long fingers, long feet, and a long torso. If we were asked to describe this person, would we need to use all these traits terms to do so? No. Why? Because we know that these traits usually go together—they co-occur. The reason they co-occur is because they are all indicators of a more fundamental trait: height! If you were trying to set your friend up with another person, you would probably tell them whether the person was tall or short. You wouldn't tell your friend that this person has long arms and fingers and a long torso (even if you may tell them about the long legs—though this is beyond the point). Your friend would know intuitively that a tall person probably has long legs, long arms, long fingers, and so on.

This is precisely why the information about the co-occurrence of these personality traits is so important. Might it be that, just as with physical traits such as height, certain personality traits co-occur because of some more fundamental, or "basic," traits? Given that unlike physical traits, personality traits are not observable, the answer to this question is not straightforward. However, according to trait theorists of personality, they do! Specifically, according to trait theory, behaviors and the traits used to describe them can be organized into a hierarchy. At the bottom of the hierarchy would be simple responses that individuals may display in any given situation, such as a student finishing an essay on time. However, these responses are not completely random. Individuals will display a similar pattern of responses across situations and over time; for instance, the student may consistently finish her essays on time. Such patterns of responses can be seen as general habits. Furthermore, individuals will also differ in the groups of habits that they possess; for instance, the student may consistently finish other assignments and tasks on time, be on time for class, and be generally organized. According to trait psychologists, these groups of habits are indicators of some more fundamental traits (just as height is an indicator of long legs, arms, fingers, etc.). These traits, they argue, can be described as basic predispositions to

23

act in particular ways. According to this state-of-the-art view of traits, every human being fundamentally differs only in such predispositions or what psychologists call basic traits. This view is called the nomothetic view of personality.

We will review evidence regarding this position throughout the book; however, at this point, we simply want you to focus on what it would mean if trait theories were correct. That is, if personality traits co-occur because of the existence of some more fundamental or basic traits, then

1. Can we identify these basic traits? And if so, how?
2. How many basic traits might there be?

Identifying the Basic Structure of Personality. As mentioned before, given that we cannot observe personality traits as we can observe length of fingers, legs, torso, and so on, the job of identifying such traits seems rather difficult. Nevertheless, psychologists have developed numerous successful methods to deal with this problem. The first of these is a statistical method, and it deals with establishing a classification, or taxonomy, of trait descriptors. In other words, it helps us to make sense out of the plethora of trait descriptors that are used to describe people. As we mentioned before, we often know intuitively which traits tend to go together. However, to identify taxonomy of basic personality traits, we cannot simply rely on intuition. We need to have precise and objective measures. This is where a method called factor analysis enters the scene. Factor analysis is a statistical tool for finding patterns of associations (co-occurrence) among a large number of variables. It does what we do intuitively, but in a statistical manner.

To demonstrate this in simple terms, imagine two variables that generally go together, such as height and weight. If we find out that you are very tall, then we could also assume that you are likely to be above average in weight, because height and weight are usually associated in this way (i.e., even if there are exceptions such as tall skinny, or heavy short, people, on average this would be the relationship). In statistical terms, the degree of association between two variables is called a "correlation." In personality research, we could, for instance, say that there is a correlation between being organized and being punctual (or a negative correlation between being organized and being late). Thus, instead of relying on intuition, we could simply measure statistically whether these traits co-occur. Of course, if we only have two variables, we need only a calculation of the correlation coefficient. However, to classify hundreds of trait terms, we would need hundreds, or thousands, of correlations. The function of factor analysis, therefore, is to find some general patterns, or factors, within a group of correlations comprising a large number of traits. Thus, sticking with the example a few paragraphs back, a researcher may find positive correlations between measures of kindness, generosity, and altruism, and positive correlations between offensiveness and aggressiveness. The researcher may also find that kindness, generosity, and altruism negatively correlate with offensiveness and aggressiveness (because we would not expect people who are kind and altruistic to also be aggressive and offensive). If researchers over time and a number of studies find that these traits consistently cluster together (correlate), then it would be possible to conclude that there is a unifying source that leads to these correlations. This unifying source is what trait psychologists would call a basic trait.

As you can imagine, factor analysis is an extremely useful tool for identifying co-occurrences between traits and, therefore, for uncovering a taxonomy of personality. And while there are several other methods psychologists use to establish which factors are basic (and we will discuss these in later chapters), to most trait theorists, the factors that are identified through factor analytic studies are, in essence, the basic structures of personality.

The Lexical Hypothesis. The assumption that basic traits can be uncovered through factor analysis itself derives from what is known as the lexical hypothesis. According to the lexical hypothesis, historically, the most important and socially relevant behaviors that people display will eventually become encoded into language. If certain adjectives we use to describe people (e.g., trustworthy, loyal, helpful) have remained in the language decade after decade, it is probably because they were necessary for describing behaviors that were important to describe. Terms that were not required, or described insignificant behaviors, would presumably have been dropped out of common usage. Thus, according to the lexical hypothesis, a systematic examination of trait adjectives might give us clues about individual differences whose description has been important enough to withstand the test of time (Goldberg, 1990).

The Structure of Personality: 16 Personality Factors. Partly based on this hypothesis, the first attempt to uncover the traits that constitute the full spectrum of personality was made by Allport and Odbert (1936). To do this, Allport and Odbert patiently worked their way through the English dictionary, which contained about 55,000 words. The researchers counted as many as 18,000 words describing aspects by which individuals could be compared. About one quarter of these (4,500) described personality characteristics (the others referred to various physical characteristics, cognitive abilities or talents, and transient states such as moods). This was of course still an enormous amount of information to make sense of. Allport himself had an ideographic view of personality (i.e., he believed that each person is unlike any other individual), and, as a result, did not attempt to uncover a more fundamental structure beyond the 4,500 trait descriptors.

The first person accredited with this endeavor is Raymond Cattell (1943). Cattell's starting point was similar to that of Allport and Odbert. Indeed, he used their initial list of traits as a foundation for his subsequent analysis. However, similar to many other trait theorists, he relied on the idea that there are hierarchical relations among trait concepts. Specifically, he believed that there is a distinction between surface traits (superficial, everyday behaviors that can be observed) and source traits (a smaller number of more basic traits that are internal and the source of the observed co-occurrence among surface traits). Cattell's ultimate goal was to uncover these underlying basic structures by reducing Allport and Odbert's lengthy list of (surface) traits. Through several laborious steps, including eliminating synonyms and antonyms and difficult or uncommon words (based on his own judgment), Cattell managed to reduce Allport and Odbert's list to only 171 trait adjectives. His next step included statistical analysis. First, he administered questionnaires to a large number of participants and had them rate people they knew on each of these 171 trait adjectives. He then made use of statistical techniques including correlational analysis and factor analysis in order to identify the intercorrelations between the 171 traits, and reduce the number further. At the end of a long and complicated process, which included both further additions and omissions of factors, Cattell was left with 16 primary factors. Cattell concluded that based on his analysis, these 16 factors, or traits, represented the basic structure of personality.

Catell's efforts to uncover the fundamental dimensions of personality were heroic. Both his theoretical and empirical work have been recognized as the building blocks to our current study and understanding of personality. Nevertheless, in modern personality psychology, his model, which includes 16 personality traits, is no longer at the forefront. The main reason for this is the finding that his 16 factors also correlated with one another. That is, despite the smaller number of traits that had been extracted through factor analysis, many of these still tended to co-occur. To many trait theorists, this indicated that there may in fact exist a simpler, more basic trait structure of personality underlying these 16 factors. This possibility was pursued by many researchers over the years to come. This included one of the giants of 20th-century psychology, Hans Eysenck.

The Structure of Personality: Eysenck's Gigantic Three.
Eysenck's theory of personality has a unique place in personality psychology, and some of its major components will be reviewed further in the next chapter. Eysenck, like Cattell, believed that personality is best investigated and measured psychometrically. He also advocated that factor analysis is the most appropriate method of identifying and representing the personality structure. Nevertheless, his approach differed from Cattell's in some important respects. Specifically, Eysenck believed that factor analysis was only a means of addressing questions concerning the structure of personality and strongly advocated the importance of having a theory in this process. Accordingly, he employed the deductive method of investigation, meaning that he started with a theory and then gathered data that are logically consistent with that theory. We will outline some of these differences in the next chapter; for now, we only need to consider one major difference between Eysenck and Cattell's data, that is, the number of basic traits extracted.

While Cattell's factor analysis revealed 16 primary factors to represent the structure of personality, Eysenck found only three (though originally he hypothesized only two). This may seem odd at first, but it has a very simple statistical explanation. Cattell's primary factors correlated with one another. Eysenck saw it a logical next step to conduct a secondary factor analysis to see whether these factors could be distilled even further to truly independent and uncorrelated traits. In his secondary factor analysis, Eysenck found that, in fact, three factors, completely independent of one another and irreducible to any others, could be extracted. These factors he referred to as "superfactors" and which are often labeled the Gigantic Three were Neuroticism, Extraversion, and Psychoticism. According to Eysenck, these factors could not be reduced any further, and therefore had to represent the most basic structure of personality.

Three traits may initially strike you as a small number to capture all the uniqueness of any one individual's personality. However, as noted above, the classification of basic traits defines a conceptual space into which many trait terms can be fitted. Think of it as analogous to the color solid, which accommodates all possible colors on the basis of just three dimensions—brightness, hue, and saturation. Like the color solid, Eysenck's three dimensions allow for an infinite variety in the personalities of different people. With such a taxonomy, however, each of those personalities can be described in a comfortably economical way.

So what do Eysenck's Gigantic Three traits actually represent? The first trait that Eysenck called Neuroticism refers to an individual's level of emotionality and tendency to worry and be moody, touchy, and anxious. Thus, the Neuroticism/emotional stability trait is a continuum of upset and distress. People high on Neuroticism are generally anxious, stressed, pessimistic, and fearful and tend to have lower self-esteem. Conversely, people who are low on Neuroticism are emotionally stable, calm, and optimistic.

The second trait that Eysenck called Extraversion assesses the degree to which individuals show a tendency to be talkative, outgoing, and energetic. Thus, the Extraversion/introversion factor represents a continuum of sociability, liveliness, and dominance. Extraverts tend to enjoy the company of others and express their feelings and emotions; they are energetic, optimistic, outgoing, and confident. Conversely, introverts (low Extraversion scorers) are resistant to interpersonal contact, reserved, and quiet; they tend to be shy and lack confidence.

Finally, Psychoticism (which was introduced much later by Eysenck) refers to an individual's level of conformity, aggressiveness, and feelings for others. High Psychoticism describes emotionally cruel, risk-taking, impulsive, and sensation-seeking individuals. They are sociopathic, which means they show little respect for social norms, and are psychologically unattached to others. Conversely, low Psychoticism (known as tender-mindedness) describes caring, responsible, and socially driven individuals more likely to conform to given rules than to defy them.

The Structure of Personality: The Big Five. If personality psychology were to advance from a preliminary classification of traits to the prediction of real-world outcomes and other psychological constructs, it would be essential to establish a consensus concerning the number and nature of traits that are necessary to describe the basic psychological differences between individuals. While both Cattell and Eysenck have made notorious contributions in this respect, the system that appears to have won the vote of most differential psychologists is the Five Factor Model, also referred to as the Big Five personality traits.

Like Cattell's 16 Personality Factors, and Eysenck's Gigantic Three, the Big Five personality framework is based on factor analytic evidence. And like the models presented above, it originated from the lexical hypothesis, that is, the assumption that the major dimensions of individual differences can be derived from the total number of descriptors in any language system. So what is different about the Five Factor Model? The answer is straightforward: a large body of research evidence.

The decades following Cattell's initial attempts to consolidate a lexical-based personality model largely consisted of trait psychologists' search for a taxonomy of personality that could represent the fundamental and truly independent trait dimensions. A now only widely quoted study conducted by Norman (1967), which drew upon earlier research conducted by Allport, Cattell, Tupes and Christal (1961/1992) and others, indicated that five factors were both necessary and sufficient to explain the fundamental structure of personality. Norman's work has since been replicated by a vast number of research studies and several meta-analyses (which estimate the average correlation in hundreds or thousands of studies). The five factors found in these studies have been shown to have good validity and reliability across research studies, varying populations, and spanning several decades. This has led most researchers today to agree on a personality taxonomy that consists of five major personality dimensions. According to the Five Factor taxonomy, the five major personality traits or factors are Neuroticism, Extraversion, Openness to experience, Agreeableness, and Conscientiousness, hence the widely used acronyms of NEOAC or OCEAN.

So what do these five factors correspond to? The first two factors of the Big Five, Neuroticism and Extraversion, are nearly identical to the ones proposed by Eysenck and will now be familiar to you. The third factor, Openness to experience, is derived from the ideas of Coan (1974) and represents the tendency to engage in intellectual activities and experience new sensations and ideas. This factor is also referred to as creativity, intellect, and culture (Goldberg, 1993). It comprises the primary facets of fantasy, aesthetics, feelings, actions, ideas, and values. In a general sense, Openness to experience is associated with intellectual curiosity, aesthetic sensitivity, vivid imagination, behavioral flexibility, and unconventional attitudes. People high on Openness to experience tend to be dreamy, imaginative, inventive, and nonconservative in their thoughts and opinions. Poets and artists (and, to some extent, psychologists and psychology students, too) may be regarded as typical examples of high Openness scorers.

A fourth factor, Agreeableness (also known as sociability), refers to friendly, considerate, and modest behavior. Thus Agreeableness is associated with a tendency toward friendliness and nurturance and comprises the subfacets of trust, straightforwardness, altruism, compliance, modesty, and tendermindedness. Agreeable people can thus be described as caring, friendly, warm, and tolerant, and have a general predisposition for prosocial behavior.

Finally, Conscientiousness is associated with proactivity, responsibility, and self-discipline. (Does this apply to you? If you're reading this book just before your exam, perhaps not!) This factor includes the primary dimensions of competence, order, dutifulness, achievement-striving, self-discipline, and deliberation. Conscientious individuals are best identified by their efficiency, organization, determination, and productivity. No wonder, then, that this personality dimension has been reported to be significantly associated with various types of performance.

How many Factors Should We Use? As you can see, there are three novel personality traits identified and included in the Big Five taxonomy that are not present—although arguably represented—in the Eysenckian model. Specifically, Eysenck's idea of Psychoticism would be conceptualized in terms of low Agreeableness, high Openness to experience, and low Conscientiousness (Digman & Inouye, 1986; Goldberg, 1982; McCrae, 1987), but Eysenck considered Openness as an indicator of intelligence or the cognitive aspect of personality rather than of temperament. On the other hand, Eysenck and Eysenck (1985) conceptualized Agreeableness as a combination of low Psychoticism, low Neuroticism, and high Extraversion rather than as a personality dimension in its own right. A large number of studies have empirically examined this relationship. In general, Neuroticism and Extraversion have been found to be overlapping dimensions in both systems, suggesting that the Big Five and Gigantic Three are assessing two pairs of almost identical traits. However, Agreeableness and Conscientiousness tend to correlate only moderately with Psychoticism ($r = -.45$ and $-.31$, respectively), and Openness has been found to be uncorrelated with Psychoticism ($r = .05$) (Chamorro-Premuzic, 2011). Thus, the systems seem to differ to some extent in their assessment of traits other than Neuroticism and Extraversion.

At this point, you would be forgiven to think that the existence of a variety of models, which include different number of factors, reflects some arbitrariness in psychologists' attempts to identify the fundamental structure of personality. However, before you are drawn to such a conclusion, you should consider that three, and at most five, factors are consistently found in studies of this kind. Rarely do researchers find four, six, one, or ten factors. These findings can not be considered statistical artifacts. For instance, in intelligence research with similar statistical methodologies, researchers consistently find a one-factor solution. And as mentioned before, this factor structure is found across a large number of research studies, in various cultures, and across genders, and different ages. Thus, whether it is three factors or five may depend on whether a researcher judges that the five factors can be condensed into three. However, researchers rarely dispute the large amount of research evidence that demonstrates the existence of a personality structure that consists of either three or, most notably, five factors.

Criticism of the Big Five. Despite its popularity, the Five Factor Model has been criticized for its lack of theoretical explanations for the development and nature of the processes underlying some of its personality factors, in particular Openness, Agreeableness, and Conscientiousness (see Matthews & Deary, 1998, for a detailed discussion on this topic). This means that, even if the Big Five factors represent an accurate description of individuals, it is not known where differences in these traits arise from.

Another more recent criticism regards the relationship among the Big Five traits. Although the five factors are meant to be orthogonal or unrelated, when Neuroticism is reversed and scored in terms of emotional stability, several studies reported all five traits to be positively and significantly intercorrelated (Chamorro-Premuzic, 2011). Although these intercorrelations are usually modest, they may suggest that personality could be further simplified to more "basic" underlying traits, perhaps even one general factor. On the other hand, differential psychologists (such as Digman, 1997) have speculated on the possibility that these positive intercorrelations among the Big Five factors may be a reflection of sociably agreeable responding (or "faking good"), as high scores on the Big Five, at least in the United States and Western European countries, are more "desirable" than low scores (remember, this rule only applies when Neuroticism is reversed).

However, the Five Factor Model has shown good validity and reliability, leading most researchers to agree on the existence of five major personality dimensions, as well as the advantages of assessing these dimensions through the NEO Personality Inventory-Revised (NEO-PI-R) (Costa & McCrae, 1985, 1992). Perhaps the most obvious advantage of this consensus is the agreement itself, which allows researchers to compare and replicate studies on personality and other variables, providing a shared or common instrument to assess personality. Thus the Big Five are the "latitude and longitude" (Ozer & Reise, 1994, p. 361) along which any behavioral aspects can be consensually mapped.

In that sense, the choice of a unique instrument to assess individual differences in personality may be compared to that of a single and universal currency, software, or language, which provides a common ground for the trading and decoding of goods, information, or knowledge. Besides, the advantage of the NEO-PI-R Five Factor Model is that it accounts not only for a lay taxonomy of personality (based on the lexical hypothesis), but also for other established systems, which can be somehow "translated" into the Five Factor system. Thus, findings on other scales may be interpreted in terms of the Big Five personality traits, just as other currencies can be converted into dollars or euros according to a given exchange rate. For example, self-monitoring, or the extent to which an individual evaluates his or her behavior and the way this may be perceived by others (Snyder, 1987), could be largely explained in terms of high Agreeableness, Extraversion, and Neuroticism. On the other hand, authoritarianism (Adorno, Frenkel-Brunswick, Levinson, & Sanford, 1950) may be partly understood as a combination of low Openness and Agreeableness.

The Person-Situation Controversy

In introducing our discussion of the trait approach, the first assumption of trait psychology was made clear: Traits are consistent patterns in thoughts, feelings, and behavior, both across situations and over time. Indeed, the large amount of research evidence and the various theories presented in the rest of the section were based on this fundamental assumption of "consistency." On the one hand this assumption is intuitive. People behave consistently, which is why we consider them to have personalities in the first place. On the other hand, intuition also tells us that we don't act the same way in all situations. For instance, even if you consider yourself shy, you are probably not shy in all situations. You may be shy in some parties but sociable in others. Alternatively, you may generally be withdrawn when you meet new people but always gregarious around your friends. Similarly, acquaintances may consider you agreeable while your friends may say you are very opinionated. You may be lazy in some aspects but hardworking in others.

These statements probably do not baffle you—they seem common sense. However, this very fact raises a fundamental question: How consistent is the hypothesized consistency in the first place? That is, are we actually sociable, agreeable, or conscientious across most situations? Or does our behavior change depending on the situation that we are in (e.g., a friend's birthday party or a family gathering), the people we are with (close friends or work colleagues), or the role that we have (employee or boy or girl friend)? This question of the relative stability of traits across situations began over 30 years ago and came to be known as the person-situation controversy.

In the 1960s, the so-called situationist movement raised a fundamental attack against the trait theory. At the forefront of this movement was Walter Mischel. In his 1968 book *Personality and Assessment*, Mischel reviewed research evidence from the literature that revealed that people may in reality be behaving much less consistently than trait theories would predict. For instance, in a now classic study concerning children's honesty, behaviors such as cheating, lying, and stealing were only marginally correlated when assessed in different settings, such as the classroom, at home, or in social settings. The study unambiguously showed that a child that was dishonest in one setting (say cheated in class) was not necessarily dishonest in another (i.e., did not cheat when it came to sports). In fact, the correlations between these behaviors in different settings rarely exceeded .3. Mischel reviewed a number of studies that indeed seemed to show the same pattern of results. Following his review, Mischel's conclusion was clear: Evidence clearly showed that behavior is largely determined by the characteristics of the situation and not the characteristics of the person.

Unavoidably, this criticism was a fundamental challenge to the very existence of the field of personality psychology. In its mild form, the argument would suggest that personality is not very important. In its extreme form, it would suggest that personality does not exist.

Unsurprisingly, Mischel's attack on the trait concept was met by a vigorous counter-reaction from trait psychologists. The reaction took several forms. Some psychologists argued that Mischel was selective in his review of the evidence. Others contested the real-world value of the findings, most of which derived from studies carried out in artificial, or experimental, settings. A third criticism comes from the difficulty in actually determining that a given behavior is a manifestation of a given trait. Burping after a meal may be seen as a sign of disagreeableness or low Conscientiousness in western cultures, but in Korea, it is a polite response. Giving someone the finger and sticking one's tongue out at the person are different behaviors, but both act to signify consistent intentions (Hogan, 2007).

Importantly, psychologists pointed out that Mischel's dismissal of the significance of personality traits' predictive power based on the correlation value of .3 (even if this correlation was not underestimated) is incorrect. According to theorists, a correlation of this size can have substantial practical utility (Schmidt & Hunter, 1998). Indeed, such effect sizes would be considered very respectable, for instance, in medical practices. One extreme example is the negative correlation of .034 between aspirin consumption and heart attack, which was enough for researchers to conclude that a monumental breakthrough had been made (Rosenthal, 1990).

There is no doubt, however, that the most important counter-argument against Mischel's claims concerned his very concept of consistency. According to critics, Mischel significantly underestimated the true predictive power of traits because of a conceptual flaw. Specifically, they argued that the studies that he reviewed seemed to show low cross-situational consistency because they usually assessed specific behaviors only on single occasions. The above-mentioned study concerning children's honesty, for instance, would assess the correlation between dishonesty (e.g., cheating) displayed on one occasion (e.g., in class) and dishonesty displayed on another occasion (e.g., in sports). Theoretically, however, traits are meant to predict behavioral tendencies rather than single instances of particular behaviors. If the single occasion of cheating in class was not a reflection of a tendency, but rather reflected a rare incident, then the study did not measure the trait of dishonesty in the first place. Evidently, it is more difficult to predict a single behavior than aggregated behaviors (i.e., tendencies). It would be difficult to predict, for instance, whether a student will be sloppy with his homework, disorganized with his future goals, and often absent from his part-time job, just because he was late to class today. However, if the student was late to most classes (assuming no unavoidable reason existed), this prediction could be made with more confidence. Thus, according to trait theory, to determine whether people behave consistently from one situation to another, the behavior in each situation must be measured not just once, but on a number of occasions.

Of course, such data are difficult of obtain. Thus, the above argument posed by trait theorists was generally regarded a theoretical one. However, research carried out in the last decade has now also provided empirical backing for these claims. This line of research involves asking participants to report their current behavior, thoughts, and feelings multiple times a day for several days. This may include questions such as "During the past hour, how well does 'talkative' describe you?" Thus in addition to a standard personality questionnaire score indicating how extraverted, agreeable, conscientious, and so on a person is, researchers obtain how extraverted, agreeable, conscientious, and so on a person actually acts on average across various situations and over an extended period of time. Thus, this provides clear data on how little or how much behavior actually varies from situation to situation and over time.

Fleeson and Gallagher (2009) conducted a meta-analysis of 15 studies employing such an impressive methodology. Their results showed that traits were strongly predictive of everyday trait manifestation in behavior, with correlations between .42 and .56. The authors' conclusion was unambiguous:

> The resulting correlations comfortably surpassed .30 and even .40. This evidence combined with the strong predictions of life outcomes (Ozer & Benet-Martinez, 2006) casts strong doubt on the contention that traits do not predict behavior or that they have a .30 to .40 ceiling. In fact, far from being irrelevant, traits appear to be necessary for a full understanding of behavior, given the large amount of variance in trait manifestation in behavior they predict. (p. 1109)

PERSONALITY DISORDERS: WHEN OUR PERSONALITY IS ABNORMAL

In the previous sections, we talked about various theories of personality, including the dispositional paradigm, which states that there are quantitative differences or variability in the degree to which people display certain personality traits. However, our discussion focused on general or normal behavioral tendencies. A distinct field of psychology that focuses on abnormal behaviors, namely psychopathology or abnormal psychology, also informs our understanding of personality, and shall be examined briefly in this chapter. Given that psychopathology is a huge area of psychology, we shall focus primarily on the specific area of psychopathology that is most relevant in relation to personality, namely, personality disorders. These refer to relatively pervasive maladaptive patterns of behavior, thought, and emotionality, which interfere with one's or others' capacity to love and work. You may think of personality disorders at the crossroads between normal and abnormal personality; people who display them are rarely institutionalized or under treatment, but they behave in ways that are quite disruptive to society.

While personality disorders and other psychopathologies are predominantly examined in clinical settings, in recent years, personality psychologists have become increasingly involved in the attempt to explain the relationship between what is "normal" and "abnormal." The argument many of these researchers hold is that people with mental illnesses, in particular personality disorders, merely represent extreme departures of normal traits, rather than being categorically different from them. Indeed, personality disorders are defined as "long-standing, pervasive, and inflexible patterns of behavior and inner experience that deviate from the expectations of a person's culture" (Chamorro-Premuzic, 2011). As you can see, the definition has clear parallels with that of normal personality, with the lone difference being the deviant nature of the behaviors.

However, despite the growing support in the field of this dimensional view (the view that posits that there is just a thin line between normality and abnormality), in its current form, psychological disorders, including personality disorders, are classified in categorical terms, that is, as either normal or abnormal. In this section, we critically evaluate these views of psychopathology and personality disorders by (a) defining what is meant by abnormality, (b) presenting the most common forms of personality disorders, (c) discussing the origins or causes of these disorders, and (d) looking at if and how they can be treated.

How Do We Know if We Are Normal?

We all know people with eccentric, extreme, or very peculiar personalities. In fact, there are probably some people in the world who think of you in that way. The behavior of film stars or iconic pop singers also appears disconnected or outright strange (anyone who has watched daytime TV will know what we mean), and if you observe people around you—at a music festival, traveling by train, or walking in the streets—you will surely think that some of them are somewhat unusual, if not abnormal. But how do we judge whether a celebrity's, a friend's, or stranger's behavior is "abnormal"? Put in other words, by what means can we decide whether someone is in need of psychological treatment? This last question is important because it would be fairly easy for anybody liberal to argue that normality is just "in the eye of the beholder" and that we should not impose the label of abnormal or clinically ill on anybody; well, if that were the case, then we would not be able to help people get better.

Before embarking on this effort, we need to first establish what we mean by abnormal behavior. Defining abnormality is not an easy task. There is no single way to determine whether a person's behavior should be considered abnormal or not. Rather, clinical psychologists use consensual criteria for making this judgment, namely, deviation, suffering, and maladaptiveness (Davison & Neale, 1998).

The first criterion, deviation, refers to the statistical frequency or "oddity" of the behavior in question, with particular reference to social norms (i.e., formal or informal rules that specify how people are expected to behave; Chamorro-Premuzic, 2011). If behavior is odd or deviant (i.e., much higher or lower in frequency than one would expect) and violates social norms, then we may consider it abnormal. Having conversations with people who are not present or staring intensely at fellow passengers on a train may qualify as examples of this, because such behavior is uncommon and violates the informal rules of society.

The judgment about oddity, however, as straightforward as it may seem, is not always a simple one to make. The first difficulty comes in trying to decide exactly to what degree behavior should be expressed to be considered abnormal, or socially inappropriate. For instance, how rigid and inflexible does a person need to be, or how many hours a week does he or she need to work to be diagnosable with obsessive-compulsive personality disorder (see the list of symptoms of this disorder below)? Of course, these judgments will be influenced by cultural, religious, and even chronological factors. For instance, a man who does not allow his wife to go to nightclubs may be considered oppressive and unfriendly in some cultures but a good person in others. Similarly, a woman choosing her career before her family would in the 1940s have been viewed by many as psychologically unhealthy, even if this may today seem absurd. Thus, it is clear that we would need to consider more than simply how deviant behavior is. Indeed, even in similar cultures like the United Kingdom and the United States there are important differences in what is expected from people's everyday or social behaviors: For instance, it is far more acceptable and common to speak to a fellow passenger in the New York underground than in the London "tube" (something that highlights personality differences between the average Londoners and New Yorkers).

The second criterion for conceptualizing abnormality takes into account whether a given behavior is associated with the suffering of the individual (Davison & Neale, 1998). A person's behavior may be classified as mentally ill if the symptoms cause him or her great distress, physically or psychologically. However, even this definition is not without its limitations because suffering (or distress) is neither necessary nor sufficient to define abnormality. Not all mental illnesses are associated with suffering, and conversely, suffering in most cases does not result from mental illness. For instance, people with schizotypal personality disorder rarely experience strong emotions and seem to display little distress even when criticized or isolated. Conversely, someone could experience an unpleasant amount of anxiety in the presence of real threats (e.g., a soldier at war, a student before an exam, a job applicant before an interview), without being considered abnormal.

A final and critical criterion for defining abnormality is *maladaptiveness*. Most behaviors that are labeled as abnormal are maladaptive (or dysfunctional) either for the individual or for society. These include behaviors that interfere with a person's capacity to carry out everyday tasks, such as studying, working, and relating to others. Freud defined normality in terms of the capacity to love and work; we could think of maladaptiveness as anything that impairs these two major life goals (career and relationship success). A common example of maladaptive or disruptive behaviors is of people with personality disorders related to the anxious/fearful cluster of Axis 2 (see below), all of which *inhibit* the individual in the action and completion of what would normally be regarded as very simple, mundane tasks. Similarly, antisocial behaviors, such as violence, aggression, and inappropriate or inconsiderate use of public space, may be labeled abnormal because they interfere with the well-being of society.

As with the other definitions, however, there are some caveats with regard to the maladaptiveness criterion for defining abnormality. For instance, it is not always easy to decide what, exactly, normal functioning entails. Indeed, even if we think of it in Freud's terms, there are just too many manifestations of love and work to pick prototypical or ideal examples for them. In fact, few people agree about the degree to which work and love should be balanced; that is, how much time and effort should one devote to his or her career and relationships? In some cultures, it is almost heretic to be an unmarried but professionally successful woman after the age of 30; in others, it is a tragedy if you are not (and this is not because of *Sex and the City*). So, precisely how much of someone's studying, work performance, relationship plans, or social functioning should be impaired by symptoms for them to be considered abnormal? Clearly, we are still faced with the elementary problem of identifying cut-off points between normality and abnormality, and still unable to overcome the relativity of the context in this definition.

As can be seen, there are issues with each criterion for defining psychological disorders. These issues are often related to the subjectivity involved in making judgments about the criteria. Yet, we must remember that the issues are not necessarily unique to psychological disorders. Indeed, there is a degree of subjectivity also in medical practices and with physical illnesses. That is, we always have to decide when a physical injury or illness is serious (or deviant) enough to require doctors' help. As with decisions about psychological disorders, this judgment can be influenced by the patient's subjective feelings of suffering (or beliefs that the injury interferes with everyday life) as much as the observable damage. And as with mental illness, feelings of suffering will be reported in varying degrees by different people; some individuals believe they need professional help even with the most mundane injuries, whereas others refuse to report life-threatening ones.

Thus, despite specific limitations, the above approaches represent useful criteria for defining the boundaries between normal and abnormal behavior. While it may be tempting from a theoretical perspective to ignore these criteria (by claiming, for instance, that abnormality is simply a socially constructed notion), the practical implications of doing so would be unfortunate. As will be seen below, personality disorders are prevalent (they affect an estimated 10% to 15% of the population; Zimmerman & Coryell, 1989) and their disruptive nature is substantial, inhibiting educational, occupational, and interpersonal functioning.

Classifying Personality Disorders

As with normal personality dimensions, classification is a necessary first step toward introducing order into discussions of personality disorders. The two dominant taxonomies for diagnosing mental disorders (in general) are the *International Classification of Diseases, Injuries, and Causes of Death (ICD)* and the *Diagnostic and Statistical Manual of Mental Disorders (DSM)*. The *DSM*, the latest revision of which is *DSM-IV* (American Psychiatric Association, 1994), represents the state-of-the-art classification system in the United States and contains a detailed list of behaviors that must be present, and the time they need to be present in order for a diagnosis to be made.

While the most widely established personality taxonomy argues for five underlying "normal" personality factors, the *DSM-IV* includes a total of 10 different personality disorders. These are, in turn, divided into three different clusters, based on the idea that these disorders are characterized by either odd or eccentric behavior (cluster A), dramatic, emotional, or erratic behavior (cluster B), or anxious or fearful behavior (cluster C).

As mentioned above, despite the dimensional view of personality disorders, the classification of these disorders remains categorical. This, of course, introduces the question of reliability of the diagnoses. With earlier editions of the *DSM*, diagnoses of personality disorders were very unreliable. More recent studies have, however, demonstrated that the inclusion of more specific diagnostic criteria, as well as the use of structured interviews to assess disorders, can markedly improve diagnostic reliability. Nevertheless, in reality, very few clinicians use structured interviews, which means that the interrater reliability of diagnoses is likely to remain relatively low.

In addition to this concern, there are at least three main issues with the categorical view of personality disorders. First, while personality disorders are supposed to be stable over time, about half of the people who are initially diagnosed with a personality disorder do not receive the same personality disorder diagnosis when they are interviewed 1 and 2 years later. Second, these individuals still display some symptoms related to the disorder, just not to a level required for diagnoses, which means that people's problems with maladaptiveness may remain, even if not to the same extent. Finally, studies show that more than 50% of people diagnosed with a personality disorder meet the diagnostic criteria for another personality disorder, known as comorbidity, which makes it difficult to interpret what actually is the cause of the disorder and which disorder is the cause of the outcome (see Kring et al., 2007).

Considering these issues, it is not surprising that many mainstream personality researchers as well as clinicians are hoping that the next revision of the *DSM* shifts to a dimensional model of personality disorders. A dimensional approach would handle the comorbidity problem, including many of the reliability problems. Furthermore, several studies, including a meta-analysis, have shown that particular combinations of personality traits can be used to explain each of the 10 personality disorders. For instance, people with histrionic personality disorder tend to be substantially higher on Extraversion, while those with avoidant personality disorder tend to be substantially lower on Extraversion (Saulsman & Page, 2004).

Despite the benefits of a dimensional approach to personality disorders, however, there are some points that need to be considered. First, although a dimensional or *continuum* view of psychopathology may be advantageous, as well as theoretically more accurate, in practice it is still necessary to define a threshold for treatment. Medical doctors, for instance, need to define a threshold for high blood pressure in order to decide when a patient needs treatment, even though blood pressure differs along a continuum. Similarly, clinicians need to have cut-offs to be able to decide when personality scores are high or low enough to meet level for diagnosis. Thus, it may still be impossible to escape the arbitrariness and subjectivity of these judgments, although, admittedly, using cut-offs may be a more useful diagnostic system than the observations of symptoms.

A final key point is that some personality disorders appear to be more than just extremes or significant deviations from the norm. For instance, people with schizotypal personality disorder tend to experience perceptual oddities that others don't experience even in mild degrees, suggesting that people with these personality disorders may be qualitatively different from other people. Thus, the advantages of the dimensional view should not lead us to underestimate the importance of classifying personality disorders.

What Causes Abnormality?

The question "How do we define abnormality?" has been around a relatively short time compared to the question of "What causes abnormality?" (which is of course paradoxical). While the former question has only formally been addressed since the early 20th century, the latter stretches back to the ancient Chinese, Egyptians, Hebrews, Babylonians, and Greeks. As with most phenomena that seemed beyond human control, such as earthquakes, storms, and changing seasons, people in these ancient times used to attribute "disturbed" behavior to the displeasure of the gods, or the possession of demons (which often led to obscure rituals and treatments such as exorcism and trephination—the cutting of a hole in people's skulls—to release the evil demons).

The belief that mental disturbances were God's punishments was, however, rejected by many prominent scholars of Ancient Greece. For instance, Hippocrates (the father of modern medicine c. 460 BC–c. 370 BC) attributed psychological illness to a physiological dysfunction. He argued that mental disorders are diseases of the brain. Conversely, Plato (c. 423 BC–c. 347 BC) contested that disorders should be understood in terms of intrapsychical conflicts. Plato was convinced that mental disorders were "all in the mind." Today, Hippocrates's and Plato's views are referred to as the somatogenic and psychogenic hypotheses of psychopathology and are still the two most dominant approaches to the causes of mental disorders, roughly corresponding to the notorious debate of "nature versus nurture."

Biological Approaches: Is Mental Illness a "Nature" Issue?
Technological developments in the past 50 years have caused an unprecedented increase in research into the *biological* causes of psychopathology. Broadly speaking, this area can be divided into the genetic paradigm and the neuroscience paradigm. The genetic paradigm deals with the question of whether certain disorders are heritable, and whether genes are "responsible"

for abnormal behavior. Through the use of studies examining identical and nonidentical twins (see the next chapter for details), research has shown that genetics clearly has an important part in the etiology of several personality disorders.

The neuroscience paradigm, on the other hand, investigates the biochemical correlates of mental illness, notably the role of *neurotransmitters*, the *structure and function of the brain*, and the *autonomic nervous system* of the mentally ill. While research in this area is advancing fast, all three aspects of the neuroscience paradigm have already been found to play a role in personality disorders.

Psychological Approaches: Is Mental Illness a "Nurture" Issue? While the somatogenic approach focuses primarily on the biological causes of mental illness, the thesis of the psychogenic paradigm is that many mental disorders have a psychological origin. There are three major psychogenic theories of psychopathology, namely, the psychoanalytic, the behaviorist, and the cognitive. We'll briefly discuss these here.

In the early 20th century, the psychoanalytic theory of abnormal behavior emerged. Its proponent, Sigmund Freud, believed that psychological disorders, including personality disorders, result from various unresolved conflicts and repressed wishes from early childhood. For instance, he argued that obsessive-compulsive personality traits are caused by fixation at the *anal* stage of psychosexual development (see the section The Psychodynamic Approach to Personality and Freud).

The second major psychological account of mental disorders, the behaviorist account, viewed abnormality as a form of learned (dysfunctional) behavior. According to the behaviorist paradigm, symptoms are merely the consequence of reinforced or punished behaviors; in this case, behaviors that would be seen as dysfunctional or disordered by society. For instance, according to behaviorists, avoidant personality disorder results from learned behavior in childhood, such as being taught to fear people and situations that others would regard as harmless.

In contrast, cognitive theorists argue that psychological disorders are the result of maladaptive perceptions and interpretations of events. For example, people with narcissistic personality disorder are thought to have a fragile self-esteem; however, unlike healthy individuals (with similar issues), they employ maladaptive cognitive biases in order to maintain an inflated self-view. These include overestimating their own attractiveness and ability, incessantly attributing success to their ability rather than to luck, and having a distorted view of how they are viewed by others (e.g., others must be jealous of me). Thus, according to cognitive theorists, the dysfunctional thought patterns cause the disorders.

An Integrative Approach. Although the psychogenic and somatogenic approaches offer us valuable information independently of each other, today the most widely accepted theory of psychopathology is an integrative perspective, often referred to as the diathesis-stress model (also known as the vulnerability-stress model) of psychopathology.

According to the diathesis-stress model (Cicchetti & Rogosch, 1996; Monroe & Simons, 1991), psychological disorders are caused by a combination of biological, psychological, and social factors. In simple terms, this model explains mental illness as a byproduct of inherited vulnerability (diatheses) and stressful life experiences (stress). For instance, Linehan and Heard (1999) argue that borderline personality disorder is caused by a biological predisposition, combined with an invalidating (i.e., disregarded, disrespected, and punished) family environment.

It should be noted that vulnerability (the predisposition or "diathesis") can have biological origins (at the level of genes, brain structures, neurotransmitters, and hormones) as well as environmental origins such as poverty or severe trauma. However, stressors are always environmental and can include traumatic experiences (such as loss of a loved one), as well as ordinary events (such as being stuck in traffic).

How Can We Treat Abnormality? Treatment of psychological disorders, including personality disorders, can broadly be divided into two approaches: the biological and the psychological. Consistent with the biological perspective, there is a wide array of psychoactive drugs that clinicians can prescribe for their patients. Indeed, the use of psychoactive drugs has increased dramatically in the past two decades. For instance, between 1988 and 2000, antidepressant use among adults nearly tripled (National Center for Health Statistics, 2004), and antipsychotic drugs are now a multibillion-dollar industry (Horne, Weinman, Barber, & Elliott, 2005).

So are these drugs effective? First, it is worth noting that most research examining the effectiveness of drug therapy has focused on the Axis I disorders of the *DSM*. Nevertheless, the available evidence shows that psychoactive drugs can be effective in the treatment of personality disorders. For instance, antipsychotic drugs (e.g., risperidone) have been found to be effective in the treatment of schizotypal personality disorder (Koenigsberg et al., 2003). A variety of drugs, such as fluvoxamine, lithium, olanzapine, and antiseizure medications (you can look all of them up on Wikipedia), appear useful in the treatment of borderline personality disorder (e.g., Hollander et al., 2001); although given that patients with this disorder often abuse drugs, there are limitations to drug therapy for borderline personality disorder.

In addition to medication, several psychological treatments have been shown to be successful in the treatment of personality disorders. For instance, one study showed that brief psychodynamic treatment reduced the symptoms of histrionic personality disorder and disorders in the anxious/fearful cluster (Winston et al., 1994). This type of treatment may involve the therapist attempting to bring to the surface the patient's specific childhood experiences that have led to current maladaptive perceptions and tendencies, before attempting to alter them. Cognitive behavioral therapists, on the other hand, aim to persuade the patient to see that it is their irrational thinking that lies behind their problematic behavior. Once the patient accepts that his or her thought processes or common assumptions (known as schemata) about things are causing the dysfunction, various behavioral techniques are offered as support. For instance, social skills training, which is one aspect of behavioral therapy, has been found to be helpful for people with avoidant personality disorder to be more assertive with others (Alden, 1989). Similarly, despite a common belief that psychopathy is nearly impossible to treat, a meta-analysis found positive therapeutic effects of studies employing cognitive behavioral techniques (Salekin, 2002).

Although this line of research is encouraging, three points should be noted in regard to the treatment of personality disorders. First, the use of antipsychotic drugs remains controversial. Drugs do not help everyone and they rarely cure a disease. In addition, they may have unpleasant side effects (in particular, the classic antipsychotics and antimanic medication). Nevertheless, while medications do not cure a disease and cannot treat everyone, they do allow many people to function and adapt to society, sometimes completely. In addition, much of modern medication does not have the side effects of classic drugs.

A second criticism relates to psychotherapy. While existing evidence is promising in regard to this type of treatment, controversy exists about the research standards in this research. In particular, the methodology used in the studies often does not allow for the effects of psychotherapy to be isolated because most of the studies do not include a control group. Thus it is not possible to know whether the improvements were due to treatment, spontaneous natural recovery, placebo effect, or some other factor. On the other hand, psychotherapy has been shown to be effective with many other Axis I disorders, providing some reason for optimism regarding the positive results found in these studies.

A final issue is the notion of stability of personality disorders, which is, of course, incompatible with the idea of treatment. Indeed, many personality disorders may be too ingrained to be changed thoroughly. While it may be unrealistic to expect complete changes to a person's underlying personality, therapists can nonetheless find ways to change certain behaviors, attitudes, and thoughts, in order to help people find more adaptive ways of approaching life.

Some Final Remarks. In the preceding sections, we have highlighted some of the main definitions or approaches to normality and abnormality. What we wanted to emphasize is that defining normality is not rocket science—there are many ways of doing it and each way has advantages and disadvantages. We also hope we made it clear that there are many more disadvantages than advantages in not defining it (this really is the worst case scenario). To recap: Unless we have certain consensual criteria—even if they are not perfect—we will never be able to provide professionals (clinicians, psychiatrists, psychologists, etc.) with a frame of reference to classify and assess problematic symptoms; this is equivalent to not diagnosing physical illnesses simply because "who are we to claim that someone is ill?" The issue, then, is quite straightforward: Either we agree on some criteria for determining who is normal and who isn't—and that means classifying behavior—or we just cannot treat people's problems, which implies not helping them cope with their suffering and disruptive lives.

That said, one clear reminder of the complexities of deciding what is normal and abnormal is the recent idea that even severe forms of mental illness could be understood as deviations of otherwise normal patterns of thought, behavior, and affect. Indeed, the only difference between being paranoid and being somewhat skeptical and difficult to fool is the degree to which the person is right about his or her suspicions and the degree to which those thoughts are uncontrollable and psychologically disturbing. Likewise, feeling extremely anxious or sad may be okay in the context of tragic or dangerous events (and you may be worse off if you are experiencing the opposite emotions in those contexts). Although researchers have still to agree on where exactly the line between abnormality and normality should be drawn, there are certainly many grey areas, which is where we conceptualize personality disorders.

CONCLUSION

We all have an inherent interest in personality. This is because personality essentially is what makes us who we are. It is what differentiates us from other people and what makes us unique. If we all behaved differently across situations and over time, that is, in unpredictable ways, then there would be no such thing as personality. Some theoretical positions indeed argue just that. However, the idea that people differ from one another in their typical ways of behaving, thinking, and feeling is as old as medicine, and most of us intuitively believe in it.

In this chapter, we have presented the most salient psychological theories of personality. They attempt to describe what personality is and how it should be viewed and analyzed. These theories differ, and sometimes substantially so, in their positions. For instance, psychodynamic theory sees personality as dynamic processes and struggles hidden beneath the mask of behavior; something that we cannot access consciously but that governs our thoughts, feelings, and overt behavior. Social cognitive theory, on the other hand, views personality as a set of cognitions—beliefs, expectancies, and goals governing our behavior. These cognitions are very much conscious and in the here and now. It follows that this theory is concerned with how social relationships, learning mechanisms, and cognitive processes jointly contribute to personality and behavior. A notable difference between these two theories is their view on the flexibility, or malleability, of personality. That is, while psychodynamic theory sees personality as essentially fixed from early childhood, social cognitive theory sees personality as flexible and as constantly evolving.

The notion of flexibility is taken even further by the behaviorist theory of personality. According to behaviorists, personality is merely current behavior determined by past experiences and the present context. This means that present and future experiences will also influence (and change) future behavior. This never-ending environment-behavior cycle essentially means that there is no such thing as "inner" stable patterns of thought, feelings, or behavior, and therefore no such thing as personality. This stand was also taken by the situationalist movement, which suggested that stability—and therefore personality—is essentially an illusion.

The behaviorist and situational theories in effect dismiss the notion of personality and directly challenge the discipline of personality psychology. Indeed, they even halted the advance of research in this field for several years during the 60s and 70s. However, they have not withstood the test of empirical investigation. Today, the view that there are consistent patterns of thought, emotion, and behavior is well established. Most psychologists in the field also agree that these stable patterns can be categorized into a few "broader" patterns of behavior.

The most widely accepted framework for classifying these patterns—the Big Five—posits five broad (or "basic") traits. These five traits are sufficient to describe the personality of any person and how he or she differs from others. The vast amount of empirical evidence in its support has persuaded most differential psychologists to conceptualize personality in terms of these five traits. Regardless of whether this framework will continue to be replicated in the future, one thing is clear: The trait approach provides a very clear answer to the question of "how," that is, how people differ from each other. If personality makes us who we are, then the trait approach to personality is certainly the most useful for telling us who we actually are, and how we differ from others.

NOTE

[1]We will give you a detailed explanation of correlations in the coming chapters, but for now we should give you a simple account of correlation, which is simply the extent to which two variables, for example, traits and behavior, are related; a correlation of $r = .1$ indicates a perfect association, whereas a correlation of $r = .0$ indicates that there is no association between the variables in question.

Why Are Some People Different From Others? Understanding the Causes of Personality

n the previous chapter, we discussed some of the major theories of personality. In particular, we examined the so-called "trait approach," which many personality experts see as the most useful approach for examining individual differences in personality. Within this approach, the Five Factor Model (FFM) has become the global language for describing both differences and similarities between people's consistent patterns of behavior, thought, and emotion; Just as we measure a region's climate in Celsius or a person's height in meters, we can describe what a person is like by reference to his or her Extraversion, Neuroticism, Openness, Agreeableness, and Conscientiousness levels (though laypeople will use less technical terms for each of these factors). Indeed, the FFM provides a rather general classification of human personality, enabling us to compare people from every culture, as well as within a given society. So, when we hear someone say "my friend and I are very similar," the FFM enables us to assess "how" (for instance, we are both sociable or extraverted).

In addition to the question of *how* people differ, however, personality researchers also want to know *why*. For example, we could ask ourselves why some people are talkative and outgoing, while others seem shy and reserved. Or, why some are relaxed before an exam or comfortable in front of a crowd, while others experience anxiety when facing those situations. These questions refer not to how a person behaves (and thinks or feels) but rather to *why* they behave the way they do. That is, what is the reason behind a person's extraverted, agreeable, or conscientious personality? Is it the way they were brought up by their parents? Is it the school they went to and the education they received? Or is it perhaps simply the genes they inherited from their extraverted and agreeable mother or conscientious father? Questions about the causes of personality allude to one of the oldest debates in psychology, namely the nature versus nurture debate.

When we reflect upon these questions, we wonder to what degree we may be biologically predisposed to act in certain ways. Laypeople tend to believe that personality simply reflects the various life experiences that we are exposed to, such that a person's character is the result of his or her life experiences. In contrast, more and more personality researchers seem obsessed with emphasizing the genetic and biological factors underlying individual differences. From twin studies to molecular genetic studies, the quest for the biological basis of personality has excited a growing number of personality psychologists and neuroscientists. As will be seen in this chapter, although there is mixed enthusiasm among the wider psychological community about the success of this enterprise, it is quite clear that nurture and nature are not mutually exclusive, but that they interact and have reciprocal effects. Around the time this book was being written, a student of psychology approached one of us after a class and asked: "Can people change their personalities?" This is an important question from the standpoint of scientific inquiry, of course. However, many people will probably also find this question to be personally relevant. After all, most of us have at least one bad habit that we would like to change (if you don't think that's your case, you may be a narcissist … or perfect). Many people would also like to change some generic aspects of their behaviors; for instance, how proactive they are, how organized they are, how confident they are, how kind or ruthless they are, and so on. These concern changing at least some aspects of our personality.

It is interesting to note that self-improvement products and services constitute a vast (and growing) market, particularly in the western world. According to a market report, the U.S. self-improvement market is worth $9.6 billion, with annual growth rates reaching 25% (Marketdata Enterprises, 2005). To some extent, most of these products and services are focused on personality change: how to change one's ways of doing things, thinking about things, or feeling about them. Some very popular self-help books will tell you to acquire new habits—habits that are common to all successful people (Covey, 1989). Others will tell you that "anyone can do it" (Bannatyne, 2007). The message here is often to be *more* determined, *more* assertive, *more* in control, *less* negative, and so on. In brief, self-help products tell us that we *can* change the way we think, the way we feel, and the way we act; they tell us that we can *change our personality.* The fact that these products and services are so popular indicates that the question of change in itself may be a very significant and personally relevant one for a lot of people. So, the question for psychological and empirical enquiry, therefore, is as follows: Can people change?

While the answer may be complex, people are often divided between one of two opinions: nature or nurture. That is, for some, personality is determined by biological factors and people cannot change. A shy person will always be shy, a lazy person will always be lazy, and a disorganized person will always be disorganized. Others believe that personality is formed through various life experiences and by the environment, which means that people can indeed change (whether they actually do is a different question). A shy person can become outgoing and assertive, a lazy person can become hardworking and determined, and a disorganized person can become disciplined and efficient. Unfortunately, however, the relationship between nature and nurture is not as straightforward. As you will see, there are additional and differing ways in which nature and nurture can interact to "form" personality (i.e., stable patterns of behavior, thoughts, and feelings), and the causality underlying this relationship is not always one-directional.

The aim of this chapter is twofold: first, to describe the main causal theories of personality, which deal with the question of *why*; that is, why people differ in various ways. Second, and following from the first point, to address the question of personality change and development; that is, whether people can change, and if so, the extent to which they actually do. In the final section, we will discuss the main factors that contribute to change.

GENES AND PERSONALITY

To tackle the first question of why personality differences between people exist, psychologists have generally occupied three different fields of investigation: the genetic, the biochemical, and the evolutionary. While these paradigms are all focused on the nature part of the argument, they are useful for assessing the relative influence of both biological *and* environmental factors on personality.

While psychologists have been interested in the biological/genetic underpinnings of personality since the times of the ancient Greeks, the greatest progress in this area has been made only in the past 50 to 60 years. The most successful and influential of these attempts have undoubtedly been in the field of *behavioral genetics*. Nevertheless, more recent research within *molecular genetics* and *evolutionary psychology* has contributed a great deal to our understanding of the biological roots of personality. Before we outline the major findings from each of these fields, however, it is useful to delineate some basic principles of the discipline of *genetics*.

Genetics as a discipline deals with the molecular structure and function of genes. Everything we inherit—traits that are common to all people and those that are unique to only one person—is passed through biological components known as genes. When we talk about inherited traits, we often refer to physical attributes, such as hair color, eye color, and height, because these are traits we can observe. Nevertheless, the discussion of heritability, as we will see, is not limited to physical traits, and extends also to psychological traits.

As everybody knows, genes are passed onto us by our biological parents. We inherit 23 pairs of chromosomes—one of each pair from each of our biological parents—and these chromosomes are made up of thousands of genes. A core function of genes is to synthesize proteins that build, maintain, and regulate our bodies. In most basic terms, therefore, genes can be seen as basic bodily components that direct the biological development of the organism. Given that around 99.9% of the genetic makeup is identical for all people (indeed humans and chimpanzees share roughly 98% of their genes), minute differences in how certain genes synthesize proteins appear to somehow snowball into visible behavioral differences between individuals (this is the bit we observe or measure). However, we should note that genes do not influence behavior directly. That is, there is no gene causing differences in intelligence or Extraversion between people. Rather, genes influence behavior and psychology indirectly, by affecting the biological functioning of the body (e.g., nervous system, hormonal regulation, etc.).

Behavioral Genetics

Now that we have outlined some basic components of the human genome, we will provide an overview of the three disciplines that have informed our understanding of the causes of personality, starting with behavioral genetics.

Behavioral genetics is an area of psychology concerned with the assessment of the relative contribution of genetic and nongenetic influences on various individual variables of difference, including personality, intelligence, and psychological disorders. It attempts to estimate the degree to which individual differences are the product of experience (e.g., learning, education, acquired values, etc.) or of "genetically imprinted" information.

One of the salient psychological traits examined in behavioral genetics research is intelligence or cognitive ability. Indeed, the link between genetics and intelligence remains one of the most controversial topics in psychology. This is hardly surprising: If we acknowledge that there are individual differences in intelligence, a natural question that follows is "Why?" Put differently, if we accept that some people are smarter than others, then the question is as follows: Are these individual differences caused by genes or by the environment?

One problem is that common sense is pretty useless when it comes to answering this question. Consider, for instance, the rather typical case of a family of four—two parents and two children. Imagine that the parents in this family are very bright and wealthy. Imagine, in addition, that the children in this family also are very bright. Would that be sufficient evidence for the fact that the children's intelligence was inherited from their parents? Although one would certainly think so in the case of height, eye color, and other physical traits, when it comes to intelligence or psychological traits, the answer could be different. Indeed, an equally plausible explanation for the higher intelligence levels of these children would be that they have received a good education because of their higher socioeconomic status. Furthermore, it would also be possible that their parents exposed them to books, quizzes, academic tasks, and other intellectually stimulating environments, which nurtured their levels of intelligence. Thus, the children's intelligence may, in actual fact, have little to do with genetic inheritance, but rather have indirectly been affected by the upbringing provided by the smart parents.

As you can see from this scenario, the question has two plausible answers—and the same problem applies to personality and other psychological traits. We could say that a person is more sociable, assertive, and determined than another, because of his or her genes. On the other hand, we could also argue that it is because they were raised in a competitive environment, where they had to fight for attention and failure was not an option. Again, logically, both arguments may be equally valid. So, how can we determine whether a psychological quality is inherited or not? This question concerns a more fundamental issue in science, namely the difference between prediction and explanation. So, while it is common sense that children are more likely to resemble their parents in personality and intelligence, the reasons for this may not be obvious. In other words, although we can predict a child's personality and cognitive ability profile from their parents' profiles, there are different explanations for that association.

The task of behavioral geneticists is to determine the relative contribution of genetic heritability and environmental influences. To do this, they employ two main research methods: twin studies and adoption studies. Twin studies provide a very convenient and scientifically rigorous way to determine biological versus environmental effects. They are often referred to as "experiments of nature" because they enable researchers to capitalize on the systematic differences that exist between identical and nonidentical twins. Identical or *monozygotic* twins develop from the same fertilized egg and therefore share 100% of their genes, whereas nonidentical or *dizygotic* twins develop from two separately fertilized eggs and share around 50% of their genes (this is the same amount as siblings share with each other, and parents share with their children). Thus, by comparing identical and nonidentical twins, researchers are able to "manipulate" (though naturally rather than experimentally) the genetic variability between individuals, while keeping constant the environmental variability (i.e., the environment that the twins shared as they were growing up). It follows that if there is a genetic underpinning for personality, then identical twins should be more alike than nonidentical twins, because they have a higher genetic resemblance. If identical twins display no more similarity to one another (in terms of their personality, IQ, or any other trait) than do nonidentical twins, then we can conclude that genes are not involved in the formation of that trait and that the environment is therefore the sole cause of individual differences in personality.

The alternative method for determining whether personality is inherited or not is adoption studies. Adoption studies are often referred to as "experiments of society" because they allow researchers to manipulate the environmental variability, while keeping constant the genetic variability. To illustrate this method, consider a child, Jasmine, who is separated from her biological parents and siblings immediately after birth. She is adopted by another family (i.e., her adoptive family). Imagine that the adoptive parents also have two biological children. After many years, Jasmine, who is now a grown woman, is reunited with her biological family. They meet for the first time in more than 20 years. Now imagine that a group of psychologists, as part of a research study, administer a personality test to Jasmine and the members of both her adoptive and biological families (i.e., parents and siblings of both families). She has not met her biological family since she was an infant. The question is as follows: Would we expect Jasmine to be more similar to her adoptive parents or her biological parents?

As you can probably see, such case studies are extremely useful for examining the relative contribution of genes and of the environment on personality differences. It follows that if environment and upbringing exert the main influence on a person's personality, then Jasmine should be far more similar to her adoptive family members than her biological family members. If genes exert the main influence, the opposite should be true.

A more robust but rather rare variation of this method involves doing research with identical twins reared apart (i.e., separated at young age). In these studies, we have biologically related individuals who share 100% of their genes but have been exposed to completely different environments for most of their lives. Again, if the environment and life experiences are central to personality, then identical twins reared apart should not be very similar to one another, or at least much less similar than they are to their adoptive family members. Any similarity between identical twins should be attributed to genetic factors (or chance).

The Relative Contribution of Genes

As discussed, the methods used by behavioral geneticists are extremely useful for disentangling the relative contribution of genes versus environment and provide a reliable method for addressing this complicated issue. In statistical terms, indicators of genetic influences are represented by the so-called heritability estimate (HE). The HE tells us how much of the variability between people's personalities is accounted for by genes. For instance, if we find that identical twins show no more resemblance to each other than nonidentical twins, or if adopted children have no resemblance to their biological parents, then we would estimate the heritability to be .0. That is, 0% of the variability in personality is accounted for by genes. If, on the other hand, identical twins were far more similar to each other than nonidentical twins, or if there was a high resemblance between adopted children and their biological parents, we would esti-mate the heritability to be closer to 1. That is, 100% of the vari-ability is accounted for by genes.

So, how heritable is personality? A good amount of research has been carried out to address this question. In a highly influ-ential meta-analysis, Zuckerman (1991) concluded that there is a substantial hereditary aspect underlying most personality dimensions, and that environmental influences on personality traits are far less important than genetic ones. In his review of the literature, Zuckerman found some consistent results; corre-lations between identical twins are always higher than between nonidentical twins. Indeed, in most studies examined, the cor-relations for identical twins were at least twice as large as those for nonidentical twins. Several other reviews and influential studies have been carried out in the past decades, and findings seem to show a consistent pattern; virtually every personality trait studied has a substantial heritability. Recent estimates of the heritability of personality traits suggest it ranges from .4 to .6 (Spinath & Johnson, 2011), that is, between 40% and 60% of the variability in personality is due to genetic factors (in case you were wondering, the heritability of intelligence ranges from .5 to .8). Given that a large portion of the variance will be accounted for by measurement error (because our measures are not perfect), the *relative* contribution of environmental fac-tors is at least somewhat smaller. Indeed, the genetic influences on personality have often been found to be quite substantial. The most compelling evidence derives from studies with identi-cal twins who grew up in completely different environments and had never met, but had almost identical vocational inter-ests, hobbies, and pets (Lykken, Bouchard, McGue, & Tellegen, 1993)! These studies are not abundant but they do remind us of the hidden power of genetics underlying many emblematic psychological traits.

At this point, we should note an important and sometimes overlooked point: HE is an estimate of the influence of genes on individual differences *within a population*. That is, it does not necessarily show the degree to which genes explain the characteristics of one specific person. For instance, although the HE of reading ability may be high, whether a person can read or not will also be influenced by whether he or she has been exposed to books and other reading material. Thus, heritability is a population estimate and only implies a statistical propensity rather than an inescapable necessity to have a particular characteristic. Second, HEs are specific to time and place. That is, different HEs for the same personality trait could be found in different populations. For instance, when environmental influences on individuals in one population are very diverse and wide (such as in large cosmopolitan cities), the HE is likely to decrease. On the other hand, when conditions within an environment are homogenous (such as in small villages), the HE is likely to increase. Thus, HE should be seen as an estimate associated with variation in a population in a given study, rather than an explanation for one particular person's behavior.

The Contribution of Environment

Although research on the heritability of personality has clearly demonstrated the importance of genes and biological factors underlying individual differences in personality differences, it has also illuminated the relative contribution of the environment. Given that genes do not explain nearly as much as 100% of the variance in personality, the same studies provide evidence for the importance of the environment (although, as mentioned before, one cannot simply subtract the genetic variance from the total variance to obtain the estimate of the environmental influence, but rather needs to take into account error variance associated with measurement issues).

Before we outline the research on environmental influences, however, we should note that behavioral geneticists distinguish between two types of environment: *shared environment* and *non-shared environment*. Shared environment entails the aspects of the environment that are the same for people within a family.

This could include being reared in the same household, by the same parents, having the same socioeconomic status, the same dog, and so on. Nonshared environment, on the other hand, would include aspects of the environment that are unique to each individual. This could include differences between how children are treated by their parents, different friends they hang out with, different schools they go to, different hobbies they have, and so on.

In behavioral genetics research, the question of the relative influence of shared versus nonshared environment has been examined in two ways: (a) by looking at the resemblance of biologically unrelated (i.e., adoptive) siblings who have been brought up in the same family (shared environment) and (b) by comparing biological siblings raised apart (non-shared environment) with those reared in the same household. In essence, if shared environment is more important, adoptive siblings reared together should show high similarities, and biological siblings reared together should be far more similar than those reared apart. So what does the evidence show? The results are quite clear: On average, the correlation for personality traits between genetically unrelated siblings brought up in the same household is nearly zero (Zuckerman, 1991). Similarly, evidence shows that biological siblings raised together seem no more similar than those raised apart (Plomin & Daniels, 1987). Indeed, the overall distribution for the relative contribution of genes and environment appears to be: around 40% due to genetic factors, 35% due to the effects of nonshared environments, and 5% due to shared environments (the rest being due to measurement error; Dunn & Plomin, 1990).

The relatively small contribution of shared environment (i.e., same household) may seem surprising. After all, the vast number of theories in developmental psychology long emphasized the importance of specific strategies for bringing up children. It should be noted, however, that while it is easy to interpret such findings as indicating that upbringing or parental styles are relatively unimportant, this is misleading. Rather, the implication is that differences between families are much less important than differences within families. In essence, the results stress the importance of differential treatment of children by parents, rather than undermining the importance of parenting. Nevertheless, there is certainly an indication that the experiences unique to the individual members of the family, such as relationships with different friends, colleagues, and teachers, may have been underestimated.

The Gene-Environment Interaction

At this point, it may seem as though we have an approximate indication of the relative contribution of genes and the relative contribution of environment—and, therefore, a relatively clear answer with respect to the nature/nurture debate. However, the relationship between the environment and genes is not that simple. So far we have examined the relative and *distinct* influence of environment and genes on personality; in reality, though, the environment and the genes interact in a more complex manner. In particular, apart from having a direct influence on personality, both the genes and the environment can have a direct influence on one another. For instance, while an environmental factor such as parenting is likely to have a direct effect on later personality, its effect is not independent of genes. This is because genetic predispositions shape the responses we evoke from the environment (e.g., our parents). That is, differences in people's genetic makeup, which influence their appearance and behavior, will bring about different reactions from others. For instance, an attractive child may evoke different reactions from parents and peers than a nonattractive child. Furthermore, although the child is more attractive than average, it is the fact that she/he will be more likely to be *treated* as attractive that in turn may boost the child's confidence (or spoil her/him). Similarly, a child with an agreeable disposition, who acts in a friendly manner, may cause parents and peers to respond differently to him/her than to a child with a disagreeable disposition. For instance, parents and peers may be more positive and responsive to one child, while being more dismissive and avoidant in relation to the other. These responses, thus, depend not only on inherent tendencies of parents and peers but also on the child's dispositional traits.

In addition to influencing how people generally act (e.g., agreeable/disagreeable), genetic dispositions also influence how they *react* to the environment. For instance, an anxious and introverted child may react uneasily to a surprise party, whereas a calm and extraverted child may react positively to the same event. Again, such differential reactions are likely to shape how others treat the person in the future (e.g., avoid surprising this person).

Finally, our genetic dispositions not only shape the environment we are in (through our general actions and reactions within it), but also influence whether we will find ourselves in a particular environment in the first place. Indeed, a person with a genetic predisposition toward Extraversion is likely to select environments that are more stimulating and social, whereas a person predisposed toward introversion may choose environments that are quiet and lonely, and so on. This is what some behavior-geneticists refer to as "niche-picking" (see Chamorro-Premuzic, 2011).

These theoretical and empirical behavioral genetics models indicate that individual differences in personality are not necessarily the result of relative and distinct environmental or genetic influences, but, rather, the result of a joint and interactive two-way process between these factors. Given this interaction between genes and the environment, one could argue that the nature–nurture debate is in essence unfounded. In actual fact, it is always both nature *and* nurture (or nature *via* nurture) that affect observed differences between individuals, and the relative contribution of each will often depend on the specific circumstances.

MOLECULAR GENETICS

So far we have reviewed studies that provide evidence for a genetic basis of personality. Yet, as you may have noticed, behavioral genetics research methods can only estimate these effects indirectly. That is, despite its label, behavioral genetics research does not conduct studies that involve biology or chemistry; in other words, it does not carry out direct investigations of the genes that are involved in individual differences in personality functioning. Consequently, genetic effects are *inferred* (via statistical probabilities) rather than observed directly.

Nevertheless, in more recent times, an area known as *molecular genetics* has achieved unprecedented progress in this area (Spinath & Johnson, 2011). By mapping behavioral differences onto particular genes, molecular genetics has attempted to find causal links between genes and personality traits. Typically, this research examines correlation between different genes and personality scores. In this so-called *candidate gene approach*, researchers usually identify a small candidate region of the genome in which the trait gene lies, before conducting statistical tests to identify the specific gene associated with the trait.

For instance, Lesch et al. (1996), in a now seminal study, identified a mutation in the serotonin transporter gene associated with individual differences in trait anxiety (Neuroticism). Furthermore, this finding has been replicated in a number of studies (mostly using NEO-PI-R Neuroticism), indicating that serotonin-mediated variation in the brain is likely to affect individuals' trait anxiety levels (Sen, Burmeister, & Ghosh, 2004). A very consistent association found in research is also that between the neuroreceptor gene, the D4 dopamine receptor, and sensation-seeking, a trait that shows considerable overlap with Openness to experience from the Big Five model, as well as the Psychoticism trait from Eysenck's model (Chamorro-Premuzic, 2011). Specifically, the length of the DNA marker for the *DRD4* genes seems to be one of the causes of higher sensation-seeking, such that longer alleles in the DNA structure are associated with higher sensation-seeking and vice versa. This indicates that sensation-seeking may be interpreted as an attempt to compensate for lower levels of dopamine.

As mentioned above, the candidate gene approach requires researchers to identify candidate genes for investigation. Evidently, this method makes the job of finding the right candidates difficult. Furthermore, it increases the chances of a significant effect of particular "unexamined" genes to be missed. While this has been an obvious limitation of previous research, some state-of-the-art methodology is now addressing these issues. In particular, some recent advances in molecular biology and genetics include techniques that make it possible to search the entire genome for genetic variants that may be related to psychological traits. These so-called *genome-wide association studies* examine hundreds of thousands gene variations that may be involved in individual differences in behavioral traits. Indeed, these studies now reveal effects of genes that have not previously been suspected of having a role in the behavioral manifestations under study. With these and other techniques, an increasing number of genes are being identified as underlying the variation in behavioral traits, and molecular genetics research continues to generate new evidence on the neurobiology of individual differences with fast pace.

At this point, it may appear to you as though researchers are close to some kind of "genetic profiling" for deducting, or "reading," a person's personality—something previously only imagined in science-fiction movies. However, this, for better or for worse, is not the case. There are several reasons for this. First, genetic profiling is a difficult endeavor—even when there is a single-gene effect in the candidate region. For instance, although it is now well known that mutation in one particular gene (the *HTT* gene) is associated with Huntington disease, it took researchers 10 years from the initial linkage finding to the identification of the specific gene (Bates, 2005).

More importantly, unlike single-gene disorders, researchers are finding that complex personality traits reflect the operation of multiple genes, each of which, individually, may account for only a small effect on personality. Indeed, one thing that molecular genetics research does seem to indicate is that we should not search for (or expect to find) specific genes for specific personality traits, or indeed for any other individual differences. Personality traits consist of complex behavioral manifestations and therefore they should be understood with complex and multiple causal linkages. Thus, it is more appropriate to see personality and its causes from a system view, where a large number of genes, additively or interactively, impact on a given trait. This does not undermine the findings of molecular genetics research, however. Even if effect sizes of individual genes may be small, in combination they can be of high value for the understanding of the genetic underpinnings of individual differences. Furthermore, with new technology fast advancing, researchers are now able to scan the entire genome in order to map these specific genes onto traits. Thus, it seems that a future where both self-report measures and genetic-profiling methods are used to assess individual differences in personality may no longer be a science-fiction-like scenario.

As seen, both behavioral genetics and molecular genetic studies illuminate the influence of genes on behavior and, in some cases, specific genes on behavior. However, as we discussed in the initial section of this chapter, the link between genes and behavioral tendencies is not direct. Rather, genes influence the development of the brain—its structure and chemistry. Thus, genes have their effects on behavior through influencing some of the key biological processes underlying brain functioning. The question, then, is precisely *what* structures and processes are influenced by genes? That is, what structures and processes of the brain directly influence behavioral tendencies and, thus, personality? This leads us to the next section.

BIOLOGICAL UNDERPINNINGS OF PERSONALITY

Research into the biological mechanisms underlying individual differences in personality predates the study of behavior genetics. Perhaps the most notable contribution in this area was made by Hans Eysenck (1916–1997). In the previous chapter, we mentioned that Eysenck postulated a taxonomy of personality that put forward three major personality factors, namely Neuroticism, Extraversion, and Psychoticism. We also mentioned that Eysenck's theory-building methods differed from Cattell's in several respects, notably Eysenck's belief that personality resulted from individual differences in people's biology or physiology. Indeed, Eysenck believed that no theory of personality could be complete unless it attempted to provide an explanation of the biological process underlying different levels of the major personality traits. A taxonomy might tell us how people differ, but a theory, he reasoned, should also explain why they do, and to Eysenck the answer was biological. If not, we risk debating statistical artifacts or socially constructed categories, falling into the trap of a social attribution: The idea that people do something because of the way they are is both circular and tautological, and could therefore not be falsified. To Eysenck, then, the real issue was to demonstrate the existence of a trait, with the empirical and material certainty that a natural scientist has when she/he demonstrates the existence of matter.

Eysenck's efforts were thus twofold. First, to identify the most parsimonious and basic trait taxonomy, using similar statistical methods to Cattell and others (e.g., administering questionnaires and using factor analysis to statistically derive to a taxonomy). Second, to identify the key biological correlates of individual differences in these traits, thus highlighting interindividual differences in brain functioning. Eysenck developed his initial theory of the relationship between personality and brain functioning to determine observed behavioral differences between people.

In regard to Extraversion, Eysenck specified a system in the brain called the ascending reticular activation system (ARAS). The ARAS is concerned with regulating the brain levels of cortical arousal. Cortical arousal refers to the sensitivity or reactivity of the brain, specifically, in how it reacts to stimuli from the outside world, such as noise, music, and people. We mentioned in the previous chapter that people process external stimuli differently, that is, they differ in how they anticipate, perceive, and interpret events. In addition, however, people also differ in the extent to which they physiologically and biologically respond to information—particularly how easily they are aroused by it.

While people will inevitably differ in their arousal levels across situations and even during the course of the day (e.g., you are probably more aroused before you go on a first date than during a psychology lecture), according to Eysenck, people will also differ in terms of their typical, or average, levels of cortical arousal. That is, some people will have higher average levels of arousal during the course of their life (or at least during extended periods of time), while others will have lower average or typical levels of arousal during the course of their life. This is where individual differences in Extraversion arise. According to Eysenck, extraverts have lower typical levels of cortical arousal—that is, they are chronically underaroused; introverts, on the other hand, have higher average levels of cortical arousal—that is, they are chronically overaroused. In other words, under equal conditions of external stimulation (i.e., in exactly the same situation), the introverted brain will be more stimulated than the extraverted brain (Gale, 1973).

Given that extraverts are more excitable and energetic than introverts, this may seem counterintuitive at first. However, the idea here is that if extraverts are more likely to seek external stimulation, it is precisely because they are trying to compensate for their lower levels of arousal. Conversely, introverts avoid external stimulation in order to *maintain*, or reduce, an already high base level of cortical arousal. This "compensatory" function is the body's natural reaction in its attempt to reach a biological equilibrium, or a steady-state of arousal, believed to be fundamental to life and health. In that sense, extraverts and introverts are the same: They both perform best under moderate levels of cortical stimulations (the only difference is that extraverts attain that optimum level by increasing external stimulation, whereas the opposite is true for introverts).

Thus, according to Eysenck, people's personalities, in particular our levels of Extraversion and introversion, are the function of some very basic survival mechanisms in the brain. What are the implications of this? Here is a point for reflection: Are you a person who likes to study with the TV on in the background? If you do, chances are you are an extravert; if, conversely, you can only concentrate in the absence of any background noise, then you are more likely to be an introvert. These Eysenckian predictions have been supported by many studies (quite a few by our friend and colleague Adrian Furnham), and highlight the biological basis of individual differences in personality. Thus, differences between the typical behaviors of extraverted and introverts (such as going clubbing or going to the library) can be interpreted as simple compensational strategies people use to find the perfect balance between their brain reactivity and environmental stimulation.

Interestingly, the theory can also be used to make predictions about people's performance. For, according to the Yerkes-Dodson law (1908)—one of the oldest laws in psychology—people's performance in anything, be it sports, academic tests, or public speaking, will be optimal at intermediate levels of arousal. In order to do well on any of these tasks, you need to be somewhat "aroused" (motivated) but not overly so. This is why you should avoid too much coffee before an interview, or Red Bull during an exam (especially if you are an introvert). True, if you are underaroused you may end up falling asleep, but if you are overaroused your anxiety will undermine your performance. In line, extraverts and introverts should perform differently depending on whether they are in a high- or low-arousal context. For instance, public speaking—a high-arousal context—is likely to benefit extraverts, whereas proofreading a long report—a low-arousal context—is likely to benefit introverts. The other factor that plays a role is your ability to execute the task; hence, very able people tend to "peak" under high stimulation (or they will be underaroused), whereas less able people do well under low external pressure (when they are rehearsing for months before the actual test).

With regard to Neuroticism, Eysenck attributed main individual differences to the limbic system, that is, the visceral and the sympathetic nervous system. Given that the limbic system is generally involved in processing emotions and information of emotional value, activity in this region is induced by emotional stimuli. Higher levels of arousability generated by emotional stimuli can be translated into experiences of intense emotions. According to Eysenck, neurotic individuals are susceptible to higher *typical* levels of arousability in this system and are therefore more sensitive to emotional information and more likely to experience anxiety in the presence of such information. Accordingly, the same event may elicit an intense emotional reaction in neurotic but not stable individuals. For instance, one student may be unable to fall asleep the night before an exam, while another may fall asleep straight away (even when their general patterns of sleep are similar and they are equally concerned by the exam). In this scenario, the former student may have higher base levels of activity in the autonomic/limbic system and as a result would experience higher levels of anxiety than the latter student.

One major benefit of Eysenck's theory is, of course, that it is subject to experimental tests. For instance, if we assume that introverts prefer low-stimulation environments and perform better in them compared to extraverts, then we can simply expose these groups to different environments and examine whether there are indeed differences in behavior and performance between these groups in these contexts. A large amount of research has been carried out to examine Eysenck's hypotheses, most notably, in relation to his Extraversion/introversion dimensions. In general, results have demonstrated moderate support for his theory. For instance, in a review of 33 electroencephalographic (EEG) studies examining differences in "arousal potential" between introverts and extraverts, Gale (1983) found that introverts showed greater cortical arousal than extraverts in 22 of the 33 studies. Geen and colleagues (Geen, 1984; Geen, McCown, & Broyles, 1985) examined whether introverts show different reactivity to stimulation than extraverts by assessing performance differences on a visual signal-detection task during low or high noise. The researchers found that introverts did better than extraverts with low noise, whereas the opposite was true in the high-noise condition.

While many other studies have provided evidence for Eysenck's arousal theory, the findings have not always supported the precise hypotheses. Furthermore, several critiques have been made in regard to the dimensional structure of Eysenck's taxonomy. One of these critiques relates to the physiological interdependence of the processes underlying the two supposedly unrelated traits of Neuroticism and Extraversion, as well as the lack of direct evidence for the biological processes hypothesized by Eysenck. In addition, Psychoticism, a trait introduced later by Eysenck, has remained the focus of a largely unresolved psychometric dispute (in the Big Five, Psychoticism is expressed as high Openness, low Agreeableness, and low Conscientiousness—people high in Psychoticism tend to lack self-control and have antisocial and impulsive tendencies). Nevertheless, some of the most interesting studies in these areas, conducted by Robinson (1996), have successfully reinterpreted Eysenck's biological theory of temperament to fit within current neuroscientific knowledge and methods.

Another influential personality theory, based initially on Eysenck's theory, Jeffrey Gray's (1934–2004) personality theory, known as the *behavioral activation system* (*BAS*)/*behavioral inhibition system* (*BIS*) personality theory. Gray developed his model after a series of animal experiments—especially rats. Like other animals, humans may respond to threatening stimuli in an active or passive way, in other words, by (actively) fighting or (passively) flying or running away. This system of response was conceptualized at three biological levels, each corresponding to parts of the brain, namely, the amygdala, the ventromedial hypothalamus, and the central gray of the midbrain.

Gray's (1981) personality theory is based on the behavioral principles of *conditioning*, that is, reward and punishment, and their long-term effects on the brain. Like Eysenck, then, Gray developed a biologically based personality theory, though Gray emphasized the developmental effects of conditioning and focused mainly on anxiety. Thus, the personality theories of Eysenck and Gray often work at different explanatory levels of the same phenomena, with Gray's model offering a more fine-grained description of the neuropsychological processes underlying individual differences in personality.

According to Gray (1982), the BAS motivates behavior toward obtaining a reward by making the individual aware of the reward and giving the "go-ahead" signal that triggers behavior. Whether the target is a box of chocolates, a packet of cigarettes, or a beautiful woman is irrelevant as the BAS causes the person to desire that "object" and direct his/her appetitive behavior toward it. The BIS, on the other hand, is an anxiety system that inhibits behaviors associated with potential punishment or lack of reward. Thus, the BIS encourages an individual to stop a particular behavior by increasing his/her level of awareness of the negative outcomes. A classic example is the fear of a snake, followed by the inhibition against touching it and, in turn, the act of running away. BIS activity is psychologically expressed in terms of neurotic anxiety and depression (Gray, 1987).

Gray argued that individuals are biologically compelled to increase activity in the rewarding system, prompted by the BAS. Any rewarded behavior feeds back positively onto the BAS. On the other hand, individuals are also "programmed" to reduce activity in the BIS, which is achieved through stopping behaviors that may lead to punishment or fail to be rewarded (leading to frustration). Failure to inhibit these behaviors will increase the activity of the BIS. Both BIS and BAS are related through the mechanism of arousal, located in the reticular formation.

The most significant implication of Gray's theory with regard to personality taxonomy is the differentiation between the two distinct dimensions of *anxiety* and *impulsivity*, comparable— yet not equivalent—to Neuroticism and Extraversion, respectively. Interestingly, correlations between Gray's and Eysenck's models indicate that anxiety is negatively, albeit modestly, associated with both Extraversion and Psychoticism, suggesting that (a) there is a conceptual overlap between Extraversion and Psychoticism, namely impulsivity (both extraverted and higher Psychoticism individuals tend to be impulsive) and (b) Psychoticism is characterized by risk-taking, while Neuroticism, at the opposite end of the scale, may be characterized by risk-avoiding (Gray, 1987). This idea is in line with a long-standing tradition in psychiatry that distinguishes between neuroses and psychoses, echoed, for instance, by Freud's psychoanalytic theory.

At the same time, Gray was generally in agreement with Eysenck about the inclusion of Psychoticism as a third major personality trait, and hypothesized this trait to be associated with the fight/flight system (Gray, 1991).

Despite the influence of Gray's theory, particularly in providing an empirically based theoretical framework for experimental research into the processes accounting for individual differences in major personality dimensions, dispositional approaches to personality have tended to focus on other taxonomies. However, Gray's theory has, perhaps like no other personality model, encouraged psychologists to combine psychometric/correlational, cognitive/experimental, and biological/neuroscientific designs to provide a comprehensive explanation of how and why people differ.

Although the biological theories of personality seem to provide a straightforward cause-and-effect view of personality and perhaps allude to a deterministic approach to the subject, such a view would be misguided. While these theories have provided us with some useful guidance as to the causes of behavior, it would be foolish to think that they provide us with the full picture or a ready-made theory of cause and effect. Brain functioning is simply not that straightforward. The brain is a system, and like all systems, it comprises several elements that interact. In this case, the number of elements of the system is so vast and the interaction between the elements so complex that a simple proposition of a specific element causing specific behavior is an erroneous oversimplification. As Zuckerman (1996) puts it: "Psychobiology is not for seekers of simplicity" (p. 128). Thus, the biopsychological theories of personality to some extent provide an oversimplified account of the nature of personality. It should be noted, however, that while this may be the case, these theories have provided us with some crucial knowledge about the potential underlying influences on our personality and character.

EVOLUTION AND PERSONALITY

In discussing the biological approaches to personality, we have attempted to provide an answer to the question of *why* people differ the way they do; that is, what the *causes* for the observed personality differences between people are. We have provided evidence to show that personality is at least partly heritable. Thus, we can be confident in concluding that personality does indeed have a genetic basis. However, we could go even further in our enquiry. We could, for instance, ask ourselves *why* there is a genetic basis to personality in the first place. That is, why is it that people inherit these specific (say three or five) traits, and why are differences between people in these traits genetic?

When we inquire about the reasons for the existence of any particular human characteristic, we inevitably refer to its evolutionary significance. *Evolution* by natural selection is the process of genetic variation found over time in one or more inherited traits within species. This variation occurs over a number of generations and genes that promote the survival and reproduction of the organism are passed on to the next generation, whereas genes that are either harmful or have no adaptive significance are gradually eliminated. Fundamentally, biological and psychological traits that have endured and exist in the human (and other) species today exist because they have been adaptive to survival and reproductive success.

For example, if we wanted to know why certain *physical* traits, such as (say) eyes, exist, we could turn to evolutionary biology. According to evolutionary biology, people inherit a pair of eyes because eyes help us see depth. Depth perception is a critical survival mechanism because it enables us to see how far in the distance objects, such as hurdles, predators, and prey, are. It is therefore passed on from generation to generation. Similarly, to answer the question of why certain personality traits (e.g., Extraversion, Neuroticism, etc.) exist, we could to turn to evolutionary psychology. However, the evolution of individual differences in personality poses a problem. A major difference with this approach is that the question here does not concern the adaptive value of the traits that are common to all humans, but rather whether the *differences* between people in such traits are adaptive. In a way, the adaptive value of variation appears to contradict an evolutionary account. After all, evolution tends to yield a single best form of any one gene, gradually eliminating less adaptive alternatives. To clarify this point, consider the case of Extraversion and Agreeableness. If we assume that Extraversion has in evolutionary sense been adaptive for, say, attracting mates and reproductive success, and Agreeableness for (say) group harmony and cooperation, then introverted and uncooperative behavior should gradually be eliminated in the species. So, how could personality *differences* between individuals be genetic?

To be sure, several authors have argued that genetically based personality differences are unlikely to be very significant. For instance, Tooby and Cosmides (1990) argue that individual differences in personality are likely to be adaptively neutral or trivial (unrelated to adaptive fitness) in relation to universal psychological capacities. Nevertheless, other authors contend that such genetically based personality variation may indeed be understood in terms of evolved solutions to adaptive problems. One such position is put forward by evolutionary psychologist David Buss. According to Buss (2009), differences in personality traits may reflect differences in adaptive strategies that are specialized for domain-specific problems. An example of such adaptive problems is the negotiation of the status hierarchy. Research has found that individuals can use different adaptive strategies to achieve hierarchically higher status, including deception/manipulation, emission of positive externalities, and industriousness strategies. In this respect, extraverts tend to use positive externalities, conscientious individuals tend to use hard work and persistence, and individuals who have low Agreeableness tend to use deceit and manipulation to advance in hierarchies. Thus, in negotiating dominant hierarchies, *low* Agreeableness may be adaptively superior to high Agreeableness. In evolutionary terms, therefore, individual differences in Agreeableness may be conceptualized as motivational strategies to cooperate or act selfishly—both of which are evolutionarily adaptive and therefore likely to endure (Denissen & Penke, 2008).

Another evolutionary account for genetically based behavioral differences is that they may be adaptive to different environments and contexts (Wilson, 1994). For instance, introverted individuals may be adaptively superior in structured and risk-free settings; whereas, extraverted individuals may be adaptively superior in social positions where greater initiative and tolerance of risk and novelty are required. This view, known as the person–environment fit, is widely acknowledged in the field of industrial and organizational psychology

(Chamorro-Premuzic & Furnham, 2010a, 2010b). Thus, by this account, individual differences in human personality may also reflect adaptive ways of specializing for different roles and activities within a social group.

Evolutionary accounts are not without their critics, of course. One major criticism of the field is that the very nature of the theory makes it difficult to test or falsify. Thus, evolutionary explanations often must be hypothetical rather than empirical. Nevertheless, most psychologists today accept that evolutionary psychology is a powerful framework for understanding behavioral patterns and variations within and between individuals. By looking at the adaptive function of behaviors from an evolutionary perspective, researchers can identify the distal causes of those behaviors and the reasons for their genetic heritability.

TEMPERAMENT

We have so far discussed the genetic, biological, and evolutionary influences on human personality. In all this, the basic argument has been that personality is at least partly and perhaps strongly influenced by our genes and biology. But does this suggest, therefore, that a person is born with a certain personality? That is, are there really personality differences between people at birth? And if so, can these be assessed and how?

Hamer and Copeland (1998) stated that people have about as much choice in some aspects of their personality as they do in the shape of their nose or the size of their feet. To imply that an infant or a baby has a personality may seem somewhat surprising. After all, behavior between babies seems not to differ a great deal. Things such as social skills, self-concept, and personal goals in life are clearly not something one can imagine to find in an infant, or even in a 2-year-old child. These behaviors are clearly learned. Similarly, it is hard to see how a trait such as Conscientiousness can be discussed with reference to a child. It would be odd to expect a baby to display conscientious behavior.

Nevertheless, we often hear parents discuss the differences they observed between their children from a very early age. Some are very energetic and will not stop moving and running around (i.e., cause trouble) despite any attempts by the parents; others will sit there quietly, rarely cause trouble, and listen to their parents. Some smile and interact with strangers, while others are shy and reserved, and perhaps even fear those they have not encountered before. Psychologists refer to behavioral tendencies at such an early age as *temperaments*. Temperaments can be defined in very simple terms as "individual differences in behavior that appear early in life" (Shiner, 1998); psychologists usually refer to temperaments as differences in personality of children below 3 years of age (Denissen, van Aken, & Roberts, 2011). But, is there evidence that children do indeed differ on behavioral tendencies at such an early age? And, how similar are these tendencies to adult personality? In other words, what is the relationship between early temperament and adult personality? For Freud, the child was the "father" of man, meaning that early manifestations of personality have pervasive effects on adult character; so, is there any evidence for this idea?

Before this question can be addressed, it is necessary to answer some other questions. First, how do we actually assess an infant's personality? Clearly, we cannot administer a personality inventory to a baby and wait for him or her to complete it. Second, the only way to understand the relationship between temperament and personality is to wait for the children under study to grow up; such studies take years and decades to complete and are hard to come by. Nevertheless, through innovative research methods and the persistence and patience of psychologists employing longitudinal research designs, the field has seen an unprecedented increase in research and we have been able to come to the bottom of many of these questions.

For instance, given that we cannot administer personality questionnaires to children and infants, researchers have had to devise different methods for assessment. Some of these methods include ratings by parents, observing infants' reactions and habituation to novel stimuli. Since babies do not display many of the adult behaviors such as socializing, working, cooperating, leading, and so on, ratings are generally made with regard to very simple and basic behaviors. These include distractibility, activity level, attention span, sensory sensitivity, patterns of sleeping and eating (and regularity of these), and reactions to various situations. Using similar psychometric techniques as with adult personality assessment (e.g., correlation, factor analysis, etc.), researchers have been able to identify the structure, or a taxonomy, of temperaments. For instance, Thomas and Chess (1977) in a pioneering study categorized babies into three different temperament types: difficult babies, easy babies, and slow-to-warm-up babies. Similarly, Buss and Plomin (1975, 1984) found three dimensions of temperament: These were emotionality (how easily the baby got distressed), activity (pace and power of motor movements and their frequency), and sociability (responsiveness to other people).

As you can see, the structure of temperaments seems to differ from the adult personality structure. Nevertheless, there appears to be a certain similarity between at least some temperament dimensions and adult personality factors. In particular, the most well-established of the Big Five personality factors, Neuroticism and Extraversion appear to be represented by Buss and Plomin's emotionality and activity/sociability dimensions, respectively. Similarly, Martin, Wisenbaker, and Huttunen (1994), upon reviewing the evidence on the structure of temperament, found evidence for additional factors such as task persistence, which is reflected by the Big Five factor Conscientiousness, and adaptability, which is reflected by a combination of Agreeableness and emotional stability. Thus, with the exception of Openness, there seems to be a clear resemblance between the structure of temperament and the structure of adult personality.

Several longitudinal studies have also demonstrated a clear link between childhood differences in temperament and later differences in adult personality. For instance, in their seminal paper, Thomas and Chess found that difficult babies had difficulties in adjusting in adulthood, whereas "easy-going" babies found it easiest to adjust in later years. Similarly, Kagan and Snidman (1999) found high-reactive infants (those who reacted to new stimuli by intense crying, arching of the back, and unhappy facial expressions) to react more fearfully, have accelerated heart rates, and have increased blood pressure, compared to the low-reactive (those who reacted to new stimuli in a calm and laid-back manner) infants, in response to novel stimuli, at 14 and 21 months. Furthermore, these differences continued to be apparent later at 4.5 years of age and 8 years of age.

Thus, the studies reviewed above provide considerable evidence for a biological basis underlying personality differences and suggest that personality is rather stable from birth to adulthood, even though development does take place (but in a similar vein for most people). Importantly, though, not all highly reactive children turn out to be more fearful in later years and not all low-reactive children end up being calm and laid-back. Correlations between temperamental tendencies and adult manifestations of personality are far from perfect, rendering any deterministic view of human behavior implausible. This raises another interesting question, namely *how much* can one change his/her personality, and do we actually do so?

STABILITY VERSUS CHANGE

From the above evidence, we can safely conclude that (a) personality has a strong genetic basis, (b) there are reliable manifestations of personality early in childhood and even infancy (called temperament), and (c) these individual differences predict later, adult, manifestations of personality. However, one question we have not dealt with so far is that of change. We noted earlier that the correlation between temperament and later personality is not 1. Not all children born with a particular temperament composition turn out to have an equivalent adult personality profile. This leaves several questions unaddressed. First, how much change is there? In the previous sections, we have alluded to the stability of personality and presented some evidence for stability from the literature. Indeed, the very definition, or at least concept, of personality rests on the notion of stability over time (and across situations). But, just how much stability is there in personality over a life span? Second, what is the nature of this stability? That is, what do we mean when we say that personality is stable? Do we mean that we have pretty much the same personality when we are old as we do when we are young (i.e., act in similar ways now as we did when we were kids)? And finally, if there is stability, does this mean that personality *cannot* change (i.e., even if one tried)? How much of our personality—of who we are—is actually in our hands?

In sum, these question refer to the nature of personality development and malleability (versus stability) throughout the life span. In order to address questions regarding development, stability, and change, we need to turn to personality studies that span several decades. As mentioned before, a number of such longitudinal studies have indeed been carried out. In terms of the degree of stability (our first question above), research findings are quite unequivocal: There is a high degree of stability in personality across the life span. That is, a highly extraverted person in their 30s is significantly more likely to be highly extraverted (than introverted) 20 or even 40 years later, when they are in their 50s and even 70s (McCrae & Costa, 2008). Highly conscientious people in their 20s are also more likely to be highly conscientious in their 40s or in their 60s and so on.

How can we tell? The research methodology psychologists use to investigate stability usually involves the administration of a personality questionnaire (or a number of them) to a sample of people at two (or more) different time periods (say 10, 20, or 40 years apart). They then measure the similarity (or correlation) between the two test scores. If the correlations are high, that is, if individuals in the sample or a population scored very similarly on the personality inventory (or a particular trait) today as they did 20 or 40 years ago, then one can conclude that personality remains very stable for that particular population over the life span.

So, what are the test–retest correlations? Research shows that, for the Big Five personality traits, correlations are around .65; this is even when tests have been administered 20 years apart (Costa & McCrae, 1994a). To put this into perspective, what this means is that if you score above average on (say) Extraversion at 30, there is about an 83% chance that you will score above average on Extraversion when you are 50 or older. We should note, however, that the longer the time interval between test and retest, the lower the stability of personality seems to be (Roberts & DelVecchio, 2000). Given the number of factors that can influence test-takers on any given day (e.g., their mood, their physical health, their fatigue, their motivation to take the test, their time and availability, etc., referred to in statistics as *measurement error*), the similarity in (or the stability of) the personality profiles obtained from these tests between such lengthy time periods are remarkably high.

To the layperson, these findings may seem quite counterintuitive. Indeed, you have probably seen very few 50- or 70-year-old individuals act like they did when they were in their 20s or 30s (in fact, other than Silvio Berlusconi or Hugh Hefner, it is hard to think of any). However, it is important to note that the stability statistics presented above do not refer to a person's personality change relative to *themselves*. Rather, it refers to *rank-order stability*, that is, how extraverted or conscientious a person is *relative to others*. In other words, it is about whether you are more extraverted or conscientious than your best friend, spouse, brother/sister, and so on now, than you were 20 years ago (not about whether you are as active at 50 as you were when you were 30; the latter is called *mean-level stability* and is dealt with below).

Another interesting question is whether people change more or less as they grow older. It is reasonable to believe that the older people get and the more control they obtain over their lives, the more they are able to change their behavior. However, evidence suggests that the opposite is in fact true. Studies show that stability *increases* as people get older (Costa & McCrae, 1994b). In fact, Costa and McCrae (1994b) stated that "by age 30, personality is essentially fixed" (p. 146), echoing William James's (1950/1890) notion that personality becomes "set like plaster," and Freud's view that adult personality is a photocopy of childhood character. Although these statements are somewhat exaggerated—research suggests that personality does indeed continue to change after 30 years of age (Roberts & DelVecchio, 2000)—there is substantial evidence to show that stability does increase with age. For instance, in a meta-analysis, Roberts and DelVecchio (2000) found that test–retest correlations increased from .31 in childhood to .54 during the college years, to .64 at age 40, and stabilizing between ages 50 and 70 with correlations of around .74 (the average test–retest intervals were around 6.7 years). These findings suggest that change is less likely to occur as you get older, a common-sense idea. Thus, the well-known saying "you can't teach an old dog new tricks" is consistent with scientific evidence.

WHY THERE IS STABILITY

Given the empirical evidence of stability, we are left with the task of explaining why stability exists in the first place—or what the mechanisms of stability are. Of course, one may argue that genetics is the obvious answer. For instance, McCrae and Costa (2008) attribute stability to the biological basis of traits. We have already noted the heritability estimates of personality, which indicate that around 50% of the variance in personality is caused by genetic factors (Loehlin, 1992). Given that a person's genetic code does not change across the life span, it is reasonable to assume that this code would continue to assert influence on a person's personality throughout his or her lives (Denissen et al., 2011).

At first glance, this may appear to be a bleak and deterministic view of personality—indicating that people have very little chance of changing or controlling their personality (even if they wanted to), just as they have little chance of changing their height. However, given that genes explain no more than 50% of the variance in personality, purely genetic explanations of stability are implausible. Furthermore, we noted before that genes and environment interact in a complex two-way fashion. Attributing stability solely to genes, therefore, is ignoring an important part of the story.

One alternative explanation for the stability of personality attributes stability to a large extent to the environment. This may sound puzzling at first given that the nature of environments seems inherently variable; such a view would also seem to be in direct contradiction to the evidence for the genetic basis of personality. Nevertheless, this account may not be as far-fetched as it appears. Indeed, it could be that particular (biologically influenced) behaviors are simply reactions, or adaptations, to particular environments. That is, although differences between people may reflect differences in the biological processes between individuals, the stability of these differences over time could be explained in terms of the stability of the environments that people inhabit. Thus, genetic predispositions determine rather stable environmental choices, which may reinforce those predispositions and "exaggerate" or amplify early manifestations of personality, but in the same direction. Think of how often you have changed your preference for food, friends, careers, and hobbies across the last 10 years or so. This is especially the case when we reach a certain age and "settle down." Settling down is simply another idiom for more stability in our environment. This could also explain why personality seems to become more stable with age. The more control people have over their lives, the less change there is in their environments. In contrast to childhood and adolescence where children regularly change environments (e.g., school, friends, girl/boyfriends, neighborhoods), in adulthood, relatively few people will have radical career or culture shifts, or radical changes in the patterns of their romantic and nonromantic relationships. The apparent stability of personality throughout the life span, therefore, may simply reflect the stability of the environment that traits react or adapt to, rather than genetic "fixedness." Importantly, by this account, changing one's environment for longer periods of time should also result in changes in personality.

Some evidence for the above derives from a rather fascinating longitudinal study on the personalities of married couples over 10 years. In this study, Caspi and Herbener (1990) found that couples who were more similar to each other in terms of their personality profiles (for instance, an extraverted pair of husband and wife) experienced less personality change than couples who were less similar to each other (for instance, an introverted husband and extraverted wife). These findings suggest that your partner's personality may have environmental-like effects on your personality development, even in adult years. So, if you want to change your personality, you may want to marry someone who has your opposite personality profile.

An interesting question one could ask is whether this explanation for the stability of personality undermines a genetic account of stability. To make this clear, it may indeed be true that extraverted persons remain extraverted (i.e., do not change), or even increase in this trait because they have inhabited stable environments that cultivate Extraversion. For instance, an extraverted person might remain extraverted because she/he has a job that requires social activity and skill, such as a sales or customer service job. Another reason for stability may be that the person has a large group of friends and therefore often ends up in various social events, which requires more Extraversion to adapt. However, one could also ask the question as to why it is that the extraverted person has a job in sales in the first place. Or, why it is that they have a large group of friends, and why they keep following them to these social events, and so on. Are these mere coincidences, or could it be that their genetic makeup, their inborn personality traits, actually predisposes them to select those "environmental niches" and avoid the ones that do not match their personality? For instance, an extravert who needs lots of stimulation (to compensate for low levels of cortical arousal or other physiological reasons) may choose jobs that provide stimulation (i.e., sociable jobs) and may surround himself/herself with people, whereas an introverted person may have a biological tendency to be overaroused and therefore choose jobs which are less stimulating (such as accountancy or research jobs), and avoid going to social events. It may be that these choices, based on matching the environment to one's personality, are in fact the source for increased stability in one's environment, which, in turn, further stabilizes personality and reduces environmental opportunities for change.

In addition, according to Roberts et al.'s (2003) *corresponsive principle*, those traits that actually select people into specific environments are the traits that are most influenced by these environments. For instance, if a person accepts a job with great responsibilities because they are highly conscientious and reliable, they will probably become even more reliable and conscientious once they have worked in that role for a while. Accordingly, not all traits will be equally strongly affected by the environment. Rather, the more characteristic traits of an individual may be affected more than the less characteristic traits because environmental niches and life experiences are "selected" by the more characteristic traits in the first place (Roberts et al., 2003).

A final source of stability is our personal identity or self-perception. As we grow older we tend to get a sense of who we are—a stable self-concept or identity (Glenn, 1990; Meeus, Iedema, Helsen, & Vollenberg, 1999). In the words of the great Oscar Wilde: "Be yourself, everybody else is taken." Indeed, we often use our identity as a reference point for our decisions (Asendorpf, 2008), because we want to stay true to that identity.

Consequently, we will tend to avoid behaviors or inhabiting environments that are inconsistent with our sense of self and our identity. For instance, if you perceive yourself to be a person that dislikes hip-hop music or hip-hop culture, you are unlikely to listen to that music, inhabit that culture, or behave in ways that represents that culture. Moreover, if you occasionally found yourself liking hip-hop music or culture, given your sense of identity and expectations that others have of you, you would be more likely to avoid than approach it. Thus, people strive for consistency in what they do and how they think of themselves, something social psychologists have argued for decades. By doing so, they also expose themselves to familiar experiences that further reinforce the stability of their dispositions.

Overall then, the above findings suggest that (a) there is considerable stability in personality and (b) there are a multitude of sources for the observed stability of personality. It is also clear from the above that the stability is chronologically dependent. In other words, we find that stability is high in older age but not necessarily in young age. Furthermore, we have so far only talked about rank-order stability. However, as we alluded to before, change can be examined both as relative to others (rank-order) and relative to oneself (mean-level). So what about *mean-level change*? How much *within person* or mean-level change is there?

This question focuses on the average level of a trait in a sample, and the absolute change in that trait expression across time. It examines whether people undergo shifts in personality during their lifetimes. We often hear that during adolescent and teenage years, people are more emotional, discontent, and rebellious; hence the saying "angry young men." With this, we refer to the personality changes of a whole population (between young age, teenage, and adult years) rather than differential changes in personality between people.

But, do people really change much during their teenage years? Are there any substantial changes in personality during a person's lifetime? And if so, in what ways do people change as they become older? To answer these questions, Roberts et al.

(2006) conducted a meta-analysis of 92 longitudinal studies examining mean-level changes in personality across the life course. The results were compelling: Significant, and sometimes substantial, mean-level changes were observed for all traits, and these changes occurred even during late adulthood, which disconfirms the "plaster hypothesis."

Interestingly, the patterns of change differed for different traits; for instance, some traits (e.g., Conscientiousness and emotional stability) increased during young adulthood (age 20–40), whereas others (i.e., Agreeableness) increased only in late adulthood (age 50–60). The general trend seems to indicate that as people get older they become more emotionally stable, more conscientious, and more agreeable, and less extraverted and less open to experience. Translating this into common language, one could say that people become calmer, less confrontational, less risk-averse, more reserved, and less open-minded, as they grow older (especially after the age of 35). It would seem that "maturity" is, at least in part, about becoming a more boring person then. But, the main conclusion is that change occurs, even if most people change in the same ways.

What Is the Source of Change?

As reviewed above, despite the stability of personality, there seems to be both some mean-level and rank-order change. So, what are the mechanisms that bring about change? This question is important because stability and change may be caused by completely different factors (or not).

To recap, mean-level change is an average change of a trait in the population, and research points to a "maturation effect" in personality with increasing age. One explanation for this effect, put forward by McCrae and colleagues, is biological and innate in nature. According to McCrae et al., personality *change* is genetically "programmed." This change is linked to adaptation to evolutionarily relevant goals, including the formation of lasting relationships and having children (McCrae et al., 2000).

As evidence for their theory, the researchers have pointed to the findings that indicate that the same patterns of personality change have been observed across numerous cultures, with each differing considerably in their political, cultural, and economic conditions (i.e., German, Turkish, British, Czech, and Spanish).

Although these findings make for a convincing argument, several authors have contested that mean-level personality change can be equally explained in terms of social influences. For instance, Roberts, Wood, and Smith (2005) point out that despite the cross-cultural nature of McCrae and colleagues' studies, the timing of major social transitions that occur across the life span in the nations examined (e.g., getting married, having children, getting a job, settling down, etc.) is relatively homogeneous, making it difficult to dissect the relative contribution of genetic and environmental influences on mean-level change. Indeed, evidence that societal and cultural conditions can bring about change has been provided by studies conducted by Twenge and colleagues. These studies have shown reliable mean-level changes on a variety of personality traits (e.g., self-esteem, depression, etc.) between young people in the 1960s and young people in more recent years (see Twenge, 1997, 2000, 2001b; Twenge & Campbell, 2001; Twenge, Zhang, & Im, 2004). Thus, although it is likely that biological changes have a direct effect on mean-level personality change and maturation, evidence seems to suggest that also nongenetic factors may have a significant impact on personality change.

The only obvious explanation of rank-order change (i.e., change in personality relative to other people) would appear to be an environmental one, as genes generally are depicted in rank-order stability (or common/mean-level change). However, research suggests that genes may in fact account for as much as 30% of the variability in personality change (Bleidorn, Kandler, Riemann, Angleitner, & Spinath, 2009; McGue et al., 1993). Although this may seem surprising, it is possible to conceive genes to produce distinct patterns of personality change over time, just as they do with the timing of pubertal changes. This can occur because gene expression is dynamic, with genes being activated and deactivated during various stages of development, which, in turn, may result in genetically influenced changes in personality throughout the life course. There is not enough research to back this hypothesis, however, and most explanations of rank-order personality change reside either with environmental influences or random occurrences.

Several environmental influences have been suggested as mechanisms for (rank order) personality change. One such is social relationships. Social relationships in childhood have often been hypothesized to have significant influence on later personality development (Bowlby, 1969). In support of this argument, Kagan (1994) provided evidence to show that parenting style (e.g., relaxed versus protective) can have a significant effect on toddlers with inhibited temperaments (i.e., whether toddlers remain inhibited in later years or not). It should be noted that, consistent with behavioral genetics research, it is the unique individual parenting style, that is, the nonshared aspect of the environment, that is shown to be the important influence in such studies.

In addition to social relationships in childhood, social relationships also in adulthood have been shown to have significant effects on rank-order personality change. For instance, a study conducted by Lehnart and Neyer (2006) shows that a person's first stable partnership has a significant impact on levels of Neuroticism (both for men and women). Specifically, it seems that after the first stable relationship, levels of Neuroticism in individuals decrease (increasing emotional stability), and that this effect is long lasting. That is, even when relationships end, people's Neuroticism levels remain low. This study initially appears to illustrate the environmental effects on *mean-level* changes. Interestingly, however, Lehnart and Neyer (2006) found that this pattern of change had different impact on different groups, depending on individuals' baseline levels of Neuroticism, as well as the point in their life they had their first serious relationship, notably, whether it was early, timely, or late (they also had a group of individuals who remained single).

The researchers found that for both groups who started off with high Neuroticism scores, a stable relationship decreased Neuroticism—but at different times. In particular, while both groups became more emotionally stable following their first relationship, timely beginners showed a linear decrease in Neuroticism, whereas late beginners showed an initial increase of Neuroticism before they had a steep decrease in the expression of this trait. Finally, those who had low Neuroticism and had their first stable relationship at an early age were not affected by this event and remained emotionally stable throughout.

Additional environmental factors have been suggested in rank-order change, such as work experiences (Denissen, Asendorpf, & van Aken, 2008; Roberts, 1997) and momentous life experiences (Franz, 1994; Harter, 1993; Lucas, 2007). It is clear, however, that change is more likely to result from long-term exposure to an environment than in brief environmental episodes. Furthermore, more change is expected when the pressure to behave in the new situation is high, and when previous responses are actively discouraged, while clear information is provided about how to behave adaptively (Denissen et al., 2011).

Taken together, the evidence on personality development change suggests that (a) personality stability may result directly from genetic influences, (b) it may result from environmental stability that is partly caused by genetic forces (indicating that genetic forces are strong predictors of stability), and (c) genetic forces may be countered by significant life events and experiences, or simply long-term exposure to environments which demand change.

CONCLUSION

In this chapter, we have examined the causes of individual differences in personality. We have documented the importance of both genetic and environmental influences on such differences, as well as the intricate interplay between genes and environment in shaping personality traits. We have further extended this discussion to examine the issue of personality change and stability. Here again, we have seen how change and continuity are the result of a complex interaction between genes and environment.

The questions addressed in this chapter are fundamental to the basic assumptions people hold about human nature. Are people born in a certain way or are they shaped by their socioeconomic, political, and familial environments? Can people change or is their destiny pretty much sealed from the moment they are born? Laypeople often hold different theories about the answers to these questions. Usually there is a divide between those who believe in the influence of nature versus those who believe in the influence of nurture. While these usually reflect different worldviews and are often based on intuition, experience, or common sense, the evidence reviewed in this chapter enables us to provide a scientific account to these questions.

Behavioral genetics research has provided us with the ubiquitous observation that genes make a substantial contribution to psychological traits. Although this may be an uncomfortable revelation to many who hold an "environmental" view of individual differences, there is now very little doubt in the scientific community that most, if not all, psychological traits are heritable. Recent advances in neurobiological research are now even enabling personality psychologists to locate specific genes and brain pathways that are related to personality traits. This research is moving at a fast pace and is perhaps the most promising avenue for providing us with the full picture of the biological underpinnings of personality. Finally, evolutionary psychology helps us to understand not *whether* traits are heritable, but rather what the *function* of personality traits and individual differences in these may be. Together, this line of research emphasizes the importance of considering biological influences (or nature) in considering explanations for individual differences in personality.

Nevertheless, even the strongest advocates of the biological basis of personality will acknowledge that genetic influences are only part of the story. In fact, the very research that has provided strong evidence for genetic influences on personality is responsible for revealing the importance of environmental factors also. As we saw earlier, it is estimated that about 50% of the variation in personality is due to environmental influences. Furthermore, the nonshared environment, perhaps surprisingly so, seems to be responsible for exerting the majority of this influence, while the influence of the shared environment appears to be only negligible.

One of the most interesting aspects of the biological research into personality is how it illuminates our understanding of the interplay between genetics and the environment. It is now clear that, far from having independent effects, biological and environmental determinants of personality are intimately entangled. Accordingly, three forms of gene–environment interactions have been distinguished: (a) the same environmental experiences may have different effects on individuals with different genetic constitutions, (b) individuals with different genetic constitutions may evoke different responses from the environment, and (c) an individual's genetic constitution influences the selection of his or her environment.

Interestingly, these same principles may also be the basis for the observed stability of personality traits over time. Thus, given that a person's genetic code remains unchanged throughout the course of life, genes may directly influence the stability, or consistency, of personality traits. On the other hand, stability is also caused by stability in one's environment. That is, personality change is small because people tend to inhabit comparable environments. Finally, one reason for environmental stability is that people select environmental niches that are consistent with their personality.

These interactions shed light on the importance of the nature of change—and the possibility of it. Evidently, with both genetic and environmental forces pushing for stability, personality is resistant to change. On the other hand, these principles also show that people are, given the right circumstances, capable of change. Indeed, even highly heritable physical traits, like weight, can be changed if the right behaviors are chosen. Thus, one point that is clear from research on personality stability versus change is that it does not allow for an extreme position. Nevertheless, the research certainly sheds light on the likelihood of change, the possibility of it, and the factors that are most likely to lead to it.

Overall, the current chapter has addressed the question of why. That is, why differences in personality between people exist. It has also enlightened us about what this means for personality change across situations and across time. It is safe to say that, while these issues are likely to continue to generate heated discussions, from a scientific perspective the nature–nurture debate is by and large resolved. It is now down to future research to expand our knowledge of the fusion between genes and environments to provide us with a better understanding, and prediction, of population-level and individual-level phenomena.

How Is Personality Assessed?

n the previous chapters, we talked about the nature of personality, covering broad themes in personality research. This included different theories dealing with its structure, its causes, and its development throughout the life span. The research reviewed above spans more than a century, and thousands of studies have been carried out to address questions concerning the nature of personality. The large amount of empirical evidence is impressive, and considerable progress appears to have been made in this field. While we have laid out empirical findings regarding the discovery of the basic structure of personality, the biological causes of it, and the change and development of it, very little discussion has been devoted to how these discoveries have actually been made. Are we to take these claims for granted? Should we even take them seriously? After all, personality is an abstract and unobservable concept; in essence, one could argue that it is not something that is subject to measurement, or even worse, that it is an illusory construct. So how do we know that we can measure this construct of personality? How do we know that we have? And, how do we know that we have accurately done so?

These are very important and very loaded questions, because they challenge the very foundations of personality psychology and psychometric testing as a whole. What's more, psychological tests, such as personality inventories, are used extensively in a variety of settings, from selection of applicants to university and organizational positions to psychiatric diagnosis. Accordingly, people's careers and even lives can be changed (and this is not an overstatement) as a result of psychometric test results. Given this, it is clearly an imperative task of psychologists in this field to provide satisfactory answers to such issues. It is their job to establish that personality is measurable, to establish that they have measured personality, and importantly, to establish that they have accurately done so. So, how can psychologists convincingly address these concerns?

To establish credibility, personality research must first demonstrate scientifically acceptable methodology. The scientific method is recognized to be the best method for obtaining valuable knowledge about any phenomenon (Kline, 1988). Accordingly, researchers have to establish some basic criteria, or standards, which personality measurement needs to satisfy for its claims to be considered scientifically acceptable. Given that personality psychology as a discipline has scientific objectives, several steps have been taken by psychologists to ensure that these standards are indeed satisfied. These include both theoretical and statistical steps, and we will discuss these throughout this chapter; however, before we embark on that, we want to ask the first basic question: Can personality actually be measured?

CAN PERSONALITY BE MEASURED AND HOW?

It is not uncommon, when we talk to people outside academia about our research and the methods of personality assessment, to be confronted with a bewildered look. Even if some don't disclose it, there generally seems to be a question mark about the way this is done, or the accuracy or validity of this research. It seems to many an unfeasible prospect. How could one possibly "measure" a person's personality? People are complex, dynamic, and one could say, chaotic. Many are difficult to read, understand, or predict. Some are worried about how others will perceive them and try hard to manage their impressions. Others are simply deceptive. With all its complexities, its dynamic and chaotic nature, there is always a sense of skepticism about attempts to quantify personality, just as with things like love or art. You often hear people say that love is not something you can describe and/or put numbers on—"It is just something you feel." The same seems to apply to the measurement of personality, at least in the mind of laypeople, but is this mainly wishful thinking?

Unlike laypeople, psychologists believe you can measure personality using reliable scientific tools. After all, if something exists, it should be subject to study. If it varies in detectable ways, it should be quantifiable. Therefore, the only thing needed is to find a valid way (or ways) of doing so. This is not a commentary of faith but is derived from our understanding of the scientific method. For instance, we would all agree that not all people are exactly the same; some people are taller, some are heavier, and some are stronger. We would also agree that people differ more than in just a physical sense; that is, they differ in the way they think, feel, and behave. Some people are friendlier, some are more aggressive, and others more assertive. When we compare people, we often say they have more or less of an attribute (e.g., friendliness, aggression, determination, etc.). These differences are differences in degree. If we acknowledge therefore that some people differ in psychological aspects in terms of degree, there is no reason as to why these aspects should not be quantifiable. All we need is to assign numbers to these degrees or variations.

Strictly speaking then, the skepticism about the prospect of measuring personality isn't justified. Indeed, the whole field of *psychometrics* (literally meaning mind measurement) is dedicated to measuring differences between people in various psychological concepts (or constructs), including personality. Accordingly, within this field (and psychology in general), the question is not really whether personality can be measured, but rather, whether it can be accurately done. So, are personality psychologists able to measure personality well? Are they able to really capture a person's character?

The answer to this question is "yes!" (with a big exclamation mark). We will review evidence for this claim below, but first, we should clarify a few points. First, there is no magic in personality assessment. Personality psychologists are not mind readers or telepathists. They cannot look at your palm or forehead and tell you who you are. Personality assessment is not standard or simple. It is not like measuring height with a tape measure. Personality assessment combines a variety of theories and methods, including common sense, probability theory, and statistical testing. The methods are often not much different from what anyone put with the task of assessing personality would eventually discover and try.

To clarify this point, suppose for instance that you (and perhaps a few of your friends) were given the task of devising a way of assessing the personality of, say, the richest person in the world (who at the time this book is being written is, according to Forbes rankings, Carlos Slim; *Forbes.com*, 2011). How would you go about doing it? In fact, if you have a minute, you may actually want to try this exercise. So, the question is as follows: How you would have measured the personality of the richest man in the world? What methods would you use?

Regardless of whether you actually attempted this task or not, it is safe to say that you would eventually have had a number of ideas, or options, in front of you as methods. Indeed, there are several ways you could do this. One way, of course, is simply to talk to them and find out as much as you could about their personality. Another way could be to ask them questions simply by using a questionnaire. You may, however, be skeptical. They may distort their story, either to self-enhance, or because they are simply delusional. So, you might decide to interview other people who know this person well and get their views of what he/she is like. Finally, you may decide that it would be useful to observe how this person behaves in a variety of situations. For instance, you could put them in various scenarios or role plays and see how they react; or put them in experimental conditions. You could, alternatively, observe their day-to-day behavior, and so on.

FOUR TYPES OF DATA

One problem (but this is also an advantage) is that there are lots of ways you could get information, or "data," about a person, and personality psychologists have divided the numerous data sources into a few categories. These data categories are (a) life record data (L-data), (b) observer data (O-data), (c) test data (T-data), and (d) self-report data (S-data). An easy way to remember these categories, or types of data, is by the acronym LOTS. Below, we briefly describe each of these categories.

L-data basically deal with a person's life history or biographical information. It involves collecting data from the individual's natural, or everyday-life, behaviors, measuring their characteristic behavior patterns in the real world. Rather than asking a person about their past tendencies, L-data often consist of actual (objective) records. This can be obtained by looking at past school/college grades, criminal records, educational attainments, and so on. It is based on the idea that past behavior is the best predictor of future behavior.

O-data consist of obtaining evaluations and information from relevant others or observers. Observers can include parents, friends, colleagues, teachers, and so on. There are a variety of ways in which observers can provide information. A common way is to provide ratings through questionnaires similar to (or the same as) those used in self-reports. The benefit of this method is that one can obtain data from different observers who see and interact with the subject in different contexts. For instance, in organizational settings, 360 multisource feedback is a common way to obtain O-data. This involves obtaining ratings from subordinates, peers, bosses, and customers (in addition to self-ratings). Other observational methods include observing participants as they go along their daily lives. This is similar to anthropological research, where people are observed in their natural environments. The observer is usually someone who is trained to make systematic observations. They attempt to obtain as much data as possible, which are then scored on a predefined set of criteria.

T-data are based on objective tests. They consist of standard stimulation situations in which the individual is unaware of what is being measured (Cattell & Kline, 1977). It basically involves examining participants' reactions to standardized experimental situations (often created in a lab), where a person's behavior can be objectively observed and measured. One example of such tests (called the Fidgetometer) involves instructing examinees to sit on a chair that is wired up to detect any movements. In this scenario, the person being examined often does not know that their movement is being measured. Even if they did, they would not know that personality traits are inferred from moving more or less (let alone which particular personality trait).

Finally, S-data involve responses based on introspection by the individual about his or her own behavior and feelings. Here, the information about the individual is obtained by the individual. This can take several forms, most common of which are self-report questionnaires and interviews (but there are others such as, for instance, written-essay form). The methods employed in S-data are the most convenient form of gathering information. This is particularly the case today, with the advent of the Internet, where surveys posted online give simple and quick access to a vast number of people.

There are also several methods that do not easily fit into the LOTS categories. For instance, some research employs diary methods, where participants are required to report specific events, or specific behaviors at specific times, or feelings and thoughts. Thus, participants in such studies are asked to keep diaries of their thoughts, feelings, and behaviors, over a set time period. This can sometimes be a highly useful method because it can provide data that may otherwise be difficult to obtain. Indeed, this was brilliantly demonstrated by studies conducted by Fleeson and Gallagher (2009), discussed in Chapter 1, which provided clear information about behavior variation across situations and time.

There are many other methods available, of course, to assess someone's personality. As you review these options, however, you are also likely to be recognizing that there are shortcomings of each. For instance, life records (L-data) are not always easy to obtain and can be biased, or even inaccurate. Asking people direct questions either through interviews or self-reports (S-data) may be subject to impression management or socially desirable answers (i.e., lying). Asking others (O-data) may seem to remedy the latter concern, but others may not actually know the person very well. In any case, it certainly cannot eliminate the possibility that they are also distorting their ratings (e.g., because they are best friends with the person being rated). Observational methods may be subject to common cognitive biases in human observers. Finally, experiments may not generalize to the outside world.

As you can see, none of these measures are perfect. Each individual data source, and methods within it, has its own flaw.

However, despite this, it is also easy to see the benefits of each method. Clearly, the information gathered from these sources will not be totally useless. It will surely tell you something about the personality of a person. In addition, there is nothing to say that a researcher needs to be confined to one data source. In principle, they can combine as many of these methods as they wish. Indeed, it is desirable, and advisable, that multiple sources are used when obtaining information about people. In this way, one can be more confident about one's conclusions, particularly if the different methods end up providing very similar profiles of the same person, if they paint a similar picture.

Nevertheless, it is not always easy to expose people to hours or days of research. Personality psychologists have therefore often had to resort to fewer, and commonly, single sources of data. A critical task for a researcher therefore is to determine which assessment method to choose. In order to do this, of course, the researcher must know which assessment method assesses personality most accurately. There are several scientific methods to establish this and researchers today generally agree on which tests are most accurate. Nevertheless, not all well-established methods are suitable for all researchers. That is, there is no universal agreement. One major reason for this is that judging which method is best is not always a question of research data, but also a matter of theoretical perspective. Thus, psychologists may employ different assessment methods because their research often rests on different theoretical ideas about what personality is, what its underlying causes are, and how it is expressed. As mentioned before, a psychoanalyst would rarely employ self-reports simply because the theory asserts that many of the causes of a person's thoughts, feelings, and behavior are not available to the person on a conscious level.

While there are different schools of thought, however, today the most commonly used source of data in personality psychology is self-reports. This may strike you as surprising. After all, self-reports, on the surface, appear to have several limitations (some of which already have been mentioned). Before you are tempted to draw any conclusions, however, let us remind you that scientific research on personality testing spans almost 100 years (even if efforts to assess personality have an even longer history that predates psychology; Boyle, 2008). Accordingly, the methods found today have gone through nearly a century's research and scientific evaluation. Therefore, the current inclination of researchers to use self-report does not reflect personal preferences, but rather years of empirical data.

For you to better understand the current status of personality assessment, it is perhaps useful to look at its evolution—that is, the different phases and stages it has passed to arrive at its current position.

A BRIEF HISTORICAL PERSPECTIVE OF PERSONALITY ASSESSMENT

Interestingly, the earliest personality measures were in the form of questionnaires not unlike those found in psychological research and practice today. However, as with intelligence measurement, the impetus for the development of personality tests came from the world of practical affairs. Indeed, a major reason for this was the success of early standardized intelligence tests. Alfred Binet had successfully introduced tests of intelligence (in 1904), which were used to classify children according to their ability, first in France and later in United States. During World War I, adjusted adult versions of these tests were soon brought into the U.S. Army, to aid in the selection of recruits (in terms of their cognitive ability) for military service. Soon after, however, a need was also recognized for tests that would identify recruits that were prone to psychological instability. To ensure army recruits were also emotionally healthy, therefore, the first standardized personality test was devised. It consisted of questions that dealt with various symptoms or problem areas (for instance, with whether a person had frequent daydreams, or wet their beds, etc.), on which "yes–no" responses could be made (Woodworth, 1919).

The measures were a success in the army. As a result, they quickly spurred interest in the application of personality assessment in other domains also. The most noteworthy of these was within clinical practices, where some researchers aspired to design a test that would provide an "objective" basis for psychiatric diagnosis. That is, they wanted to develop a test with items (i.e., test questions) that could distinguish between groups known to have different psychiatric disorders, as well as patients from people in general. The best-known test of this sort was the Minnesota Multiphasic Personality Inventory (MMPI; Hathaway & McKinley, 1940), which appeared in 1940. Similar to the tests used in the army, the MMPI was a self-report inventory consisting of true–false statements. The achievement and popularity of the MMPI were enormous and still remain today (in fact, with its revised version [MMPI-2], the MMPI is thought to be the most widely used personality inventory in history; Boyle et al., 2008).

Given the practical usefulness of the MMPI, similar tests with nonclinical populations soon followed. The aim of researchers again was to distinguish between groups, but this time between nonclinical personality characteristics. One of the best known of these was the California Psychological Inventory (CPI, Gough, 1957). As with the MMPI, the CPI was designed with practical purposes in mind. Specifically, it was aimed at high school and college students. The CPI tested for various personality traits such as dominance, sociability, tolerance, and so on and was useful for categorizing people into different groups, for instance, dominant versus submissive pupils. As with the MMPI, the CPI was (and still is) a highly popular inventory in applied settings (even if the academic community has largely dismissed the test on empirical grounds). This is one reason as to why it has long been known as "the sane man's MMPI" (Thorndike, 1959).

An interesting historical observation is that around the time these self-report measures were being constructed, other personality tests that differed substantially in their method-ological and theoretical foundations were also appearing. These included the now infamous Rorschach Inkblot Tests (Rorschach, 1921), the Thematic Appreciation Test (Murray, 1943), and the Objective Analytic Test Battery (Cattell, 1950). These tests con-trasted radically from self-report inventories, such as the MMPI and the CPI. While self-reports clearly relied on people's sub-jective evaluations of themselves (as well as their honesty and self-knowledge), these latter tests were designed to eliminate the subjective element in testing. The notion here was to design tests that would actually measure a person's personality rather than asking him or her about it. Thus, akin to intelligence tests, advocates of this line of research wanted to design objective measures of personality. This division between subjective and objective measurement of personality has a long-standing his-tory, and tension between advocates of each remains even today. Nevertheless, the desire to create convincing objective measures of personality traits is no doubt shared by all researchers in the field (even the skeptics of such measurement).

Perhaps, deriving from this tradition, more recent assess-ments of personality have increasingly included objective measures. This "renaissance" of objective measures no doubt has come as a result of technological improvements in various areas such as software and computers, medical equipment, and technological advances in experimental settings. For instance, psychologists are now able to, and increasingly do, use physi-ological measures to assess personality, including examining genetic, biological, and neurological markers (see Chapter 2 section on Genes and Personality for more details). Positron emission tomography (PET) scans, functional magnetic reso-nance imaging (fMRI) scans, and electroencephalography (EEG) measures are becoming increasingly popular in psycho-logical research on personality.

Nonetheless, as mentioned before, today self-reports remain at the forefront of personality assessment. With so many other options, you may be wondering why that is. As mentioned above, however, the choice of self-reports is not a matter of personal preference but rather reflects the simple fact that this method has met the scientific criteria better than other methods. The criteria in question are the cornerstone of personality assessment; they are the means by which personality psychologists determine whether they have assessed personality accurately or not (or rather how accurately). Accordingly, the next section will be devoted to their nature and description.

HOW CAN WE DETERMINE WHETHER PERSONALITY IS ASSESSED ACCURATELY?

We mentioned earlier that a fundamental aim, or one might even say obligation, for personality psychologists is to determine whether they, through the various methods mentioned above, are actually able to capture people's personalities. That is, they need to determine and demonstrate that they are assessing personality accurately. This is, of course, an empirical question. It is not down to your or our opinion about whether a certain data source or assessment method seems to be more suitable than another for assessing personality. There are ways to demonstrate this scientifically. The criteria that any personality test (or indeed any other psychometric test) needs to meet to be considered useful, or fit for purpose, are *reliability* and *validity*. A good test of personality is one that is both highly reliable and valid. Given their importance for psychological research of personality, we will discuss the meaning of these terms in detail below.

Reliability

Suppose you went on a weighing scale in the morning and found that you were 165 pounds (or around 75 kg). Imagine that you did the same the morning after and found that you were now 130 pounds (or around 60 kg). The following morning the scale seems to suggest that you are now 200 pounds (or around 90 kg). You would obviously throw the scale away. It is clearly unreliable. At least two of these values have to be wrong, which means you cannot take any of them at face value. Even if the scale got it right one of the occasions, you would still not find it fit for purpose. This is because it is inconsistent—it does not consistently show the same values (which it, of course, should).

In psychometric testing, similarly, reliability refers to the consistency of a measure. It refers to the extent to which observations are dependable. This consistency (or reliability) can refer to three aspects of the test: the test's internal consistency, test–retest reliability, and interrater reliability. Should a test be lacking in (or score low on) one or more of these components, it would be considered to be unreliable. The extent to which the measure is lacking in one of these components is reflected by the "measurement error," that is, the amount of error there is in the measure's ability to capture (or assess) what it is supposed to capture (be it weight, height, or personality). Thus, for a measure to be considered reliable, it has to have high internal consistency, high test–retest reliability, and high interrater reliability (although this latter point can depend on other factors, as you will see below). We will deal with each of these components below.

The aspect of reliability—internal consistency—refers to how much association there is between the items that are measuring the construct in question. It is essentially the correlations between the items of the test. For instance, imagine we wanted to measure a person's intelligence and gave the person a five-item measure to complete. Of the first three items, one is on arithmetic, one on vocabulary, and one on picture completion. However, suppose that the last two items consisted of measuring how fast the person runs and how much weight this person can lift. Now, regardless of whether these two items (running speed and power) is part of your concept of intelligence or not, we are likely to find little or no correlation between these and the other three items of the test (which do correlate with one another). In this scenario, we have little internal consistency between the test items. Similarly, in a personality questionnaire that aims to measure, say, ambition, we may have items (or questions) asking about a person's tendency to persist on tasks, their reactions to competition, or their eagerness to advance. If we then included questions about the person's tendency to visit art galleries, to daydream, to read scientific magazines, and so on, we would not expect the test to be internally consistent. Many of the items of the test would not be associated with one another. If different parts of the test are measuring different variables, it is hard to see how it could be a good test. Thus, internal consistency of a test is necessary for a test to be reliable and therefore useful.

The second aspect of reliability, test–retest reliability, refers to the extent to which observations (for instance, score on a personality scale) can be replicated. It is what we illustrated with the weight scale example. Does the scale give identical readings each time you are on it, or does it give different values? In terms of personality measurement, test–retest reliability refers to the similarity of test scores between different occasions. That is, the correlation between test and retest scores is the index of the test's reliability. If a group of people, for example, take a test of Extraversion on two different occasions, say, a few weeks in between, it is expected that they should score approximately the same on the second occasion as they did on the first (assuming that there will be no change in the construct being measured, i.e., in people's actual Extraversion levels). If there was no consistency between the scores, that is, if the test gave different scores to people at these different occasions, then no trust could be placed on the scores. It should be noted that we are referring to test–retest reliability in terms of rank-order consistency (see section on Stability Versus Change for a reminder of rank-order stability). So, a person scoring similarly means that they score similarly relative to others. That is, it is perfectly possible to have high test–retest reliability even when a significant mean-level (or absolute) change has occurred in that particular trait (for instance, test–retest reliability of IQ scores remains high, even if people become more intelligent as they move from childhood to adolescence).

The final component of reliability concerns interrater reliability. Interrater reliability refers to the amount of agreement, or consensus, between two or more raters. For instance, if you rated yourself as a very funny person but your partner completely disagreed, interrater reliability would be low. Commonly, interrater reliability involves ratings by others (often referred to as judges). For instance, how much agreement is there between your friends that Brad Pitt or Angelina Jolie is beautiful? If beauty is in the eye of the beholder, of course, there should be low interrater reliability between your friends' judgments. That is, there would be little consensus on how attractive they found Brad or Angelina. If, on the other hand, they mostly seemed to agree (and a guess would be that they do), we would say that the interrater reliability is high.

This is also the case with regard to personality. In job interviews, a panel of interviewers generally want to rate you on different personality traits—how ambitious you are, how agreeable you are, how socially skilled you are, and so on. If the interviewers disagreed on how reliable or friendly you are, for instance, there would be little value in this method of assessment. As before, at least one judge would be wrong, which in essence would render all the ratings futile. Thus, interrater reliability is crucial for a personality test to be considered reliable.

It should be noted, however, that there could be value in having low interrater reliability. For instance, in some instances, such as in 360 multisource feedback, interrater reliability is not necessarily expected. This is because different people may have seen different parts of the ratee's personality, and thus, the ratings would be considered to be complementary and provide different sources of information (rather than reflecting disagreement).

Sources of Unreliability ("Error")

Several factors can influence the reliability of a measure. In technical terms, we would say that there are many sources of "error" in measurement. These can include factors internal to the person, such as mood state, motivation, physical state, and so on, or external factors, such as test-taking conditions and the nature of the test itself. It is obvious to see how internal factors could influence tests' reliability. For instance, if a person completes a test on subjective well-being just after he or she won the lottery, they would probably respond differently than they would have just a few hours before (and even some time after the win, as positive effects may wear off with time). Thus, in this situation, we could not rely on the test score of subjective well-being. The test score would be unreliable.

Sometimes error in measurement may result from factors inherent to the test. One source of error is the number of items included in the test. For instance, if you wanted to test whether a person is conscientious, you could simply pose the question "Are you a conscientious person?"—"Yes" or "No"—in a questionnaire. This makes sense; however, you would probably also recognize that there would be several sources of error in this type of questionnaire (even if the person was being honest). A person may respond "Yes" because they see themselves as more conscientious than, well, "not conscientious." However, in essence, they may still not be very conscientious. The test doesn't tell us how conscientious they are. Thus, although the test is not wrong, there will be quite a bit of error in the test because it has not been able to capture how conscientious that person actually is.

If we, on the other hand, asked two or three questions (e.g., "Are you conscientious with regard to your university assignments, at work, at home, etc.?"), and perhaps gave them a rating scale from 1 to 5 on which they could indicate their agreement, then we would have a better estimate of how conscientious they are. In essence, the more questions you ask about different behaviors related to Conscientiousness, the fewer sources there would be for error. This is why personality questionnaires usually comprise dozens and sometimes hundreds of questions. However, we should note that the remedy isn't always simply to include more items to increase reliability. A large amount of items may lead to fatigue, boredom, anger, or other possible mood states in test-takers, which, as mentioned before, are themselves sources of error.

The Practical Importance of Eliminating Error

Error, and thus unreliability, in measurement can have serious implications, particularly in applied settings. It is therefore critical that psychologists and practitioners try to minimize the sources of it. Suppose for instance that we are selecting applicants for a job, based on their scores on Conscientiousness. Here, we inevitably need to decide a cut-off score for selection versus rejection. Imagine that the average Conscientiousness score for all candidates is 50 and a first candidate scores 75, whereas a second scores 55. Should we hire the first candidate based on this score? Initially, this would certainly seem like a reasonable decision. However, crucially, the decision would also be dependent on the reliability of the scale that we are using. If we have a scale that is highly reliable and people score the same each time they complete it (so the first candidate would score 75 and the second 55 on every occasion), then this decision would be correct. However, if we have a test with low reliability and people score rather differently on different occasions (for instance, if there is a reasonable chance that the scores reverse, i.e., the first candidate scores 55 and the second 75, on a second occasion), then this decision would be incorrect (because we do not know what the candidates' "true" Conscientiousness levels are).

As you can tell, this issue is a worrying one. If you are applying for a job, you would certainly not want to be the one having an "unlucky" test day. Such a revelation may also evoke serious skepticism in you toward psychometric testing in general. However, you do not need to draw any such conclusions. Psychometricians have inevitably found a way of dealing with this issue and there is a statistical way to eliminate this problem. In plain language, to be able to make a selection decision based on psychometric scores, we need to know the standard variability of the scores, that is, how much disparity we can expect on individuals' test scores in general, or, on average. This is what psychologists call standard error of measurement. We do not need to dwell on the statistics for calculating the standard error. Instead, we will give you a simple explanation. First, we know that in a normal (bell-curve) distribution, 68% of all scores will fall between the mean (average) and ±1 standard deviation (i.e., the average departure of scores from the mean). In all, 95% of scores fall between the mean and 2 standard deviations (note that we can generalize this observation because most, if not all, human traits show a distribution that looks like a bell curve). For instance, IQ tests have a mean score of 100 and a standard deviation of 15. This means that 68% of all people score between 85 and 115 and 95% of all people score between 70 and 130.

We can then apply this same formula to our example above. Imagine that our test of Conscientiousness has a standard error of 5. This would mean that there is a 68% chance that a candidate's score will fall within ±5 points of their current score, and 95% chance that it will fall within ±10 points of their current score on another occasion. Thus, in the above scenario, a standard error of 5 would mean that the first candidate's score would, 68% of the time, fall between 70 and 80, and 95% of the time between 65 and 85. The second candidate's score would, 68% of the time, fall between 50 and 60, and 95% of the time between 45 and 65. Thus, as you can see, if we know that the standard error in the sample is 5, and we know that the first candidate scored 75, and the second 55, we can be confident that there is about 95% chance that our decision to select candidate 1 would be correct. This is a pretty good bet.

The good news is that standard error can be calculated fairly easily. Interpretations of scores (and selection decisions) can, subsequently, be made by taking this formula into account. Once calculated, an employer can decide that differences between two candidates' scores would have to be beyond the specific error boundaries to be considered enough to make a selection decision. This would certainly minimize the probabilities of getting it wrong. The takeaway message from this example is, however, that for all practical testing, it is essential that the test be highly reliable. A test with low reliability can be highly detrimental in practical use and would, in general, be considered to give a poor indication of a person's real, or true, personality.

We should finally note that even a highly reliable measure can sometimes be of little use. This is because very high levels of reliability may indicate that we are measuring rather narrow and psychologically trivial variables. For instance, it is easy to increase the internal consistency of a measure by asking an essentially paraphrased version of the same question over and over. This may give us very little information about the overall trait we are trying to assess. Thus, very high internal consistency may simply indicate that the test is so specific that it is of little psychological interest (Cattell & Kline, 1977).

In addition to being consistent, therefore, we need to determine whether the test in question is, in fact, also a useful one. This is where the next criterion for establishing the quality of a test comes in, namely, validity.

Validity

Validity essentially refers to the usefulness of the test. It assesses whether the test measures what it claims to measure. As mentioned above, the main task of personality psychologists is to demonstrate that the assessment methods they use are, in fact, measuring specific personality traits, and that they are accurately doing so. These concerns are evaluated by looking at tests' validity.

To illustrate, suppose that a woman wanted to investigate whether she was pregnant or not, but used a thermometer to do so. Now, this measure could be perfectly reliable, but it would no doubt be useless. It measures some variables consistently but those variables are not related to pregnancy; it is an invalid measure of pregnancy. Thus, although reliability is an essential component of a test, validity is arguably even more important (although, of course, if a test is not reliable, or consistent, it is difficult to see how it could be valid).

Given this definition of validity, however, you may be wondering how one could actually demonstrate what a personality measure is measuring. It is easy to validate a thermometer or a pregnancy test. We can feel as the temperature gets higher and lower; if a thermometer doesn't respond to these temperature changes, it is invalid. We can see whether a woman is pregnant or not (well, we can tell for certain after birth); if the pregnancy test repeatedly tells you something different from what you observe, it is invalid.

However, how do you demonstrate whether a personality test measures what it claims to measure? This is an important psychometric issue, since it is often difficult to even agree on what a psychological construct is in the first place (think of the notorious difficulty in agreeing on what intelligence is). Furthermore, things in psychology are not as observable as things in physics or chemistry. This difficulty has led psychologists to develop a number of different ways for assessing validity.

A very basic, and obvious, way to determine whether a measure is valid is to examine its *face validity*, that is, to simply check whether it looks valid. For instance, in personality questionnaires, this would involve verifying that the questions look relevant. As the old proverb goes: "If it walks like a duck, quacks like a duck, and looks like a duck, it must be a duck." Of course, face validity has no inherent connection to "true" validity. You may have a toy thermometer that looks exactly like a real thermometer, but is useless for indicating temperature. Face validity is good, insofar as it increases the probability that test-takers will take the test seriously (well, also that they will take it in the first place). However, very high face validity can also mean too obvious a test, or, a test easier to fake.

A related type of validity is *content validity*. This refers to whether the test measures all aspects of the construct being measured. For instance, a test of intelligence shouldn't just measure mathematical ability. Content validity can be examined, for instance, by having experts in the field (of, say, intelligence) inspect whether the test seems to represent a comprehensive measure of the construct. If the test doesn't cover all domains of a construct, it cannot be valid. Although mathematical ability is one aspect of intelligence, few would equate intelligence with merely a talent for mathematics. We should note, however, that with psychological constructs, no expert can tell us that a test is, in fact, valid just by looking at it—even if the content looks valid.

A more rigorous, and arguably more scientific, way of assessing validity is by looking at tests' *concurrent validity*. Concurrent validity can be empirically demonstrated by showing that the measure correlates highly with other measures of the same construct. For instance, if you have designed a new measure of impulsivity, you want to make sure that this measure is related to other already empirically established measures of impulsivity. If it does not correlate with any of these well-established measures, it is difficult to argue that this is in fact a measure of impulsivity. If there are substantial correlations between the new test and other tests of impulsivity, then it could be said that there is convincing evidence of validity. Of course, although concurrent validity involves statistical evidence for the validity of a new measure, there is an obvious question: If there already is an established measure for a construct, then why design a new one? This logic is accurate. However, one reason for new tests can be that they are simply better able to predict relevant outcomes.

In essence, quite separate from face, content, and concurrent validity, a key question relating to all psychometric tests is as follows: Does it provide practically useful information? A test may appear good, seem to encompass all the right components of a construct, and correlate well with other measures assessing the construct. However, if it does not yield information that enables psychologists to predict criteria that the construct should predict, then of what use is it? For a test to be considered worthy of attention, it needs to be associated with certain external criteria or real-life outcomes. For instance, if we have a measure of trait anxiety, we should, in essence, be able to use it to distinguish between people with anxiety disorders and people suffering from depression. If we have a measure of Agreeableness, we should be able to predict who will be less likely to have conflicts at university or work. These are called criterion-related or *predictive validity*. If we cannot predict outcomes, then clearly these tests do not capture the variables that we want to capture—and serve no real purpose. If we, on the other hand, can distinguish between groups based on the test, or predict who will act in what way, then the test would be of great practical value.

There are two other aspects of validity. These relate to the practical usefulness of a test beyond other available tests. If, for instance, we develop a new test of, say, emotional intelligence (EI), we would want (or need) it to yield information that is different from what we can obtain from existing ability or personality tests. This is called *discriminant validity*; it assesses whether a test measures a construct that is actually distinct from existing constructs. If the test has no discriminant validity (i.e., the correlations are very high), then we would have to conclude that the test either does not capture the distinct construct in question, or that this construct does not exist.

In addition to discriminant validity, we would also want the test to be able to predict external criteria beyond existing tests. To keep with the example above, if we, for instance, gave job applicants a test of intelligence (IQ test) and a test of personality (say the Big Five), would it matter if we also give them an EI measure? That is, will the EI measure give us information about how the person will perform at the job, beyond that of what is already obtained by the IQ and personality measures? This latter type of validity is referred to *incremental validity* and is, as we will see in the next chapter, of vital importance in applied contexts, and particularly within occupational psychology.

It should be clear from the above that various types of validity criteria are needed to establish whether a personality measure is accurately assessing the construct it is attempting to assess. Any one of these methods individually will not do. Thus, Cronbach and Meehl (1955) suggested an inclusive way of measuring tests' validity, namely, through *construct validity*. Construct validity refers to the extent to which results obtained from the tests fit into a theoretical network; it is the combination of all the findings. For instance, to establish the construct validity of a self-report measure of general anxiety, we would not only correlate it with individuals' feelings of anxiousness before a test, but a range of other criteria, such as the likelihood of receiving treatment for an anxiety disorder, the likelihood to be stressed in dangerous situations, physiological indices of anxious arousal, and so on. We would also have to show that the measure is related to other self-report measures of anxiety, is not correlated with tests not measuring anxiety, and is not correlated with ability tests (such as IQ). If all these criteria have been satisfied, however, we would be confident that we are indeed measuring anxiety, and we are accurately doing so.

As you can see, there is a highly rigorous and scientific process involved in demonstrating that personality traits (or indeed any other psychological traits) can be measured, are measured, and are measured accurately. This process is derived from scientific methodology. If we want to have confidence in personality tests, and make practical judgments based on these tests, we need to first establish that they show good psychometric properties. If a test shows good reliability and validity, we can be confident that we are indeed able to measure the personality trait in question, and that the test is practically valuable. Thus, although personality may be a complex, unobservable, and even chaotic, phenomenon, to the extent that tests show high reliability and validity, they can be said to be measuring personality with good accuracy.

Of course, so far we have only specified that a test would be considered valuable and an accurate estimate of a personality trait (or traits) if it shows good reliability and validity. We have not actually shown that assessment methods are, in fact, reliable and valid, nor have we specified the types of measures that may be more or less valid in assessing personality. Much of the criterion-related validity estimates, that is, what personality predicts, will be discussed with reference to self-report inventories in the next chapter. In the rest of this chapter, we will focus on describing in detail the different kinds of assessment methods in personality research, and critically evaluating the strengths and weaknesses of each. This will, in essence, also give you a better idea as to why personality psychologists so often prefer to employ self-report inventories.

TYPES OF PERSONALITY ASSESSMENT

In our example above, in which we asked you to consider methods for assessing the personality of the world's richest man, we illustrated the numerous options that are potentially available for personality psychologists. We also noted that the choice of personality assessment is guided not only by common sense or preference, but also by theoretical and statistical considerations. Thus, psychologists may employ different assessment methods depending on their theoretical perspective of what personality is, what its underlying causes are, and how it is expressed. Here, we will describe the various methods that personality psychologists have tried and tested throughout the years. Some of these methods have only recently emerged; many others have been used from the very early days of personality assessment.

Traditionally, it has been useful to divide the various assessment methods into three different categories: projective methods, self-report methods, and objective methods; however, as will be seen, not all methods fit into one of these categories, and we will review several other methods of assessment beyond this classification. Below, we will start by describing some of the more intriguing measures for assessing personality, namely, projective tests.

Projective Tests

If you have seen a Hollywood movie featuring psychological testing, chances are that it was the Rorschach Inkblot Test. The Rorschach Inkblot Test is one of the most well-known psychological tests, and indeed, one of the few (if not the only) personality test known to the general public. It is from the family of *projective tests*, which at their core are designed to obtain information about a person's innermost thoughts and feelings that he or she may or may not be consciously aware of. They do so by presenting people with ambiguous stimuli, or open-ended and unstructured tasks, such as completing unfinished sentences, interpreting events presented in pictures, or describing what they see in inkblots. They are referred to as "projective tests" because they require participants to project their feelings, thoughts, and perceptions in their interpretations of these stimuli. The assumption is that when people are presented with an ambiguous stimulus, whose meaning is not clear, differences in interpretations must reflect differences in inner psychological properties.

These tests are based on a theoretical perspective quite opposite to that of self-reports. Unlike self-report assessment, which in essence must assume that people know themselves and their own personalities (hence, why they can report it), projective tests assume that people are often not conscious of, or otherwise not willing to admit, many of their underlying psychological tendencies.

They would (evidently) therefore not be able to report these to interviewers or on questionnaires. Accordingly, the only way to access these parts is through techniques that require projection. There are numerous projective techniques; however, given space limitations, we will only review the most widely used (and the most popular) of these: the *Rorschach Inkblot Test* (or simply Rorschach; Rorschach, 1921) and the *Thematic Apperception Test* (TAT; Murray, 1943).

The Rorschach Inkblot Test

The Rorschach was designed by Swiss psychiatrist Hermann Rorschach (1884–1922) and consists of 10 symmetrical inkblots presented on cards. These come in black and white, or colored. Respondents are asked to report what they see, and subsequently (after all 10 blots have been presented) about what parts of the blot they used, and which attributes were most important.

The most important part of the test from a methodological perspective is the scoring. Numerous different scoring systems have been developed, focusing on a large number of elements of the response. These include the portion of the blot that is used (e.g., the whole blot or just parts), the specific attributes of the blot used (e.g., the color), and the content of the response (e.g., images of death, sex, animals, etc.). Some systems may, for instance, interpret (score) using parts as opposed to the whole blot as indicating rigidity and compulsiveness. Using the colored parts of the blot may indicate emotionality and impulsivity. Scoring some content, such as seeing sex organs or people engaging in sexual acts, may be obvious; however, others are inferred. For instance, seeing a wild animal may be interpreted (scored) as reflecting an examinee's conflict with his or her father.

While fascinating in its appearance, several problems have been identified with the Rorschach (some of which are common to all projective tests). An obvious problem is that scoring often requires subjective judgment, or interpretation, by the examiner. This means that different examiners may interpret the same responses very differently. Second, there are major inconsistencies among all the various scoring systems (Kline, 1992), which complicates the issue of interrater reliability even further. Finally, critics have pointed out that there is no psychological theory that justifies the assumptions made in the Rorschach test, or indeed any other projective method (Kline, 2000; we will consider this issue further when we evaluate the TAT).

These criticisms directed at the Rorschach have been empirically confirmed. Research has found little or no relation between individual Rorschach indices and external criteria. Indeed, in a seminal review of the validity of this test, Hunsley and Bailey (1999) noted that it is "the most reviled of all psychological assessment instruments" (p. 266). Furthermore, even when specific scoring systems have been able to improve the reliability and validity of the Rorschach (e.g., Exner, 1986), they have not done so beyond quicker and cheaper alternatives (such as self-reports), making it difficult to justify their use.

Thematic Apperception Test

The other major projective test is the TAT, developed by Murray (1938). Like the Rorschach, TAT involves the presentation of cards to participants. However, rather than inkblots, TAT consists of pictures depicting human beings interacting in various scenes. The scenes are ambiguous and open to interpretation (for instance, a man with a firm grip of a woman's arm), but they are less ambiguous than mere inkblots. The examinee taking the TAT is then asked to describe what is happening, what the characters are thinking and feeling, what may have led up to the scene, and what the outcome will be. The responses are interpreted and analyzed for recurrent themes that supposedly reflect important aspects of a respondent's personality, motives, and conflicts. For instance, an image depicting a man having a firm grip of a woman's arm may be interpreted as a scene of violence or a scene of passionate love. From participants' responses, different personal characteristics, such as power motivation, achievement aspiration, or affiliation orientation, can be extracted. What is extracted will depend on the nature of the response—for instance, the type of relationship depicted, motives and feelings attributed to characters, assumed causes of event, expectations of positive/negative ending to story, and so on.

Interpretations made by psychologists can often be appealing, intriguing, and even make complete sense (more so with the Rorschach, because the latter does not provide any obvious reference point that is offered by the TAT images). However, as with the Rorschach, a major problem with these interpretations is their subjective nature. Given there is no standard way of interpreting responses (even if several systems are available for scoring, these do not eliminate subjectivity of interpretations), different raters may often interpret responses differently. Given that at least one of these interpretations will be wrong, we cannot attribute credibility to any one of these interpretations. This also makes it difficult to determine whether the personality and motivational facets that are suggested by these interpretations, and the TAT, are actually real.

As with the Rorschach, the TAT has not fared well in studies assessing its reliability and validity. Although some studies have found TAT to be useful for identifying some personality and motivational characteristics (e.g., Atkinson, 1958;), correlations with several relevant motives as well as external criteria have often been poor. For instance, one key motive measured by TAT is Need for Achievement (nAch)—a variable strongly associated with entrepreneurial activity (McClelland, 1961; Rauch & Frese, 2007). However, studies have found little correlation between the TAT and objective or psychometric measures of nAch. Furthermore, while psychometric measures of nAch show significant associations with entrepreneurial activity (Rauch & Frese, 2007), the TAT has no validity at all in the prediction of this criterion (Hansemark, 2000).

The number and variety of projective techniques are remarkable (cf. Lilienfeld, Wood, & Garb, 2000). Overall, however, it is clear that evidence for the reliability and validity for these tests is scarce. Although the tests show some validity for limited purposes, when systematic research has been carried out, the results have been disappointing. In a recent review of the validity of all projective techniques, Lilienfeld et al. (2000) had a damning conclusion. They wrote:

> We conclude that there is empirical support for the validity of a small number of indexes derived from the Rorschach and TAT. However, the substantial majority of Rorschach and TAT indexes are not empirically supported. The validity evidence of human figure drawings is even more limited. With a few exceptions, projective indexes have not consistently demonstrated incremental validity above and beyond other psychometric data. (p. 27)

Given this review and that the ethical implications of relying on projective indexes in applied settings are not well validated, it is clear that projective techniques do not meet the criteria for personality assessment we discussed above. That is, they are not reliable, nor valid, methods for assessing personality; they do not capture personality accurately. Some researchers point out that this finding is not surprising. For instance, according to Kline (1993), projective techniques are based on thin theoretical grounds. While these tests share the psychoanalytic notion of projection of unconscious and inaccessible motives and drives, the use of projection (e.g., the scoring systems) and the assumption that subjects identify with the main characters in images (e.g., project onto inkblots) are quite different from that of psychoanalysis. Furthermore, there is no indication in general psychological theory to suggest that the inherent assumptions of projective techniques should be correct (i.e., that unconscious feelings and thoughts should "jump out" when a person is confronted with ambiguous stimuli, such as inkblots, or that a person should identify with characters in drawings). Thus, despite their inherent appeal and continued popularity in some circles of psychological assessment, the lack of reliability, validity, and theoretical rationale behind projective techniques has meant that there is now a rather general skepticism in personality as well as mainstream psychology about their use.

Objective Tests

Apart from their objective of discovering hidden sexual drives or dark repressed motivations, projective tests appeal to laypeople also because they have one important objective element: They attempt to assess personality without asking the person directly for his or her own opinions about it. The desire to assess personality objectively is not in need of any rationale. Anyone interested in assessing personality, be it academics and practitioners applying these in research or practice or examinees in organizational or clinical settings being assessed, would rather that this assessment be done objectively. After all, the best form of knowledge is, as mentioned before, objective knowledge. Objectivity is the essence of science. If personality assessment is to be considered scientific, then objectivity should be at the forefront of this endeavor. This is so obvious that it does not really need mentioning.

Despite this, however, one does feel that this sometimes needs repeating. After all, psychologists' preference for self-reports in personality assessment is notable. With this in mind, it is necessary to ask why this is so. To address this question, below we will describe and critically evaluate various objective tests and discuss the current state and projected future of this field.

As mentioned before, attempts to find objective measures of personality stretch back to the very beginnings of psychology. Although the efforts of some early pioneers in this non-questionnaire area is well documented (e.g., Thornton and Thurstone; in Hundleby, Pawlik, & Cattell, 1965), the most important protagonist of this field of research was undoubtedly

Raymond Cattell. Cattell believed that self-reports (as well as other sources of data) have several serious limitations: They are susceptible to both voluntary (e.g., faking) and involuntary (little, or biased, introspective knowledge) biases. He argued that it is therefore a vital task for personality psychologists to make progress with objective tests or T-data.

The Objective Analytic Test Batteries

Cattell (1957) defined an objective test as a test that can be objectively scored and in which individuals being measured are unaware of what is being measured. This description of tests reflects Cattell's concept of personality as the totality of behavior. According to Cattell, personality characteristics should be inferred from what a person does rather than from what the person says. In the 1950s, with this perspective in mind, Cattell and his colleagues launched a research program, assembling a broad sample of nonquestionnaire behaviors that could be used in tests as indicative of personality traits. Once these behaviors were composed and tested, the researchers attempted to elucidate by factor analysis the number of objectively derived personality dimensions. By the mid-1960s, Cattell had listed over 500 objective tests comprising more than 2,000 personality variables (Cattell & Warburton, 1967). These were later combined into a battery (collection) of tests known as the *Objective Analytic Test Batteries* (Cattell & Schuerger, 1978).

It is, of course, beyond the scope of this chapter to describe even a small percentage of these tests. Suffice it to say that advocates of such techniques attempted to derive certain personality characteristics based on how a person reacts to, or responds in, these tasks. For instance, one example is Thurntone's early attempt to measure—objectively—individual differences in persistence. To do this, Thurntone (as reported by Hundleby et al., 1965), in addition to self-reports, measured factors such as amount of time spent on an unsolvable perceptual ability test, time spent in breath holding, strength of hand grip, number of familiar words written in a word-building test, and more. This may give you an idea of the variety of tests now classified as part of the Objective Analytic Test Batteries. Other examples of these tests include speed of tapping, speed of reading when asked to read at one's usual rate, selection of acceptable versus deviating book titles, faster speed of social judgment, larger number of things disliked, number of admissions of minor wrongdoings or frailties, longer estimates of time to do tasks, and amount of movement when seated in a chair.

Although these tests seem to provide an appealing alternative to self-report assessment, their use has been rather limited outside a small group of researchers (mostly colleagues of Cattell or those otherwise influenced by him). Indeed, Cattell's research program was practically abandoned throughout subsequent decades. Kline (1993) notes that, as a consequence of this, the validity of these tests is virtually unknown. So, why were these tests abandoned? Several reasons have been listed, including low face validity (see section Validity), difficulties in constructing objective tasks, and difficulties in administration of these tests. These explanations essentially indicate that tests included in the objective analytic test battery were, quite simply, impractical. There were, nevertheless, other, and perhaps more serious, problems. A major such concern, for instance, was the personality structure extracted by these tests. Schuerger (2008) recently noted that "even under the very good conditions under which the [Objective Analytic] Kit research was conducted, the factor structure might be considered well demonstrated for only six of the hypothesized factors" (p. 543). In addition, research has shown that factors that were extracted, in some cases, loaded on ability tests.

Recent Developments in Objective Measures of Personality

In recent years, there has been an increased interest in alternative methods for objectively assessing personality. One compelling example is the *Implicit Association Test* (IAT). The IAT is based on recent approaches to the study of "implicit" cognition. According to social cognition research, people have two different systems of information processing, the reflective and the impulsive system (Strack & Deutsch, 2004). While the reflective system is rational and consciously accessible (for instance, consciously reflecting on whether one is extraverted or not when asked), in the impulsive system, information is processed automatically. Specifically, this processing occurs by spread of activation between concepts that are linked in the memory. For instance, for you, the concept of "party" may be closely linked, in memory, with the concept of, say, "fun"—and less closely linked with the concept of "anxiety"; the concept of "exam," on the other hand, may be closely linked with the concept of "anxiety," and less closely linked to the concept of "fun." Similarly, people also have personality trait–self-concept linkages in memory, such as, for instance, the concept of "I" being closely linked with the concept of "talkative" and less closely linked with the concept of "shy" and so on.

IAT is a computer-based method for assessing these automatic associations that exist between concepts in a person's memory. The strength (or closeness) of linkages is measured by the time it takes for people to react to associations between specified concepts. For instance, during the test, participants may be asked to associate as fast as possible a target, such as "me" or "others," with an attribute, such as "outgoing" or "shy," by pressing a response key. They are exposed to such associations through a series of blocks that alternate in the presentation of the target and attribute (e.g., "me" + "outgoing," "me + "shy," "other" + "outgoing," "others" + "shy," etc.). The notion is that some personality attributes will be more strongly associated with the "self" in memory than others (Asendorpf et al., 2002). This should therefore be "detected" in the IAT by observed differences in respondents' reaction times. If a person, for instance, is quicker in combining "me + outgoing" and "others + shy," than he or she is in combining "me + shy" and "others + outgoing," then one could conclude that the person's self-concept is more closely associated with the personality attribute of "outgoing" than "shy."

It is worth noting that IAT concepts presented to participants are not dissimilar to those presented in self-reports. For instance, rather than asking a person how assertive he or she is on a scale from 1 to 5, IATs may present the concepts of "me" and "assertive" and record the person's reaction time to this combination, compared to, say, the reaction time for the combination "me" and "compliant." The fundamental difference between these techniques (and in essence what makes one a subjective and the other an objective test) is that the speed at which the IAT tasks are carried out (often milliseconds) does not allow for introspection. This makes reflective, and therefore subjective, judgments (including faking) highly unlikely. One could, therefore, argue that IATs are essentially an objective (or less subject to conscious "intrusion") form of gathering self-reports. Another way of putting it could be to say that they are like self-reports with a lie detector attached to them. This is, of course, the gold standard for personality assessment. This raises the question as to whether there is evidence to demonstrate that IATs may indeed be as valid alternatives as the theory that they are based on claims.

First, it should be noted that the application of IATs in personality assessment (and in general) is relatively new (Greenwald et al., 1998). Nevertheless, some recent studies have provided support for the validity of IAT measures. For instance, Steffens and Konig (2006) found that an implicit measure of Conscientiousness predicted conscientious behavior in an experimental task better than the questionnaire measures of the same trait. Interestingly, this study did not find any association between the IAT measure of Conscientiousness and the self-report measure of Conscientiousness. Furthermore, in a recent meta-analysis, Greenwald, Poehlman, Uhlmann, and Banaji (2009) found compelling evidence for the predictive validity of IATs. In particular, IATs outperformed explicit measures (e.g., self-reports) in the prediction of behaviors, or "judgments," such as stereotyping and prejudice. Such judgments are assumed to be made below conscious awareness; therefore, the validity of IATs to predict them makes theoretical sense. Finally, research has shown that IATs have both additive (Schnabel et al., 2006), interactive (McGregor et al., 2005), and double dissociative or "distinct" (i.e., IATs predicting spontaneous, while explicit measures predicting controlled, behavior; Asendorpf et al., 2002) validity in predicting criteria.

It is clear that implicit measures of personality are intriguing research tools for personality psychologists. They also seem to have practical usefulness in predicting behavior, sometimes beyond explicit measures. Their main appeal, as with other objective measures, is that they seem to tap into the inaccessible parts of personality—aspects of a person's self-concept, which he or she may not even be aware of. As yet, however, they have not been widely researched. Furthermore, there remain several critical points these tests need to address. For instance, while IATs usually meet internal consistency standards, investigations of their test–retest reliability are less encouraging. Furthermore, meta-analysis has demonstrated that IATs have low concurrent validity. For instance, studies find little convergence between supposedly identical constructs measured by IATs and self-reports (Schnabel, Asendorpf, & Greenwald, 2008). IATs also show low association with other implicit measures, such as priming procedures. This indicates that IATs may predict unique variance but are unlikely to capture the broadest aspect of personality. Given that they do show evidence for incremental validity, one can argue that IATs may be complementary to self-reports—though they are unlikely to replace them. For instance, while Greenwald et al.'s meta-analysis found IATs to predict implicit judgments made below the level of consciousness (e.g., stereotyping and prejudice), explicit measures outperformed IATs in domains requiring reflection, such as brand preferences or political candidate preferences. Finally, there are doubts about the explanations of IAT effects. For instance, it remains unclear whether IAT participants respond to the actual (semantic) meaning of the attributes presented or simply on their positive and negative "tone" (e.g., shy = negative, confident = positive; cf. Schnabel et al., 2006).

Psychophysiological Measures

Other significant steps in objective testing have been made within the field of *psychophysiology*. Psychophysiological measurement attempts to increase our scientific understanding of the physiological functions that contribute to personality differences. One aim of psychophysiological measurement is to elucidate the biological processes underlying factor-analytically derived dimensions of personality. We have already outlined some of the research in this area in Chapter 2. However, as with other objective tests, a second objective of these measures is to actually eradicate subjectivity and cognitive biases completely. In a sense, they are attempts at measuring personality directly, rather than indirectly through self-reports or investigations of explicit behavior (which is essentially what other objective tests reviewed above attempt). Furedy (2008, p. 295) uses the metaphor "Psychophysiological Window on Personality" to exemplify this field. Given that people have limited control over much of the recorded biological signals in physiological measures, this seems a promising method for achieving the latter objective.

Although many techniques in psychophysiology have emerged only in the past couple of decades, today there are a large number of physiological tests available. Neuroimaging techniques are among the most popular of these; they include MRI, fMRI, PET, and EEG. Personality researchers often have to make informed (and cost-effective) choices among these measures, and the specific neuroimaging technique used in a particular study will often depend on the specific theoretical question. For instance, a researcher interested in how various brain structures relate to individual differences may employ MRI in order to generate detailed images of the brain (e.g., DeYoung et al., in press). Conversely, studies concerned with brain activity may use fMRI (e.g., Canli, 2004) or PET (e.g., Johnson et al., 1999), whereas researchers interested in measuring brain processes as they occur (Wacker et al., 2006) may prefer to use EEG. Not all physiological techniques measure brain activity, however. Other measures employed in research include salivary cortisol, which relates to hypothalamic pituitary axis stress response, body temperature, blood pressure, heart rate, skin conductance, and eye-blink startle response.

These techniques can, in addition, be used in two different experimental designs: recording biological signals under pure resting conditions or in response to tasks or challenges presented in the laboratory. The first approach involves the measurement of base levels of neural activity that may underlie personality differences. For instance, as discussed in the previous chapter, Eysenck's personality model of Extraversion posits that introverts and extraverts differ in their "natural" levels of cortical arousal. These differences should therefore be detectable with measures of resting brain blood flow using fMRI or electrical activity in hypothesized brain regions using EEG (as was done by Gale, 1983).

The second approach involves the measurement of brain activity during laboratory tasks. For instance, one of Cattell's measures included in the objective analytic test battery assessed startle response (such as pupil dilation) to a gunshot. Other examples include measuring differences in brain activity while participants are exposed to words with different connotations, such as strong negative (e.g., vomit, rape, murder, etc.) versus positive (e.g., win, happy, love, party, etc.). Indeed, much recent work has employed this latter approach, looking at various indexes, such as the magnitude, timing, and topography of changes in brain activity of participants, while they engage in experimental tasks.

So, what evidence is there for the reliability and validity of psychophysiological measures of personality? First, research has shown that significant and reliable correlations exist between physiological measures and personality traits measured by self-reports. For instance, people higher in Neuroticism have been shown to have larger startle modulations to fearful scenes than emotionally stable participants (Caseras et al., 2006). These findings have also been confirmed with fMRI responses (e.g., Canli et al., 2001). Similarly, extraverts have been found to have faster habituation of the startle reflex as measured by various physiological measures (Blumenthal, 2001). Furthermore, extraverts compared to introverts also tend to show higher reactivity in the brain when presented with stimuli associated with rewards (Cohen, 2005). A number of additional studies such as these show that there are indeed significant correlations between physiological measures of brain activity and self-reported personality traits.

On the other hand, the magnitude of these correlations is not always very strong. Thus, a large part of the variance between physiological measures and self-reports is not shared, meaning that the different measuring paradigms will tap into substantially different constructs. A question one might ask, therefore, is which method of assessment better captures the personality constructs in question. To address this, we need to first examine the reliability and validity indices of physiological measures. In terms of reliability, the results of research on psychophysiological measures have been mixed. For some measures, test–retest reliabilities have been found to be high (e.g., Smit, Posthuma, Boomsma, & De Geus, 2007). Other studies, however, have shown poor test–retest correlations of physiological responses (e.g., Anokhin et al., 2007). These discrepancies are often due to the difference in methodology and the question a researcher is trying to address in the study. Regardless, it is clear that the overall reliability of psychophysiological measures remains to be addressed.

In regard to the validity of psychophysiological measures, the literature is much less developed. Indeed, surprisingly little is known about the predictive validity of these measures. While some studies have provided preliminary validity evidence in regard to psychopathology, very few have actually examined the ability of psychophysiological measures to predict more common behavioral outcomes, such as career or relationship success. Thus, while there is clearly an increased enthusiasm among researchers about the use of psychophysiological measures in personality assessment, a lot of work remains to be done before any firm conclusions can be drawn in regard to their usefulness. A final point, which physiological research will need to address, is whether there actually is a causal relationship between brain areas detected by these measures and trait manifestations. In essence, there is nothing to say that a brain area that is activated during a particular task is not merely a "by-product," or "side effect," occurring concurrently while the actual causal, yet distinct, brain areas are doing all the work.

Taken together, while recent years have seen a renaissance of objective measures of personality, questions still remain in regard to their reliability, validity (usefulness), and, on some occasions, theoretical rationale. Nevertheless, with the rate of technological improvements in software and computer developments, objective personality measurement is certainly not an unimaginable ordeal. Furthermore, given the scientific aim of objectivity in measurement, the quest for objective assessment of personality traits is likely to continue. It remains to be seen, however, when and whether these measures will be adequate alternatives to more established methods of assessment (e.g., self-reports). Until reliability and validity analysis of objective measures are established, they can, at best, be seen as complementary to these methods.

Self-Reports

We have alluded to self-report measurement of personality throughout this chapter. We noted that self-reports are the most commonly used methods for assessing personality today.

The interesting thing about self-reports, and particularly personality questionnaires, is that most people seem to find them poor alternatives for assessing personality. They do not have an intuitive appeal. Questionnaires seem easy to fake (and it is not difficult to think of situations in which people would want to fake). Furthermore, even when people don't want to fake, one could question their self-knowledge. You would probably not find it hard to think of someone you know who thinks they are someone they are not.

Despite these apparent limitations, personality psychologists extensively employ these tests. Clearly, then, they must have merit for assessing personality; or else psychologists must be doing something wrong. We will evaluate the merit of personality inventories below. We will start by describing the various features and types of self-report inventories before critically evaluating their usefulness, or accuracy, for assessing personality.

The majority of personality psychologists see personality scales as scientific and technical measuring instruments. A main reason for this is that these scales can be used to gather structured information from people concerning personality and other psychological characteristics. That is, the key feature of self-report inventories is that they are standardized. They consist of a standard list of questions or statements, a fixed set of response options, and standardized scoring systems. Everyone taking the particular personality questionnaire in question gets the same questions, the same number of questions, and the same response options. Everyone's score is calculated through the same principles, or formula, often called the "scoring key."

Today, there are a vast number of personality inventories available, both within academia and outside it. Although most share some common features, they can generally be differentiated in a few basic ways. First, personality inventories may differ in the number of attributes they measure; some assess single characteristics, others assess multiple attributes. For instance, a measure such as the Core-Self Evaluations (Judge & Bono, 2001) measures a person's self-perceptions on a single scale. On the other hand, the NEO-PI-R (Costa & McCrae, 1990) measures five different traits.

A second way in which personality inventories differ is in their response format. Some inventories include a Yes/No response format. For instance, the item "Must you be in plenty of time if you have to catch a train?" (Eysenck & Eysenck, 1975) can only be answered as either a "yes" or a "no." Others include True/False (e.g., "I regularly feel sick before exams"; MMPI; Hathaway & McKinley, 1951), Like/Dislike, and Forced Choice. The most common response format, however, is a rating scale, which may differ on a continuum from, say, "strongly agree" to "strongly disagree." Thus, the measure of entrepreneurial tendencies and abilities (Ahmetoglu, Leutner, & Chamorro-Premuzic, 2011) item "I am quick to spot profitable opportunities" may be answered as "strongly agree," "agree," "uncertain," "disagree," or "strongly disagree."

In addition to differences in number of attributes measured and type of response format, personality inventories can differ in the approach taken to their development. Most common test construction involves both theoretical considerations and empirical analysis. Sometimes, however, they are simply based on the validity of items, without any theoretical conceptions. For instance, items in the MMPI were chosen not because their content seemed relevant to the trait in question, but because the item could discriminate between different psychiatric populations. That is, an item was kept in the MMPI if it could differentiate between people with depression and people with anxiety (and eliminated if it couldn't). Indeed, hundreds of such scales have been developed using this approach (Kline, 2000).

Most commonly, researchers first have a theoretical conception of the trait(s) in question before constructing a personality inventory. For instance, a researcher in leadership may have a theoretical conception of charismatic leadership—what this construct constitutes, and what sort of statements a person has to agree with to be considered a charismatic leader. Based on this concept, the researcher then usually assembles (writes) a large number of items for "piloting." The items are thus administered to participants (usually in the form of questionnaires) and analyzed for their efficacy.

Efficacy of items can be judged in several ways: First, they need to be able to discriminate between people's responses. Is there enough variability between responses or does pretty much everyone agree (or disagree) with this item? For instance, 99% of people will agree with the item "Do you have a good sense of humor?" (Hogan, 2007). Conversely, very few would disagree with the item "I prefer to have autonomy in my life." Such items are pretty much useless as they give no information about individual differences.

Second, individual items need to correlate well with the total score. An item that does not correlate with the total score usually measures a different variable. For instance, in a test of say, self-confidence, each item should correlate with the person's overall level (or score) of confidence. If it doesn't, it probably doesn't measure self-confidence. This relates, as mentioned above, to the internal consistency of a scale. In addition, an item should not measure more than one variable, or the researcher could have a mixed test. An item that correlates with, for example, both self-confidence and achievement motivation (two related but distinct concepts), would render the test less reliable.

If items are discriminating and internally consistent (i.e., they all correlate well with the total score), and are univariate (measure only one variable), usually the test will be reliable. Of course, as mentioned earlier in addition to reliability, the validity of the test needs to be established. In this respect, the construct validity of the questionnaire should be demonstrated by methods already mentioned above (i.e., predictive validity, criterion validity, and concurrent and discriminant validity).

What Makes Personality Inventories So Popular?

One reason for the widespread use of personality inventories is undoubtedly the "convenience factor." Questionnaires are easy to administer and score. Data can be collected from a large number of people at the same time, even without an examiner present. Today, web-based surveys make it easy to reach large, diverse, and arguably more representative, samples, quickly and without much effort. Researchers can, in addition, give instant feedback to test-takers about their personality, which is often an effective way of enticing participants. Thus, compared to other assessment methods reviewed above, which can be cumbersome (and very costly), personality measures are highly practical.

Nevertheless, ease of data collection is hardly the main reason for the popularity of this method. Ultimately, the key advantage of personality inventories is that they are highly suitable for reliability and validity analyses. That is, simply by following the principles outlined above, of the test-construction process, researchers are able to increase a test's reliability, determine its validity, and establish its norms. This can be done with self-reports far more readily than with other available methods. Good personality scales often take months, if not years, to devise, pilot, and standardize. During this process, revisions are made in order to increase reliability and validity. Items are eliminated until a test enables researchers to compare individuals fairly and with confidence. Large samples can be, and usually are, tested, which enables standard scores, means, and variability around the means to be established. Thus, self-reports are considered scientific and technical measuring instruments because they go through a rigorous scientific construction process. The rationale is simple. If criteria in each step of the process are scientifically validated, eventually one will have a scientifically validated tool for measuring personality. Thus, self-report questionnaires per se may not be good tests. Indeed, there are a vast number of self-report tests that are very poor indicators of personality traits. This simply means, however, that they have not met the required standards during test construction. The bottom line is that good self-report inventories are good because they have been and can readily be made so. Compared to other methods, this process is relatively easy.

Why Are They So Unpopular?

Despite benefits of self-reports, however, there is a prevailing skepticism to the use of such tests, especially in applied settings (but also in general). The reason is not very complicated and has been mentioned before: Self-reports are vulnerable to what are known as *response biases*. Several forms of response biases exist. Some are much more serious than others.

For instance, one common response bias is known as "yea-saying"—some people tend to agree with most responses, regardless of their content. One reason for this can be that the items are ambiguous. Another is that people are simply acquiescent by nature. Nevertheless, there are also people who tend to disagree with most items; this is known as "nay-saying." Another response bias is the tendency to endorse extremes. Some individuals tend to either strongly disagree or strongly agree with most items. Conversely, some individuals have a greater tendency to avoid extremes. They seem to be uncertain with regard to most items. Yet, others simply respond in a random manner. They simply don't care, or are otherwise not motivated to respond in a true fashion.

These are systemic biases. They can make interpretations about people's "true personalities" difficult and weaken test validity. However, test-developers have usually been able to deal with these response biases by taking steps in the test construction. For instance, "yea" and "nay-saying" can be nullified by having both positive and negative statements about the attitude in question (also known as "reverse scoring"). For instance, "I get stressed out easily" and "I am relaxed most of the time" are two items from the International Personality Item Pool (IPIP; Goldberg, 1990), which require the participant to disagree and agree, respectively, to be responding in an emotionally stable direction. Avoiding ambiguous items is another way of reducing "yea" and "nay-saying." Although it is difficult to avoid people's tendencies to endorse or avoid extremes, careful item construction can minimize these effects. Similarly, while carelessness can be difficult to eliminate, it can easily be detected. If internal consistency of a scale has previously been established, participants who respond inconsistently or in contradiction to themselves on items (thus lowering internal consistency) can be eliminated from the analysis.

Response biases, such as the ones outlined above, can generally be cancelled out by test-developers. However, as mentioned before, there is one bias that seems particularly serious when it comes to evaluating the robustness and actual value of personality questionnaires: faking. Faking is the tendency of people to dishonestly present themselves in an overly favorable (or overly unfavorable) light. It is no doubt the most obvious criticism of self-report inventories. The criticism is there because it is usually easy to "see the point" of items in questionnaires and to identify good from bad responses. So, can self-reports be valid given that people can distort their results? And, how much can we trust self-report scores when people's necks are on the line, for instance, in job applications or clinical interviews?

The question of faking has been investigated by personality psychologists for over 60 years. We will review in detail the literature on faking in Chapter 5; however, suffice to say at this point that although faking is a valid issue in personality research, it is not a decisive problem. The data from a vast amount of research show that people do not fake as much as one would imagine, and that being able to fake in turn may be a desirable personality trait in itself. Nevertheless, there is still an ongoing debate between advocates and critics of self-reports about the issue of faking in personality assessment, and we will critically evaluate both sides of the argument in Chapter 5.

Other Ratings

It has been suggested that one of the ways of overcoming faking is to obtain ratings from others. As mentioned above, these ratings may be done by peers, bosses, subordinates, and so on. Thus, if there is high agreement between self and other reports, one may conclude that the person isn't lying. Other reports are popular methods for assessing personality. Indeed there are those who argue that other reports are even more valuable than self-reports (e.g., Hogan, 2007). There are two reasons why this may be the case. First, others may actually know you better than you know yourself. Secondly, what you think about yourself (your identity) is arguably less important than what others think of you (your reputation). You may "deep inside" believe that you are a great leader or a very warm person but unless others (e.g., your peers or the person you fancy) agree, what you think will matter very little for outcomes.

An important question, of course, concerns the convergence between other ratings and self-ratings. Do other ratings converge with self-ratings? Research has shown a remarkable consistency in identifying the structure of personality, with the Big Five dimensions of personality emerging also with other ratings (Digman, 1990). Studies have also found clear convergence when comparing self-reports with ratings of knowledgeable others, suggesting that people are not completely oblivious to others' views and are honest. Nevertheless, the effect size of these correlations is often moderate, which means that significant differences between self and other ratings do exist. This discrepancy could be interpreted in several ways. The most obvious is that while people are not entirely dishonest, they do self-enhance to a degree. Differences may also reflect some limitations in introspection. However, increasingly, researchers suggest that ratings from different sources are complementary rather than indicative of measurement error. That is, reliable differences in ratings may simply reflect distinct information that each source receives by the ratee. Each source, in turn, would provide unique information through their ratings. As a result, a more complete picture of the person can be obtained. Indeed, research shows that other reports and self-reports explain unique variance in the prediction of relevant criteria (Chamorro-Premuzic & Furnham, 2010a, 2010b).

Whether other-reports can remedy faking is difficult to judge. However, it is clear that obtaining other reports, in addition to self-reports, may provide researchers with more information than each method may by itself. Of course, one limitation with other reports is that they are often not easy to collect. Moreover, it has been pointed out that the accuracy of other reports seems to depend on the level of familiarity between the rater and ratee. The level of familiarity may, in addition, itself be related to distortion in ratings.

Interview Methods

Another self-report method is the interview. Interviews are one of the oldest methods for assessing the personality of other people. In applied settings, it is still one of the most widely used (Chamorro-Premuzic & Furnham, 2010a, 2010b). In fact, it is estimated that 90% of employment selection decisions involve interviews (Cook, 2004). Interviews are also highly popular in clinical settings. Advocates of the interview argue that this method provides an opportunity like no other to obtain rich and detailed information about a person. First, interviews allow people to express themselves freely and answer a question in an elaborate way. This is not possible with self-report questionnaires, where responses are fixed. Second, interviews provide information not only about the content of the response, but also allow the interviewer to assess nonverbal behavior, appearance, mannerisms, and so on, which are impossible to capture in questionnaires. Finally, this method allows greater scope for maneuvering; for instance, an interviewer can, at will, explore further a particular response, focus on an issue in greater depth, or prompt the interviewee to provide additional information about a particular event.

Of course, how much flexibility there is in an interview may vary quite substantially. It has long been common practice to differentiate between what has been called structured and unstructured interviews (though, strictly speaking, they are really on a continuum from completely unstructured to rigidly and inflexibly structured). The ultimately unstructured interview is a little like an informal discussion, where interviewers ask whatever questions come to mind and interviewees follow up with answers in an intuitive and whimsical way. Crucially, questions are open-ended and attempt to avoid "leading" the interviewee's answers into any specific direction. Given its theoretical orientation, psychoanalysis often takes the form of unstructured interviews. This allows the interviewer to dig deeper into the recesses of the patient's mind to uncover unconscious conflicts, motives, and drives.

The structured interview, on the other hand, is preplanned to ensure every candidate receives exactly the same questions, in the same order, and at the same pace. Structured interviews also employ rating scales, use checklists for judgment, allow for few or no follow-up questions (to limit interviewees' response time and standardize it), and leave little autonomy for the interviewer. In that sense, totally structured interviews are little more than standardized personality questionnaires. Researchers tend to favor structured interviews, in order to obtain more standardized and less biased information about people. It is probably true to say, however, that most interviews are unstructured or semi-structured (Chamorro-Premuzic & Furnham, 2010a, 2010b).

Interviews undoubtedly provide a richer source of information than most other assessment methods. This could explain its popularity and widespread use in applied settings. Indeed, research has shown, for instance, that people applying for jobs not only approve of interviews, but often expect them (Chamorro-Premuzic & Furnham, 2010a, 2010b). They may even be surprised and disappointed if they are not asked to give them. Given that many people see interviews as fair and good methods of assessment, the question of how reliable and accurate interviews are in assessing personality is of utmost importance.

A large amount of research has been carried out to address this question. Results in the field have led to a number of conclusions. The first is that interviews, and particularly unstructured ones, show poor reliability. For instance, in a meta-analysis, Conway et al. (1995) found reliabilities of .53 when observers watched different interviews of the same candidate. This is substantially below the accepted standard of .7 for test reliability. Furthermore, different interviewers watching the same interview frequently show low levels of agreement. That is, interviews often also have poor interrater reliability. Given the flexibility of interviews in general, this is perhaps to be expected. There are several sources for low reliability. One is individual differences between interviewers. Interviewers ask different questions, record and weigh answers differently, and may have radically different understandings of the whole purpose of the interview. Furthermore, their personal backgrounds and life experiences affect the questions asked, how answers are interpreted, and the format or process of the interview. In addition, interviewees may react and respond differently to different interviewers, who differ in appearance, age, personality, interpersonal style, and so on.

Apart from individual differences between interviewers, sources of unreliability may derive from common cognitive biases. For instance, studies looking at the process of selection interviews have shown all too often how prior knowledge about the interviewee (based on the application form or curriculum vitae [CV] of the candidate) can strongly influence the interviewer, before the interview even occurs (Harris, 1989). Research also shows that interviewers make up their minds too quickly based on first impressions (superficial data, Cook, 2004). Equally, they overweigh or overemphasize negative information or bias information not in line with the algorithm. A final source of unreliability is that interviews, which are often face to face, make people even more concerned about managing impressions. Thus, socially desirable responses (i.e., faking) may be even more likely in interviews than in self-report measures.

Given the numerous sources of error in interviews, it is unsurprising that research finds mixed and often unsatisfactory results also with regard to the validity of interviews. A sufficient number of meta-analyses have been done to examine the validity of interviews. Studies looking at vocational outcomes, for instance, show that interviews often provide very little unique information about a candidate and show little incremental validity over established personality tests in the prediction of future job performance (Schmidt & Hunter, 1998). Similar conclusions are also reached in clinical settings.

Despite their limitations, interviews can still provide valuable information. This is particularly true in clinical settings where patients may have little awareness of their symptoms and are, therefore, not able to report these in questionnaires. Furthermore, in organizational settings, interviews can be designed to be more reliable and accurate. Most reviewers have seen that the single, simplest way to improve reliability is to introduce consistency and structure to the interview. Studies also show that it is possible to increase an interviewer's reliability by different, but important, steps, including doing a job analysis, training the interviewer, having structured interviews, and having behaviorally based and anchored rating scales (Chamorro-Premuzic & Furnham, 2010a, 2010b). If used in conjunction with other methods, interviews can indeed work well. However, it is probably fair to say that laypeople and practitioners have overrated the usefulness of interviews compared to other methods for assessing personality, such as the questionnaire methods.

Other Methods for Assessing Personality

Although we have reviewed the most commonly used methods for assessing personality, several other methods exist. These include the diary methods (where people keep a diary of their everyday behavior over a period of time), case studies (where a psychologist gets in-depth information about a person through lengthy conversations and tests), life history records (objective information obtained through records and reports about a person's past behaviors), behavioral observations (where people are observed in experimental settings or in their everyday life), narratives, and more. Although these methods are used in research, they are often done so for very specific purposes, by researchers with particular theoretical orientation and in a minority of studies. A major reason for this is that they are often not very practical, can be cumbersome to employ, and, in general, show lower levels of reliability and validity than standardized and empirically validated self-report questionnaires.

What About Astrology, Graphology, and So On?

Before we conclude this chapter, we want to say a few words about some assessment methods that seem to have won the hearts and minds of the general population but are rarely subject to scientific discussions. The most popular of these no doubt is astrology. Astrology is any of several traditions or systems in which knowledge of the apparent positions of celestial bodies is held to be useful in understanding, interpreting, and organizing knowledge about reality and human existence on earth. It is probably useful to talk about methods such as astrology, simply because people often use them to make inferences about other people's character and personality. Indeed, chances are that you will occasionally be asked about your zodiac sign by someone you have recently met at a party or a social event (we can certainly attest to this). It seems that people are prepared to make instant judgments about your personality based on the month you were born, or zodiac sign, sometimes regardless of your actual behavior.

Making judgments based on zodiac signs may often be a fun exercise. This is also undoubtedly the most handy personality assessment tool out there; it takes virtually no time and there is no test that needs completing. However, there is evidence to show that people (i.e., aside from astrologers) actually believe in astrology (Hamilton, 1995) and do accept the personality descriptions it offers (Glick, Gottesman, & Jolton, 1989). For example, Hamilton (1995) found that undergraduates presented with one-paragraph descriptions of the characteristics of their own astrological sun sign and an alternative sun sign, chose their own sun sign paragraph as a better representation of their personality than the alternative sun sign description. Van Rooij (1999) found that participants presented with individual trait words associated with the personality descriptions of each of the 12 sun signs chose the traits of their own sun sign as more personally descriptive than the traits associated with the other 11 signs. Thus, more than being mere amusement tools, it is likely that astrological readings have real-life implications. This could involve simple (but important) things such as people deciding their compatibility as partners based on their zodiac signs. However, it could also involve important decisions made in applied settings, such as an employer's evaluation of an employee's personality or a clinician's evaluation of a patient's symptoms. The significant implication is that, even if the inferences made are invalid, they may bias judgments or have self-fulfilling effects. It is of practical interest therefore to examine the empirical grounds of astrological readings.

There have been several scientific investigations of the reliability and validity of astrology as a tool to assess personality. For instance, Eysenck and his colleagues examined relationships between astrological and "Giant Three" personality factors of Extraversion, Neuroticism, and Psychoticism (Gauquelin, Gauquelin, & Eysenck, 1979; Mayo, White, & Eysenck, 1978). A couple of studies have even reported associations between these established traits and astrological factors (e.g., Gauquelin, Gauquelin, & Eysenck, 1979). Indeed, more recently, Sachs (1999) attempted to put astrology on a scientific footing by using statistical methods to explore associations between the zodiac and human behavior (in particular, criminal behavior).

While some studies have found significant correlations, however, many other results have failed to support the role of astrology in personality (van Rooij, 1994). For instance, Clarke, Gabriels, and Barnes (1996) explored the effect of positions of the sun, moon, and planets in the zodiac at the moment of birth and found no evidence that tendencies toward Extraversion and emotionality are explained by such signs. Even when whole charts are used in "matching tests," astrology seems unreliable and invalid. Furthermore, astrologers seem no better at identifying different personality profiles (e.g., highly extraverted versus highly introverted people) than random guessing (Dean, 1987). They also fail comprehensive tests when they themselves provide the required information (Nanninga, 1996). In a comprehensive review, Kelly (1997) concluded that:

> The majority of empirical studies undertaken to test astrological tenets did not confirm astrological claims, and "The few studies that are positive need additional clarification." (p. 1231)

Various authors have similarly dismantled Sachs' (1999) "scientific" claims, leading at least one group of authors (von Eye, Lösel, & Mayzer, 2003, p. 89) to claim that:

1. If there is a scientific basis to astrology, this basis remains to be shown, and;
2. If there exists a link between the signs of the zodiac and human behavior, this link remains to be shown too.

Finally, it is worth noting that very few, if any, psychometric studies on the structure of personality have found 12 factors of personality indicated by the zodiac signs. Most studies converge (as discussed in Chapter 1) on five or three factors. In addition, astrology is proposing a typological perspective of personality, which contrasts with the dispositional view. According to the dispositional theory of personality, people do not differ in terms of which category they fall in (e.g., extravert or introvert) or which trait they possess (e.g., introversion or Extraversion), but rather in terms of how much they possess of each trait (e.g., how extraverted; Chamorro-Premuzic, 2011). In this (nomothetic) paradigm, which has represented the state-of-the-art approach to the study of individual differences for the past 50 years, traits cannot form psychological categories or types, such as those proposed in astrology.

It is worth noting that several methods, in addition to astrology, such as graphology, phrenology, physiognomy, and, certainly, projective tests, are still in use in applied settings, despite the lack of any scientific merit for their effectiveness. This is perhaps a testament to the naivety, ignorance, and perhaps desperation of laypeople and many practitioners. However, it may simply be because people are more accepting of information that is ambiguous, general, and positive (known as the *Barnum effect*). These features are inherent in many of the tests mentioned. What is clear is that while astrology and other methods have stood the test of time, they have consistently been shown to be both unreliable and invalid methods for assessing personality.

CONCLUSIONS—WHICH IS BEST? HOW TO CHOOSE?

We started by asking: "Can personality be assessed?" The answer is "yes." The question then becomes how well? This, in essence, asks how reliably and how accurately can we measure personality. Clearly, there is more than one method one can employ. Some seem more intuitively appealing and compelling than others. It is clear that many people want objectivity. However, objective tests with acceptable reliability and validity levels are yet to be found. Projective tests may be compelling and interesting, but they are virtually useless. Even the interview, which is perhaps the most common method for assessing personality, is shown by research to have poor reliability and relatively low validity. Self-report inventories have little intuitive appeal. They seem easy to fake and work out. They also seem subjective in nature. Yet, they are also the most amendable to improvements in reliability and validity. Thus, psychometric tests are suitable for meeting the demands of good scientific work. They are concerned with sound quantification and place great emphasis on sampling, research design, and statistical analysis. For instance, tests such as the NEO-PI-R (McCrae & Costa, 1999) or the EPQ (Eysenck & Eysenck, 1975) have been validated extensively throughout the years. They show high internal consistency, test–retest reliability, cross-cultural consistency, and high construct validity. They are, in addition, able to predict a large amount of real-life outcomes better than any other available methods. We will review these in the next chapter; however, suffice it to say that the rationale behind the use of self-reports is far beyond the "convenience" factor. Good self-report instruments have been found to be highly reliable and valid for the assessment of personality. Thus, they are the most accurate instruments currently possessed by researchers for measuring personality, and they are scientifically proven to be fit for the job.

Despite the validity of self-reports, they are by no means the only methods worth using. Several other methods have shown to have acceptable reliabilities and incremental validity over self-reports. Thus, it is advisable that researchers try to use multiple methods. Further advances in measurement should also soon make it possible to assess personality objectively. This is not necessarily an either-or scenario. We may well need each type of measure, self-report, and objective to assess personality accurately. What is clear, however, is that currently personality psychologists are able to measure personality and are able to do so fairly accurately. As Meyer et al. (2001) conclude:

> Data from more than 125 meta-analyses on test validity and 800 samples examining multimethod assessment suggest four general conclusions: (a) Psychological test validity is strong and compelling, (b) psychological test validity is comparable to medical test validity, (c) distinct assessment methods provide unique sources of information, and (d) clinicians who rely exclusively on interviews are prone to incomplete understandings. (p. 128)

This statement is a testimony to the incredible progress that has been made in the measurement and assessment of personality. The sophistication of psychological measurement will no doubt continue to improve and contribute incrementally to our understanding of personality. Their informed use will hopefully also increase in applied settings to make more informed and rigorous decisions about people and their likely behavior.

Does Personality Matter?

n previous chapters, we discussed the theories, causes, and measurement of personality. We outlined the classification system that people use to describe other people. We explained the intimate interplay between genes and environment in forming personality traits and behavior. We also discussed how this interplay can help explain stability of personality parallel to the capacity to change it. The amount of research and public interest in the nature of personality is truly astonishing. Both researchers and laypeople have a strong interest in this concept, but why is this distinct interest there? Why do we want to understand our own and other people's personalities? In other words, why do we care about the concept of personality?

The answer is quite simple: We care because we believe that our personality has a strong impact on our lives; and this belief is even stronger when it comes to considering the personality of other people. Indeed, we believe that personality plays a strong role in shaping our lives, and that it will continue to have a central role in shaping our future. Although we may not always be aware of this, we probably all believe that our habits and typical ways of interacting with people will have an impact on our future. If we are right, then personality tests should predict the most important life outcomes: relationships, work, learning, health, and happiness. This section examines these issues.

The current section deals with some of the fundamental questions people have asked for centuries: Why are some people more successful than others? Why are some better leaders than others? Why are some better at making friends and influencing people? Why are some better at attracting and keeping romantic partners? These questions partly concern self-reflections (e.g., am I going to be successful or find the right romantic partner?); but they also concern predicting other people's behavior (e.g., is this person a competent leader or a reliable partner?)

An understanding of the basic ways in which people differ and the cause of such differences is essential for addressing the above questions. Fundamentally, however, we need to refer to the issue of validity of psychometric tests (described in Chapter 3) in order to evaluate whether personality predicts important outcomes in life. The current chapter therefore looks at the (criterion or predictive) validity of personality tests in explaining differences between people's current life circumstances and future paths.

There is an abundant amount of research of this kind, and it covers a wide range of outcomes that personality may predict. Here, we focus on some of the most relevant and widely researched areas. These include the effects of personality on (a) social attitudes and religious beliefs, (b) antisocial behavior, (c) educational and career achievements, (d) romantic relationships, (e) leadership, (f) health outcomes, and (g) happiness. Before we move on to review this literature, however, it is necessary to provide an outline of the basic statistical principles and procedures psychologists use to assess the psychometric validity of personality tests.

TESTING PERSONALITY THEORIES: CORRELATION, REGRESSION, AND STRUCTURAL EQUATION MODELING

The beginnings of personality research were characterized by the use of precarious methods of data collection and personality theories were often derived from *introspection, observations,* and *case studies.* However, modern approaches to personality can be distinguished from such theoretical or speculative approaches in that they are based on systematic gathering and analysis of quantitative data. As discussed in Chapter 1, dispositional theories of personality were derived from large datasets, which were generated by the use of self-report inventories. Accordingly, theories and hypotheses about the relationship between personality and various life outcomes can be examined through statistical tests, such as Pearson's correlation coefficients (see below). This systematic and predominantly quantitative process enables researchers to validate personality inventories and, consequently, test personality theories (or models). Below, we outline some of the more basic, as well as the more complex, statistical methods of data analysis used by personality psychologists.

Correlation

The statistical test of correlation is widely employed to assess the extent to which two variables are related to each other. The most widely used correlational test is the *Pearson Product–Moment Correlation Coefficient,* simply known as the *Pearson correlation.* This coefficient is represented by the lower-case letter r and takes its name from Karl Pearson (1857–1936), a famous British statistician. Although Sir Francis Galton may be credited with developing the theory of correlation in 1888 (Galton, 1888), Pearson's (1896) statistical test was one of the first to provide robust scientific instruments for the study of individual differences.

In simple terms, the Pearson correlation is a measure of the extent to which two variables (e.g., x and y) change together. It assesses whether (and to what extent) changes in one variable are predictable by changes in the other. For instance, when people make statements such as "the more you exercise the better you feel," "nice guys finish last," or "the less you drink the less you get in trouble," they are inferring correlations between variables. That is, in each of these statements it is hypothesized that one variable is predictable on the basis of the other. For instance, in the first statement, as one variable (exercise) increases so does the other (feeling well); in the second, as one variable (niceness) increases the other decreases (probability of attracting a female mate); and in the third, as one variable decreases (drinking) so does the other (getting in trouble).

Correlations can also be distinguished on the basis of their direction—positive or negative, ranging from –.1 to +.1. In the above statements, the first and the last are positive. The first, because both increase together, and the last because both decrease together (the product of two negative numbers is always positive). The second is negative because the variables are inversely related. The name negative correlation can sometimes be misleading, commonly interpreted as meaning no correlation. No correlation is, however, when the two variables are not related at all; that is, changes in one variable are not predictable from changes in another. For instance, two unrelated variables may be running speed and Extraversion. Given that changes in one are not predictable by the changes in the other, we can say that there is *no* (rather than negative) correlation between the two variables.

Of course, this kind of discourse on correlations is more theoretical than empirical. Saying that two variables are correlated doesn't tell us much; we also need to establish whether this relationship is significant (i.e., that it is not simply a chance event) and the strength of the relationship. Strength and significance are not the same thing; a strong correlation may be nonsignificant and a weak correlation may be highly significant.

When we make a correlational statement (e.g., the more hard-skinned the person, the better a leader he or she is), however, we generally assume that the covariation is not a chance occurrence (i.e., that it is significant). Therefore, the magnitude of the correlation is of key importance.

As we mentioned above, the value of r can range from −1.00 (perfect negative relationship between two variables) to +1.00 (perfect positive relationship between two variables), with an intermediate value of 0 (no association at all between two variables). Here, the implications of a correlation of .8, for instance, will be very different from those of a correlation of .1 because one covariation will be highly predictable, whereas the other will be barely above chance level. Correlations reaching ±1 (i.e., perfect or nearly perfect), however, are rarely found in psychological research. For instance, even when test–retest correlations are measured—that is, a person takes the same test twice, with only a few weeks in between—they rarely exceed .6 to .7 (and this is with reliable tests). More frequently we find r values close to 0, indicating weak or no association between two variables. The general consensus in psychology is to consider $r > .70$ and $< -.70$ as indicating a "strong" or "high" relationship, while r values ranging from .30 to .70 and −.30 to −.70 are typically regarded as "moderate," and r values ranging from .00 to .30 and .00 to −.30 are usually taken as indicators of a "weak" or "modest" relationship (Cohen, 1988).

Given that we will be discussing the predictive power of personality inventories, it is important to understand the practical meaning of the various values. Say we wanted to predict the relationship between two variables, X and Y. A correlation of .0 means that our ability to predict changes in Y based on changes in X is no better than chance. That is, our prediction would be wrong 50% of the time (and right 50% of the time). Another way of putting it is to say that X explains 0% of the variation in Y. On the other hand, if we had a correlation of .3, our ability to predict changes in Y by variations in X would increase by 15% (a simple way to think about this calculation is to divide the correlation by two; for more detail on this calculation, you can refer to Rosenthal & Rubin, 1982). Although 15% might sound like a limited ability to predict something, it is certainly an improvement on a 50/50 bet. For instance, if we knew that someone is above average on variable X, a .3 correlation would allow us to predict that they would be above average 65% of the time in Y. That is, we would be correct almost twice as often as we would be incorrect. That's not a bad bet. Even with a very weak (but significant) correlation of .1, we would be able to predict covariation of variables with 10% more accuracy (55% versus 45%). A relatively strong correlation of .6 would allow us to be correct 80% of the time. This is just to put things into perspective.

Of course, the significance, or strength, of a correlation cannot tell us anything about the *causal* direction underlying this correlation; that is, which variable, if any, influences which. The notorious quote "correlation does not mean causation" is something psychology (and other) students get to hear on a regular basis. This simply means that, even with a very high correlation, we would not be able to tell whether Y causes X, or X causes Y, or whether another variable (Z) causes both to change simultaneously.

Statistically, there is no scientific solution to this problem: Causational tests seem to exceed the explanatory scope of correlational designs. For example, knowing that time spent on watching violent movies is positively correlated with violent behavior cannot tell us whether one variable truly *affects* the other, and, if so, which one affects which. Journalists and the media would, of course, be quick to soak up such correlational findings as evidence for the detrimental effects of violent movies on society. However, one could equally argue that people with violent dispositions simply prefer more violent movies (you can refer to Chapter 2 for a detailed explanation of the interaction between dispositions and environmental preferences). Some associations may, in addition, be the result of another "linking" variable. For instance, even if we know that there is a perfect correlation between two thermometers—one indicating Celsius and the other Fahrenheit—we would not propose that variation in one causes variation in the other. Evidently, they both vary together because of a common causal factor, namely, heat.

Finally, it is also possible that the relationship between two variables is *mediated* or *moderated* by other variable(s). For instance, research has shown that people who score higher on Neuroticism tend to score lower on IQ tests (Furnham, Moutafi, & Chamorro-Premuzic, 2005). While a direct relationship would indicate that more neurotic individuals are less intelligent, studies looking at the mechanisms behind this relationship have found that this link is a function of (or mediated by) another variable, namely, test anxiety (Moutafi, Furnham, & Tsaousis, 2006). That is, higher Neuroticism leads people to be more anxious in test circumstances, which, in turn, impairs their IQ test performance (rather than there being a direct cognitive link). Indeed, when test anxiety scores are taken into account the negative correlation between Neuroticism and IQ disappears (full mediation) or decreases (partial mediation).

In moderation models, the effect of one variable on another is contingent upon a third variable. For instance, although there may be a significant correlation between IQ and leadership performance (Judge et al., 2002), this relationship may be moderated by a third variable—stress. Specifically, when there is low stress, high IQ may be beneficial for leadership performance. However, under high stress, high IQ may be detrimental for the performance of a leader (Fiedler & Garcia, 1987).

As can be seen from these examples, causality can be interpreted in various ways and may be affected by a number of factors. More sophisticated designs, such as longitudinal studies, can provide "chronological" data that may help us interpret the causational paths underlying correlations.

Regression And Structural Equation Modeling

Although correlations are widely used in psychological research, psychologists have more sophisticated methods at their disposal for assessing relationships between variables. For instance, when more than two variables are considered, the statistical method of regression enables us to *predict* one variable (the criterion) by another set of variables (the predictors). It also allows us to assess the degree to which a predictor and a criterion are related, when controlling for other predictors. For instance, IQ and educational level may both significantly and strongly predict future job salary (i.e., how much a person will earn). Yet, since these two predictors are likely to show a substantial degree of overlap, the prediction of one may be stronger than the prediction of the other. Thus, regression analysis can tell us which one is the strongest predictor in the model, when all predictors are considered simultaneously; it allows us to test the incremental validity of predictors (see Chapter 3 for a theoretical discussion of incremental validity).

Structural equation modeling (SEM) allows for even more sophisticated analyses to be conducted. For example, while regression analyses distinguish clearly between a set of predictors and a criterion, SEM can treat a variable as predictor and criterion at the same time. Thus, with SEM, we may test a *causal chain*, or whether x affects y and y affects z at the same time. Furthermore, SEM allows us to test mediations (Baron & Kenny, 1986), that is, whether the relationship between x and z may be a function of y (as with the Neuroticism–IQ link we discussed above). It also allows for tests of moderation, that is, whether the relationship between x and z is dependent on y. Of course, mediational and moderational effects can also be tested through regressions (i.e., by entering each predictor in different steps or blocks first, and then regressing one predictor onto another). Unlike regressions, however, SEM can simultaneously treat the same variable as predictor and criterion. A real advantage of SEM, therefore, is that it allows hierarchical models to be tested against alternative models. It should be noted, however, that the hierarchical nature of SEM does not mean that we are able to crack the issue of causality. Although SEM specifies causal models, it does not always guarantee that the causal direction is correct. Indeed, models may often fit equally well when the causal direction is reversed. Nevertheless, with careful theoretical and statistical considerations, a rigorous researcher is often able to provide the *most likely* causal model through the use of SEM.

Personality and Social Implications

he 2011 U.K. riots resulted in millions of pounds worth of material and industrial damage. Three people were killed. Every year, thousands of people are injured or murdered, directly or indirectly, because of conflicting religious and other social convictions. Such convictions are becoming increasingly salient in today's society. Social attitudes, beliefs, and behaviors are often attributed to social factors, such as parenting, schooling, culture, and the media. Rarely do we think of such attitudes and behavior with respect to inborn dispositional traits. Yet, an increasing amount of research suggests that political and religious attitudes and behavior may be closely related to individual differences in personality. In this chapter, we review the literature that shows how personality influences what is traditionally seen as social and cultural phenomena, such as political attitudes and religious beliefs, and prosocial and antisocial behavior. We start our discussion with political attitudes.

PERSONALITY AND POLITICAL ATTITUDES

In order to explain the antecedents, or causes, of political attitudes, we must first define the concept of political attitudes. A common distinction in the literature is that of right- versus left-wing attitudes. Researchers have found that right- and left-wing attitudes comprise several components. For instance, right-wing attitudes are thought to encompass right-wing authoritarianism, conservatism, and social dominance. Authoritarianism has been explained in terms of a set of behaviors, including showing excessive conformity, intolerance of others, and rigid and stereotyped thought patterns. Conservatism is thought to represent tendencies to resist change and to play it safe. Finally, social dominance is believed to involve individual discrimination, institutional discrimination, and behavioral asymmetry. These concepts are related yet separate constructs, and conceptual distinctions can be made between them. For instance, right-wing authoritarianism involves rigidity and lack of cognitive complexity; however, these individuals are often passive. In contrast, those who are high in social dominance orientation are more socially aggressive and hostile. Conservatism, on the other hand, involves tender, versus tough, mindedness and may therefore overlap with both these dimensions.

Right-wing attitudes have been explained in various ways. For instance, psychodynamic theory sees authoritarianism as an interaction of various conscious and unconscious mental or emotional processes involving submissive tendencies toward authority, which are caused by a strict upbringing (Adorno et al., 1950). Social psychologists view conservative attitudes as predominantly resulting from social forces; for instance, conservative people are argued to be heavily influenced by traditional institutions and their parents' values. Discrimination and social dominance are also explained from a social perspective, involving in-group and out-group principles (or forces). That is, individuals who are similar (physically or psychologically) to the members of the group tend to be "placed" within an in-group, whereas individuals who are different to these members are placed within an out-group.

Despite this traditional explanation of social attitudes, researchers within the field of differential psychology have pointed out that personality may operate as a strong influencing factor of such attitudes. Accordingly, it has been argued that certain personality characteristics may "predispose" people to hold more or less of right- or left-wing attitudes. Research investigating the relationship between personality and social attitudes has confirmed this hypothesis. Specifically, studies examining the role of the Big Five personality traits in political convictions have found significant and consistent links between several personality traits and right-wing attitudes.

According to this research, the strongest personality correlate of political attitudes is Openness to experience. As one would expect, this trait is negatively associated with *conservatism* and *authoritarianism* (a construct put forward by Adorno, Frenkel-Brunswick, Levinson, & Sanford, 1950). For instance, Riemann, Grubich, Hempel, Mergl, and Richter (1993) and Van Hiel and Mervielde (1996) reported correlations in the order of –.57 and –.42, respectively, between Openness and conservatism in European samples. Similar results have been reported for larger U.S. samples. For example, McCrae (1996) reported a correlation of –.35 between Openness and authoritarianism, while Trapnell (1994) reported more variable correlations of Openness with conservatism (from –.18 to –.64) on one hand, and authoritarianism (–.29 to –.63) on the other. Some predicted a quadratic relationship between Openness and political ideology, such that extreme attitudes (both left and right) are associated with lower Openness scores (Greenberg

& Jonas, 2003; Wilson, 1973). Thus, higher Openness would be associated with moderate political views and more critical attitudes toward authority: "questioning authority is a natural extension of an open individual's curiosity" (McCrae & Costa, 1997, p. 837). However, Stone and Smith (1993, p. 154) argue that political psychologists tend to "base their case on intuitive evidence...concerning apparent similarities between regimes of the far left and far right, rather than on a system review of the empirical data on any personality and ideology." There is also evidence for the negative relationship between Openness and prejudice, including racial discrimination. Thus, having an open mind would dispose people to be more tolerant toward other groups and perceive them as equal (Flynn, 2005). As you will recall from Chapter 1, Openness is characterized by intellectual curiosity, aesthetic sensitivity, vivid imagination, behavioral flexibility, and unconventional attitudes. According to the literature, therefore, people who hold right-wing attitudes tend to be less perceptive, sophisticated, knowledgeable, cultured, artistic, curious, and analytical.

CONCLUSION

Political attitudes are often seen as malleable, shaped by past experiences or the environment that a person has encountered. Yet, research shows that personality is a significant and consistent predictor of such attitudes. This suggests that personality will shape the way a person reacts to past experiences and environments, by influencing the type of attitudes that are absorbed and rejected, and the extent to (or intensity by) which these attitudes are absorbed or rejected. Such findings are interesting because social attitudes and prejudice have almost universally been explained in terms of social or cultural processes, such as in-group versus out-group membership. However, as the research above shows, central to differences between people, in terms of the political attitudes they hold, are dispositional personality traits, such as Openness to experience.

PERSONALITY AND RELIGIOUS ATTITUDES

Pretty much every known culture to mankind has some form of religious conviction. Religion is a universal aspect of society and, it seems, human nature. It is also arguably the most dominant social factor to have influenced modern history. Today, religion is, as ever, at the forefront of newspapers, radio, and television. Religion may have different meanings as well as consequences. From an individual difference perspective, it has been studied in terms of differences in *religiosity*. Since the 60s, psychologists have attempted to capture the concept of religiosity, as well as investigate individual differences in this construct.

Two main aspects of religiosity have emerged through research; these are religious orientation and religious coping. Religious orientation can be separated into intrinsic and extrinsic orientation toward religion. Intrinsic orientation comprises strong feelings, strong personal beliefs, and strong commitment toward religion. It is the more common view we have of religiosity, as something internal and emotional, which influences a person's way of being and thinking. An extrinsic orientation, on the other hand, reflects a person's use of religion for purposes of protection and consolidation, as well as participation and social status. It is a more practical and perhaps indirect way of using religion, where religiosity is a means to an end rather than an end in itself.

As with political attitudes, religious attitudes are socially learned. People have no genes for Christianity, Islam, or Judaism. Religious attitudes clearly need to have been taught to the person by his or her family, friends, or society. Nevertheless, there are often substantial differences between people in how religious they are, even within the same families and (homogenous) social environments. So, it is not impossible to conceive that these individual differences in religiosity are the result, not of differences in the social environment that people are exposed to, but rather of dispositional traits.

Several theorists argued that this may indeed be the case. For instance, according to Hans Eysenck (1916–1997), religiosity reflects tender-mindedness, such that tender-minded individuals are more likely to have stronger religious orientations. Given that low Psychoticism comprises attributes such as empathy, responsibility, and, in particular, conformity, Eysenck hypothesized this personality dimension to be inversely related to religiosity.

The link between religiosity and Psychoticism has been investigated in a large number of studies. This research has largely confirmed Eysenck's hypothesis in that Psychoticism has been found to consistently and strongly predict religiosity, with the findings generalizing across cultures and denominations (Saroglou, 2002). Furthermore, Psychoticism has been found to be inversely related to both religious orientation and religious coping. This personality dimension, in addition, predicts the frequency of religious activity, for instance, how often a person attends church or engages in personal prayer. Empirically, the (negative) relationship between low Psychoticism and religious orientation is well established; but it is also rather interesting. It suggests that people who are more religious are less aggressive, less impulsive, less unfriendly, less insensitive, and less antisocial. Perhaps this explains why the majority of people with a religious orientation often feel misrepresented by the minority of those that capture the attention and coverage of the media as a result of violent and aggressive extremist acts.

Less research has looked at the Big Five personality factors in relation to religious orientations. However, this trend has been shifting. Initially, studies suggested that high Agreeableness and high Conscientiousness were related to religiosity, confirming the religiosity–low Psychoticism relationship found in the literature (given that the Five Factor Model [FFM] explains

Psychoticism as low Agreeableness and low Conscientiousness). Recently, a meta-analysis conducted by Saroglou (2002) showed that there were associations also between other Big Five factors and religiosity. Saroglou classified religiosity into four types roughly corresponding to: (1) intrinsic religiosity, (2) extrinsic religiosity, (3) spirituality, and (4) religious fundamentalism (the intrinsic and extrinsic distinction corresponding to the traditional view of religiosity). While previous research with Eysenck's PEN model had revealed mixed results in regard to Eysenck's *Neuroticism* and *Extraversion* dimensions, Saroglou found all Big Five traits to be related to religiosity. The results of the meta-analysis showed that Extraversion was related to intrinsic religiosity and spirituality, Neuroticism was negatively related to intrinsic religiosity and positively related to extrinsic religiosity, and Openness to experience was positively related to spirituality and negatively related to fundamentalism.

Saroglou postulates that the link between Extraversion and religiosity may be explained by differences in the present-day expressions of religiosity, whereby religiosity today arguably takes a more expressive and social form than in the past. However, he is also quick to point out that the Extraversion facets of gregariousness, warmth, and positive emotionality are all conceptually related to religiosity, suggesting that there may also be a more direct link between these constructs.

The negative link between Neuroticism and spirituality poses an interesting question in regard to the causality of this relationship. That is, does spirituality lead to emotional stability or are emotionally stable people more likely to find spirituality? This is an intriguing research question given that the former scenario may be an important one, both in terms of explaining religiosity and also in terms of psychological interventions. Longitudinal studies may help to explicate this enquiry. It is also interesting to note the positive link between Neuroticism and *extrinsic* religiosity, which corresponds to Freud's notion of religiosity as an obsessive act. In particular, Freud explained religious practices as analogous to obsessive actions, serving

173

as defensive, self-protective measures to repress unconscious desires and impulses. Finally, the negative link between Openness and religious fundamentalism is in line with studies on Openness and political attitudes, which indicate that open individuals have moderate political views and are more critical toward authority.

CONCLUSION

The literature presented above indicates that personality plays an important role in forming religious attitudes. This is found both in relation to Eysenck's PEN model and the Five Factors of personality. Furthermore, Saroglou's meta-analysis indicates that similar patterns of the religion–FFM associations may be found across countries and denominations (e.g., United States, Canada, Poland, and Belgium). This is an important point for consideration. Currently, explanations for religious convictions and their links to various behaviors (e.g., a U.S. or U.K. citizen seeking military training from terrorist bodies abroad) are regularly based on societal or contextual factors, and sometimes on the content of the religious teachings themselves. In contrast, research into the psychology of religious personality seems to confirm the hypothesis that religiosity corresponds to individual differences in dispositional traits. This research suggests that personality often acts as a filter or an amplifier with respect to religious convictions (i.e., thoughts and feelings), as well as influencing the way religiosity may be manifested in behavior. It is also of interest to note the traits that religiosity is associated with. Religious persons and, in particular, those who possess intrinsic religiosity and spirituality tend to be more agreeable, more emotionally stable, less aggressive, impulsive, and antisocial. These are characteristics not always associated with religiosity, perhaps because religious connotations are overshadowed by atrocities that a very few unrepresentative groups commit in the name of religion. Regardless of these associations, the evidence clearly points to the fact that models of religious and political convictions need to include individual difference variables such as personality, in order to explain social behavior and attitudes.

PERSONALITY AND SOCIAL BEHAVIOR

Social attitudes, be it political, religious, or otherwise, may not always influence social behavior; and even when there is a relationship between attitudes and behavior, one could ask the question as to how much of this relationship results from common underlying factors. Psychologists have studied the causes of social behavior for decades. Although social behavior is an all-encompassing concept, the focus in this section is between prosocial and antisocial behavior.

Psychologists have generally made a distinction between these two concepts. Prosocial behaviors include altruism, volunteerism, community involvement, and social services, whereas antisocial behaviors include crime, substance abuse, and truancy. Accordingly, prosocial and antisocial behaviors are not viewed as two opposite extremes of the same dimension, but rather as two different factors (even if negative correlations would be expected). For instance, a person may not act prosocially, but that does not mean that he or she engages in antisocial behaviors.

Predictably, there has been wider interest in antisocial than in prosocial behavior, though recent years have seen an upsurge in studies examining the link between personality and prosocial behavior (Ozer & Benet-Martinez, 2006). Prosocial activities have obvious positive, and important, implications for society. Nevertheless, it is easy to see substantial differences between people in terms of their willingness to get involved in helping others. So, what makes some people more prosocial than others? Why do some people volunteer or engage in charity work, while others do not?

According to research, the most important personality correlates of prosocial behavior are Extraversion and Agreeableness (Carlo, Okun, Knight, & de Guzman, 2005). Studies suggest that extraverted and agreeable individuals have a general tendency to help others and are more motivated to engage in altruistic behaviors, such as volunteering and charity work.

These findings are not difficult to explain. For instance, one of the lower level facets of Extraversion is sociability. Thus, individuals high on Extraversion have a higher interest in people and are, as a result, more likely to help them. Similarly, Agreeableness comprises facets such as altruism, modesty, and helpfulness; these are all conceptually related to prosocial behavior. In support of these findings, Penner, Fritzsche, Craiger, and Freifeld (1995) suggested that prosocial behavior is the result of two salient components: (a) *empathy*—a dimension strongly related with Agreeableness and (b) *helpfulness*—a dimension correlated with Extraversion (Penner, 2002).

Although prosocial behavior has important social outcomes, the benefits of such behaviors are no doubt overshadowed by the costs of *antisocial* behavior. This may explain why the literature is dominated by research focusing on the causes of antisocial behavior. Destructive behavior in the workplace, rioting, assaults, shoplifting, and other antisocial behaviors are costing millions of dollars for organizations and communities every year; violent and aggressive behaviors destroy individuals' and families' lives.

Needless to say, preventing antisocial behavior is of imperative public interest. For a problem to be prevented and solved, however, its causes must be identified and understood. Explanations for antisocial behavior vary. Learned, sociological, and demographic influences have evidently been implicated to have a strong impact on such behavior. Statistically, antisocial behavior is predictable with clear demographics: males who are young, poor, uneducated, and belong to the minority are more likely to offend than others (Egan, 2011). Accordingly, one perspective is bluntly sociological (and, to some extent, political). In poor communities, the struggle for survival is harder; in such conditions, survival motives may overshadow communal and egalitarian ones, resulting in higher rates of antisocial behavior. Poor communities are the result of hierarchical societies with the top having undue influence on the bottom. Therefore, antisocial behavior can be considered a societal phenomenon.

Although "engineered demographics" is one way of explaining antisocial behavior, major individual differences in offending exist *within* these groups. That is, not all young men who are uneducated and a minority engage in antisocial behavior. In fact, such acts are committed only by a very small percentage of people within that society. The statistics show that even in criminal cohorts, an estimated 6% of the people are responsible for *most* of the offenses (Farringdon, Barnes, & Lambert, 1996).

There are two ways of explaining individual differences between those who offend and those who do not (within a homogenous society). One is through environmental, or learned, processes. These may include intergenerational deprivation, parenting, and other communal contagion. For instance, a child may be raised in a poor family, where struggle for survival often takes an aggressive form. To gain sufficient resources, parents, siblings, and relatives may engage in violent or criminal acts. In addition to social and communal influences, therefore, family members may act as antisocial or criminal role models, teaching and reinforcing antisocial behavior. Accordingly, in this model, learning and reinforcement are the source of antisocial behavior.

The other account of antisocial behavior posits dispositional factors and heredity. From an evolutionary perspective, heritability of antisocial behaviors may sound counterintuitive because evolution only promotes genes that are beneficial for survival of the group. On the other hand, it is theoretically possible that violent acts may have been evolutionarily adaptive. For instance, in hunter–gatherer societies, violence was found both between tribes and within them. Such violent acts included not only aggressive fights for resources between tribes, but also violent warnings to in-group members who threatened group cohesion. Furthermore, in unpredictable and dangerous times, aggressive, opportunistic, and promiscuous behavior may have been more effective for surviving than agreeable and reflective behavior, as quicker "fight" or "copulation" responses may have been necessary to gain resources and mates. Such tendencies will, consequently, have been passed on from generation to generation because they promote survival.

Based on these arguments, there is good reason to expect antisocial behavior to be heritable. Research supports this hypothesis. Behavioral genetics research indicates that genes account for about 41% of variation in antisocial behavior (with nonshared environment accounting for 43%) and that this heritability becomes stronger with age (Bergen, Gardner, & Kendler, 2007; Jacobson, Prescott, & Kendler, 2002). This does not mean that there are specific genes for stealing or assaulting people, of course. As discussed in Chapter 2, single-gene effects are rare in research. Rather, genes have their effects indirectly by directing the development of biological mechanisms. Thus, more commonly, biological mechanisms have been implicated in antisocial behavior. These include sex hormones (i.e., testosterone), neurodevelopmental disorders (e.g., *attention deficit hyperactivity disorder* [ADHD], child conduct disorder, oppositional-defiant disorder), specific information-processing impairments (e.g., failing to learn associations between negative stimulus and negative consequences), and genetic vulnerability to addiction, indirectly associated with antisocial behavior (Egan, 2011).

The above accounts link antisocial behavior directly and distinctly either to environmental or biological processes. As mentioned before, however, the nature–nurture interaction is rarely an either-or phenomenon. Rather, it is always nature *and* nurture, and the influence of either can depend on the other and differ across time. Indeed, longitudinal studies examining the interaction between genetic and environmental factors have found biopsychosocial processes to strongly predict the onset of antisocial activity. For instance, persons with *combined* obstetric *and* poverty-related concerns are twice as likely to commit violent acts or theft as groups who have either poverty or obstetric concerns alone (Raine, Brennan, Mednick, & Mednick, 1996). Similarly, although maltreatment increases the risk of conduct problems, this risk increases by 24% if the child is also at high genetic risk compared to a mere 2% increase if the child is at low genetic risk (Jaffee et al., 2005). Caspi et al. (2002) found that maltreated children with high levels of the gene for metabolizing monoamine oxidase A (which metabolizes neurotransmitters such as dopamine, noradrenalin, and serotonin) were nine times less likely to commit a violent crime than peers who had a low level of this gene. Lastly, a dysfunctional family environment can help to explain variability in antisocial behavior; however, the effect of a dysfunctional family environment is substantially stronger for children with a genetic susceptibility for such behavior.

While these findings demonstrate the environmental influences involved in antisocial behavior, they arguably present a stronger argument for a genetic basis of such tendencies. It is clear that genes and environment are intricately interlinked in influencing the onset of antisocial behavior, and models attempting to account for such behavior can exclude neither of these factors nor their interplay.

Given the genetic basis for antisocial tendencies, it is only natural to ask how they relate to broader dispositional tendencies, such as the basic three or five dimensions of personality. Research on the personality correlates of antisocial behavior stretches back several decades. Eysenck and Eysenck (1976) hypothesized that the Psychoticism dimension of the PEN model, which includes facets such as tough-mindedness, hostility, aggression, coldness, egocentricity, impulsivity, and low empathy, is a good proxy for the development of antisocial tendencies. This premise has been supported by research. For instance, in a recent meta-analysis, Cale (2006) found that a disposition for Psychoticism strongly predicted antisocial behavior, with a mean effect size of .39. Cale also found a relationship between *Neuroticism, Extraversion,* and antisocial tendencies, but these relationships were substantially smaller, with *Extraversion* being the weakest predictor (mean effect sizes: *Neuroticism* = .19, *Extraversion* = .09).

The relationship between *Psychoticism* and antisocial behavior is unsurprising. People high in *Psychoticism* are highly argumentative and may be inappropriately assertive. They are verbally more aggressive and more prone to resort to violence to resolve conflicts. Consequently, they are more likely to provoke conflicts, which, in turn, augment the probability of antisocial conduct. Despite the theoretical (and empirical) relationships between *Psychoticism* and antisocial behavior, the use of the *Psychoticism* construct to predict such behavior remains controversial because of its weaker psychometric properties, in comparison to other personality dimensions. Thus, more contemporary research has increasingly focused on the relationship between the Big Five dimensions and antisocial behavior.

As would be expected from the literature on *Psychoticism* and antisocial tendencies, research conducted with the Big Five has identified low Agreeableness and low Conscientiousness as the strongest predictors of such behavior. Another important correlate of antisocial tendencies is Neuroticism. Interestingly, Extraversion seems less important for predicting such behavior, which emphasizes the idea that prosocial and antisocial behaviors are not two opposite extremes of the same dimension but, rather, two different factors (Krueger, Hicks, & McGue, 2001).

The negative link between Conscientiousness and antisocial behavior highlights the fact that conscientious individuals have a higher sense of morality and self-control, which is the tendency to suppress impulsive, risk-taking, and physical behaviors (O'Gorman & Baxter, 2002). Indeed, low Conscientiousness predicts adolescent conflicts (Conger & Ge, 1999), substance abuse (Walton & Roberts, 2004), vandalism and theft (Heaven, 1996), criminal acts (Wiebe, 2004), and even suicide attempts (Verona, Patrick, & Joiner, 2001).

Agreeableness is, perhaps, the strongest personality predictor of antisocial behavior. For instance, Miller, Lynam, and Leukefeld (2003) found that facets of Agreeableness were consistently related to a variety of outcomes, including stability, variety, and onset of conduct problems, aggression, and antisocial personality disorder symptoms. Buss and Perry (1992) also found Agreeableness to be the single best predictor of general aggression (a factor comprising verbal aggression, anger, physical aggression, and hostility) and to have a relationship with physical aggression that no other dimension of personality had.

Longitudinal studies have also shown that personality can predict not only past but also future antisocial behavior. For instance, Samuels et al. (2004) found that the big five traits could predict criminal behavior and offenses (e.g., violent arrests), across a time frame of 12 and even 18 years. The researchers found that people who had been arrested more frequently were higher on angry hostility, depression, and impulsiveness (all facets of Neuroticism), and lower on trust, straightforwardness, compliance, and modesty (all facets of Agreeableness). Those who had committed violent arrests, in addition, were lower on gregariousness (facet of Extraversion) and Openness to feelings, respectively (facet of Openness). Offenders were also higher on the excitement-seeking facet of Extraversion and lower on the Conscientiousness facets of competence, dutifulness, and deliberation. Samuels et al. (2004) found that the overall effect size of personality for predicting offending was .5, even after controlling for demographic and biographic factors, such as age, sex, race, substance misuse, or a diagnosis of personality disorder.

Overall, the literature on antisocial behavior seems to demonstrate a consistent pattern. While demographic and biographic variables have influence on antisocial behavior, persons with high Neuroticism, low Agreeableness, and low Conscientiousness seem particularly prone to these tendencies. It is clear that there is an intricate link between sociological and dispositional influences on the onset of antisocial behavior. For that reason, models attempting to account for such behavior can exclude neither of these factors nor their interplay. For instance, while alcohol is often seen as a trigger to hostility, alcohol-related violence is very much moderated by the personality traits of Agreeableness and Conscientiousness (Egan & Hamilton, 2008).

Personality and Personal Implications

ow important is personality for our personal lives? This is perhaps a question to which the answer would, for many, intuitively be "quite a lot." As we mentioned at the outset, this is one of the fundamental reasons why people are interested in personality psychology: We want to know what, and how big an, effect our character has on our personal lives. For instance, we know from experience that people frequently contemplate their own and their partner's personality when they are thinking about their love life. We think about our (and their) preferences, the aspects of our character that are desirable, and the aspects that may be undesirable in relationships. This may be the case also with family and friends. Importantly, we believe that our personality does have an effect on outcomes of such personal matters. But how far does this effect stretch? We may believe that personality characteristics impact relationships—but can we also then assume that they impact our happiness? What about our health? In this chapter, we review the literature that shows how, and the extent to which, personality impacts our personal lives. We start our review by discussing an intuitive but most intriguing topic of romantic relationships, before moving on to some less intuitive but no less important personal issues, namely, health and happiness.

PERSONALITY AND ROMANTIC RELATIONSHIPS

We all want to be in a satisfying and healthy romantic relationship. The obsession with finding the "right one" is a testament to this desire. Everyone wants to be happy and we know that relationships are highly important for achieving this. Indeed, research indicates that healthy romantic relationships play a key role in fostering emotional well-being and physical health (Berscheid, 1999). As Freud famously said, mental health consists of the capacity to "love and work" (Arbeit und Liebe), so at least half of our happiness may depend on having a fulfilling relationship.

A 12-year-old neighbor of one of the authors once asked: Do you find destiny or does destiny find you? Often people wonder whether fate will introduce to them the "right one." They also differ in how actively they seek destiny. Should, or can, one do anything about finding that person—"the right one"? And, if one believes in finding destiny, then what do men and women want? What is it about some persons that make them more successful in relationships, both in terms of initiating them and in terms of maintaining them? Why are some couples happier than others?

The study of personality and romantic relationships attempts to address these questions by looking at the influence of people's character on a relationship's success. We should note that this area of research is relatively small within individual differences. Traditionally, psychologists have focused on sexual attractiveness, often only examining physical attributes (Swami, Stieger, Haubner, Voracek, & Furnham, 2009). Nevertheless, in the past 10 or 15 years, an increasing number of studies have investigated the effect of personality traits on our love life, and this research is growing steadily.

Reviewers have noted that "attraction of a suitable partner, propensity to establish a relationship intended to be permanent, and maintenance of that relationship may have related etiologies [causes] and that these etiologies may have their roots in personality" (Johnson, McGue, Krueger, & Bouchard, 2004, p. 285). At this most basic level, an individual-differences approach to romantic relationships seeks to establish whether there are certain traits that make relationship *initiation, satisfaction, and maintenance* more likely. Key questions in this research are: (1) Why are people attracted to some but not others, that is, what traits are involved in the initial attraction of a suitable partner, (2) Why are some couples happier in their relationship than others, that is, what traits are involved in achieving a happy relationship, and finally (3) Why do some relationships break while others last, that is, what traits are involved in enduring relationships. Below, we will review research dealing with each of these questions.

Love At First Sight? Personality And Initial Attraction

Typically, psychologists have viewed nonphysical factors in interpersonal attraction as trivial in understanding *initial attraction* (Swami & Furnham, 2008). Nevertheless, several authors have suggested that interpersonal attraction is multi-faceted and should be expanded to include variables such as conversational skills, sense of humor, expressive movements, facial expressions, body language, and so on (e.g., Rucas et al., 2006). Furthermore, individual difference factors involved in the process of early attraction may reside both with the *observer* and the *observed*. Thus, the question is: Are there certain psychological traits on the part of the observer and the observed that influence interpersonal attraction? While the latter seems more obvious than the former, both are plausible scenarios.

The Observer

It seems likely that the observer's personality should influence interpersonal attraction (Swami, 2007); however, very few studies have empirically tested this possibility. Nevertheless, some exceptions exist. For instance, Wood and Brumbaugh (2009) conducted a study with 4,308 participants and reported that each of the Big Five personality traits was associated with preferences for target photographs of women and men. In another study, including almost 1,000 participants, Openness to experience was found to correlate with the perception of a wider range of body sizes as being physically attractive (Swami, Buchanan, Furnham, & Tovée, 2008). The authors suggested that this association might be expected given that Openness reflects an acceptance of unconventional societal norms. This trait may, consequently, serve to widen the pool of potential partners. Research has also reported significant associations between two of the other Big Five traits, Agreeableness and Extraversion, and body size perceptions in a potential partner (Swami, Buchanan, Furnham, & Tovée, 2008). In addition, an interesting study found Neuroticism to be significantly associated with a preference to be in a relationship where the male is taller than the woman (Swami, Furnham, et al., 2008). The authors proposed that this finding may reflect more neurotic individuals' desire to avoid negative emotions associated with breaking conventions or social norms related to height.

It should be noted, however, that despite such findings, there are studies that have found no significant effect of the observer's personality on initial attraction (e.g., Ahmetoglu & Swami, 2012; Swami et al., 2010), and the reported significant associations in studies of this kind have generally been weak (reported rs between .10 and .28). Nevertheless, there is a good reason to believe that an observer's personality should have a significant effect on initial attraction, and some empirical research supports this. To get a complete picture of initial attraction, thus, we need to examine physical and psychological features, including those of the observer. There is therefore a strong need for further research in this area.

The Observed (The Target)

More research has been done on the personality characteristics people desire in others. The literature suggests that personality information provided, or obtained, about a person may have a causal influence on how attractive that person is perceived to be. A common research method for examining this effect is to present personality information concurrently with physical information (e.g., pictures) about potential partners. For instance, Gross and Crofton (1977) had participants rate the physical attractiveness of potential partners based on a profile containing personality and physical information. They showed that both the attractiveness of the target, as well as the favorability of the personality profile, had an influence on ratings of physical attractiveness. In another study, Lewandowski, Aron, and Gee (2007) showed that positive personality information can change participants' ratings of opposite-sex facial attractiveness seen in photographs. The researchers showed that when positive personality information was provided in conjunction with facial photographs, targets were perceived as more desirable as friends and dating partners, compared to when no (or undesirable) information was provided. Personality information has also been shown to moderate the effect of body size on attractiveness. That is, positive personality information may compensate for less attractive physical traits such as (larger) body size (Swami, 2010).

Other studies employing different methodologies have also shown that personality influences attractiveness. For instance, Friedman and colleagues (Friedman, Riggio, & Casella, 1988; Riggio, Friedman, & DiMatteo, 1981) found that Extraversion and exhibition are positively correlated with ratings of attractiveness in initial encounters. Interestingly, studies report that people may infer personality characteristics from physical attributes and that this information may in itself influence perceptions of attractiveness. For instance, Little, Burt, and Perrett (2006) found that faces that are perceived to possess desired personality traits (e.g., Extraversion) are rated as more attractive than faces that did not possess that trait. Similarly, Ahmetoglu and Swami (2012) showed that men who use more expressive body language are rated as more dominant, and consequently, as more sexually attractive. Traits such as dominance, hyper-masculinity, and sensation-seeking have all been found to relate to initial attraction and courtship success (Renniger, Wade, & Grammer, 2004), providing clear evidence that traits of the observed individual affect relationship initiation (Bogaert & Fisher, 1995).

Overall, this literature suggests that personality differences, both in the observers and the observed, influence initial attractions between individuals, suggesting that the notion of "love at first sight" may be even more complicated than commonly believed. But what happens after initial attractions—or love at first sight? Does personality influence whether the love story has a happy ending or not? Below, we review research examining the influence of personality on a relationship's success.

The Secret of a Successful Relationship

What is the secret of a successful and happy relationship? Is it enough to have love? What makes love last?

Discussions on love and relationships are common among friends, relatives, and colleagues and have long been a favorite topic of poets and songwriters. Often, people will converge on the notion that a relationship's success is all about finding the perfect match. While that may be the case, one could ask oneself if some people actually tend to match more readily with others *in general,* while others find it hard to find anyone matching. In other words, could it be that some people are inherently more prone to be happier and last longer in relationships (while others are destined to fail in most)?

Understanding the factors involved in a relationship's success is increasingly falling within the purview of the psychological sciences (Griffiths, 2007). Developmental psychologists have long highlighted the importance of upbringing, in particular, implicit observation and imitation of parental relationships (Booth & Amato, 2001), as a constituent of romantic relationships. For instance, Conger, Cui, Bryant, and Elder (2000) reported that supportive upbringing during childhood predicted less hostile relationships in adulthood. Indeed, a recent study (Donnellan, Larsen-Rife, & Conger, 2005) has shown that parenting styles can predict romantic relationships, even when the personality (of the child) is taken into account. Researchers have also pointed to sociological, economic, or chance factors as important in influencing a relationship's success.

In recent years, however, an increasing number of psychologists have argued that individual differences in personality may play a pivotal role in whether a relationship is successful or not. This literature covers the associations between personality and various relationship outcomes, including the relationship's length (i.e., how long the relationship has lasted) and its quality. So, can personality traits predict relationship satisfaction and stability?

Although the research only stretches back a couple of decades, there is strong evidence to suggest that personality factors do influence a relationship's quality and length (Bradbury & Fincham, 1988). In particular, a number of studies have reported a negative association between Neuroticism and relationship or marital quality (e.g., Barelds, 2005; Heaven, Smith, Prabhakar, Abraham, & Mete, 2006; Watson, Hubbard, & Wiese, 2000), as

well as a positive link between Neuroticism and marital dissolution (Kelly & Conley, 1987). Whereas this link has sometimes
been interpreted as a mere artifact of neurotics' negative self-
bias (neurotics are more pessimistic and thus generally more
likely to report negative ratings of anything), there is wide consensus that Neuroticism is, in fact, detrimental for relationships
(Bouchard, Lussier, & Sabourin, 1999). Furthermore, a recent
study defined competence in romantic relationships as "the set
of behaviors that enable an individual to form an enduring
romantic union that is mutually satisfying to both partners"
(Donnellan et al., 2005, p. 563) and considered Neuroticism
as the most important threat to these behaviors. The authors
concluded that neurotics' predisposition to easily experience
anger, distress, and anxiety is "relatively destructive for relationships" (p. 572).

Agreeableness is another relevant trait in understanding the
dynamics of relationships and has been negatively associated
with both marital dissatisfaction (Botwin, Buss, & Shackelford,
1997) and negative partner interactions (Donnellan, Conger,
& Bryant, 2004), and positively linked to conflict resolution in
romantic relationships (Graziano, Jensen-Campbell, & Hair,
1996). This association is intuitive given that agreeable individuals are more likely to positively perceive others, are more
responsive in social interactions (Tobin, Graziano, Vanman, &
Tassinary, 2000), and are more likely to control their negative
emotions and use constructive (rather than coercive) tactics in
conflict situations (Jensen-Campbell & Graziano, 2001).

Our own research (Ahmetoglu, Chamorro-Premuzic, &
Swami, 2009) shows that personality also influences your relationship style, that is, the degree to which you tend to be intimate, passionate, or committed in relationships (see Chapter 5
for a bit more detail on types of relationship styles you may
adopt). In addition, it demonstrates that the style you adopt in
a relationship will have consequences on the outcome of that
relationship, such as how long the relationship lasts. In a study
we conducted in 2009, we examined over 16,000 people in

regard to their relationship style and their personality profile. We found that extraverted persons tend to be more passionate in their relationships, whereas conscientious people tend to favor intimacy and commitment. Agreeable individuals, on the other hand, tend to adopt what Sternberg (1986) calls a "consummate love" style; in other words, they tend to be intimate, committed, and passionate.

Importantly, we found that two out of three relationship styles were significantly related to how long a relationship has lasted. As one would expect, our results showed that a tendency to be committed to the partnership was predictive of longer lasting relationships. Interestingly, however, a passionate relationship style was negatively related to the relationship's length. That is, if you tend to be more passionate, your relationship is likely to end quicker—and this is a function of how extraverted you are in the first place. Such findings suggest that your personality and the love style you adopt may have an independent effect on your relationship in terms of how long it lasts, regardless of whether you have found a suitable partner or not.

Compelling evidence on the influence of personality on a relationship's success derives also from longitudinal studies. Personality traits have been found to predict not only concurrent relationship outcomes, but also future ones. For example, Newman, Caspi, Moffitt, and Silva (1997) found that temperament measures at the age of 3 predict a relationship's quality at the age of 21. Likewise, Robins, Caspi, and Moffitt (2002) showed that positive emotionality measured at age 18 predicted the quality of a relationship at age 26. Finally, personality traits assessed by the Multidimensional Personality Questionnaire (Tellegen, 1982) measured in late adolescence have been found to predict aspects of romantic relationships in early adulthood (Donnellan et al., 2005).

What about the perfect match hypothesis? A prevailing theory of the perfect match hypothesis, known as the similarity-attraction theory, suggests that two individuals are more likely to form (and successfully maintain) romantic affiliations if they share similar characteristics, such as political and religious attitudes, socioeconomic background, level of education and intelligence, and personality. Indeed, most dating sites use this theory in their advertising. While this is a common presumption also among lay people, studies that have examined the similarity-attraction hypothesis in relation to personality and romantic attraction and maintenance have returned equivocal results, with consensus now suggesting that the effects of personality similarity are weak at best (Caspi & Herbener, 1990; Gattis, Berns, Simpson, & Christensen, 2004).

Conclusion

Overall, the research reviewed above shows that your partner's and your own natural dispositions have an important role in whether the relationship is satisfying and enduring, and this is independent of whether you match or not. It should be noted, however, that despite these impressive findings, the literature is relatively small and few longitudinal designs have examined the role of all Big Five personality dimensions, with most studies comparing between positive and negative emotionality. Clearly, the available research only begins to scratch the surface of what may be termed the "personality of love," and much future work remains to be done in uncovering the associations between personality, love dimensions, and particularly relationship initiation, maintenance, and dissolution.

Nevertheless, the insights obtained from the available research may have important implications both in personal and in professional terms. For instance, Neuroticism and low Agreeableness consistently emerge as predictors of negative relationship outcomes, and this is the case also across relationships with different partners (Robins et al., 2002). Knowing that your (current or potential) partner's and indeed your own personality, as opposed to social or contextual factors, may have a stable influence on your relationship could result in different coping strategies and more cognizant approaches to conflict resolution.

Furthermore, insights generated by research may prove useful also for the formulation of relationship advice or interventions that promote more stable relationships through changes in personality dimensions (e.g., teaching individuals how to adopt more conciliatory tactics in conflict situations). Regardless of the application, research into individual differences in relationship initiation and success teaches us a valuable lesson about internal influences on success in romantic relationships.

PERSONALITY AND HEALTH

So far in the chapter, we have discussed the effects of personality on the captivating issue of romantic relationships. One could argue that the impact of character on love and relationships is intuitive. In choosing a partner, we inevitably base our decisions on more than just looks—indeed, the character of the person we choose is often more important in this decision. By the same token, our character may either facilitate or inhibit the success of a relationship. It is normal to think that the character of both partners will play a role in the initiation and maintenance of a relationship.

In this section, however, we will discuss the possibility of our personality affecting an arguably less obvious outcome, namely, our health. We say less obvious because when contemplating about our health, more often than not, we think of physiological rather than psychological factors. For instance, we know that some people are more prone to illness, while others seem immune to it. Some people are quick to recover, while others remain ill for prolonged periods. Indeed, some live longer, while others die young. While this is a fact of life, we would rarely attribute such health issues to psychological causes. More commonly, we would talk about a person's genetic makeup (e.g., her parents lived long too), or their upbringing and lifestyle (e.g., she had a great diet and did a lot of sports), as factor influencing his or her health. It is less common to hear people talk about how conscientious, or emotionally stable, someone is when his or her health is at issue.

One reason for this, of course, is that health-related factors are more often than not treated in medical rather than mental health hospitals, and by medical doctors rather than psychologists. The most common health treatment is simple medication (e.g., aspirin). Given that the treatment is physiological, we naturally infer the causes to be physiological. If a person has high blood pressure, we would hardly assume this to be associated to that person's personality or character, but is it possible that physiological factors such as blood pressure are indeed associated with personality?

Although this may seem unusual at first, such a hypothesis was proposed as far back as at the times of the ancient Greeks. Hippocrates, for instance, argued that personality characteristics such as anxiousness, anger, or depression related to fluctuations in the blood and were associated with different types of diseases. The relationship of personality and physical factors is also clearly implicated in modern research on temperament (Shontz, 1975; reviewed in Chapter 3). While these approaches discuss the association of personality and physiology in terms of the effect of the latter on the former, more recently, researchers have started to examine it in the opposite direction also, in terms of the influence of personality on physiology (Alexander, 1939). For instance, hypertension, which is the diagnostic label for elevated blood pressure of unknown origins, has been understood as a direct cause of individual differences, such as particular reactions to conflicts, frustration, and repression (Shontz, 1975). For instance, Jorgensen, Blair, Kolodziej, and Schreer (1996) note that "persons with [hypertension] have been described as passive, unassertive, submissive, and prone to suppress anger and hostility" (p. 294). Studies on subjective evaluations also suggest that low self-efficacy can induce physiologic activation and psychological distress (Bandura, 1986). Thus, it has become clearer that the study of modern conceptions of health requires the examination of not only the physical but also psychological as well as social factors—a so-called biopsychosocial model of health.

What are the ways that these different processes operate within this model? That is, in what way might personality influence health? According to Contrada, Cather, and O'Leary (1999) there are three ways by which this process can occur. The first is through the *intrinsic characteristics* of personality traits, which may be associated with psychological processes. For example, low Agreeableness, and, in particular, its lower order dimensions of anger and mistrust, may lead to higher activation of the sympathetic nervous system and, in turn, enhance the chances of coronary artery disease (Smith & Spiro, 2002). The second is through *risky behavioral choices*, such as smoking, unhealthy diet, and substance abuse, which may threaten individuals' health. For instance, research shows that unhealthy behaviors are more typical in individuals with low Conscientiousness scores. The final way personality may influence health is through *preventative behaviors and reactions to* health problems. For example, conscientious individuals will be more likely to visit the doctor if they sense health problems, and take a more proactive approach to treatment of illness (e.g., take all prescribed medication, adopt beneficial behaviors).

Studies examining these hypotheses have accumulated in the past few decades. Research has shown that personality traits consistently predict broad indicators of physical health, such as absence of illness and longevity (Caspi, Roberts, & Shiner, 2005). For instance, in an early meta-analysis, Friedman and Booth-Kewley (1987) found personality traits, such as hostility, anxiety, depression, and aggressiveness, to predict various disease outcomes.

A major data source for research examining the relation between personality and health has been the longitudinal research project of the Terman Life Cycle Study, which began in 1922 (Terman, Sears, Cronbach, & Sears, 2002). Terman and his colleagues started this project at Stanford by assessing the personality characteristics of over 1,500 children. Data for these children were subsequently collected in consistent periods of 5 to 10 years. Incredibly, researchers were able to follow-up most of these children even after 70 years. These data provided information about health and mortality rates of participants, and crucially, about how these rates related to scores on personality inventories that were assessed when participants were children.

In an early examination of these data, Friedman et al. (1993) found that children high on Conscientiousness (as rated by their parents) were at a lower risk of mortality. Interestingly, this finding generalized even when the researchers looked at each individual decade on its own. Subsequent studies replicated this finding, and a meta-analysis of 20 such studies reported significant and negative correlations between Conscientiousness and mortality. Astonishingly, the data revealed that the more conscientious participants lived about 2 to 4 years longer than their less conscientious counterparts. This remarkable relationship has been explained in terms of the differences between more versus less conscientious individuals tendencies to engage in risky behaviors, follow treatment recommendations, and use coping strategies successfully, as well as of career and social relationships, and engagement in broader prosocietal activities.

Although other personality traits have also been related to health outcomes, such links have been more complex and inconsistent. In particular, facets-level traits have been found to relate to health differentially. For instance, evidence has shown that the Extraversion facet of dominance is predictive of heart disease in males but not in females (Ferraro & Nuriddin, 2006; Rasul, Stansfeld, Hart, & Smith, 2005). Similarly, this facet has been found to relate negatively to health in environments where dominance cannot be established (Manuck, Kaplan, Adams, & Clarkson, 1988), and when it is manifested in more aggressive forms (harming healthy relationships; Smith et al., 2008). However, Kern and Friedman (2011) argue that the effect of dominance on health may depend on the context, such that dominance may be adaptive in stable environments, and if combined with Agreeableness.

Another facet of Extraversion—sociability—has also differentially been linked with health. For instance, in Terman's study, sociability was found to predict physical health, but only in women. Given that sociability promotes social ties and thereby social support, it is generally taken as a facet beneficial for health. Nevertheless, there may be exceptions to this rule. For instance, highly social individuals may be drawn to social situations involving alcohol, drugs, promiscuous behavior, and less sleep, which may have negative effects on health, such as morbidity and mortality (Ploubidis & Grundy, 2009).

One facet that has yielded consistent positive effects on health outcomes, however, is activity. This link seems intuitive in that people who score highly on activity are more likely to take on physical pursuits and be more engaged in life, which results in greater positive arousal, energy, and mental state (Martin et al., 2009).

Studies examining the relationship between Agreeableness and health provide evidence for the effect of this trait on subjective reports, but the effects on objective criteria such as physical health and longevity are mixed (Friedman, Kern, & Reynolds, 2010). Agreeableness may also interact with Conscientiousness in relation to health. Specifically, a combination of high Agreeableness and high Conscientiousness promotes health; however, it may increase the risk for individuals low on either of these traits. Kern and Friedman (2011) suggest that a moderate degree of Agreeableness is most likely to be optimal for good health.

One subfacet of Agreeableness that has received ample attention in research is hostility. Hostility has consistently been linked to negative health outcomes. Numerous studies have found this subdimension to relate to health issues such as heart disease, illness, and mortality risk (Suls & Bundy, 2005). Meta-analyses have shown that high hostility is associated with higher body mass index (BMI), more alcohol consumption, smoking, and markers of heart disease, suggesting that the link between this dimension and health may partly be a function of dysfunctional behaviors. Another explanation is that hostility leads to poor social ties, which, in turn, leaves hostile individuals with little social support when care and encouragement may be needed.

Several meta-analyses have also shown Neuroticism to be negatively related to health outcomes. These include higher incidents of illness and coronary heart disease (Rugulies, 2002) and increased risk of mortality (Roberts et al., 2007). Such findings can be partially explained with respect to common biological pathways underlying both Neuroticism and various illnesses. This relation can also be environmental, however. For instance, research shows that neurotic individuals are less likely to engage in healthy behaviors and more likely to engage in smoking, alcohol use, and other risky health behaviors, which are more proximal causes of illness and disease. Furthermore, anxious individuals have a tendency to interpret events as more negative and stressful and cope worse than less anxious individuals (Vollrath, 2001). Such response styles may, in addition, lead to the long-term changes in the physiological system, further increasing stress responses and elevating natural anxiety levels. Thus, the result can be a negative spiral of occurrences.

Interestingly, some studies have also found effects of Neuroticism on health in the opposite direction (that is high Neuroticism leading to better health). For instance, studies show that high Neuroticism may lead to more protective behaviors (because neurotic individuals may be more attuned to health symptoms), which, in turn, may result in higher objective health outcomes (regardless of subjective ratings). Indeed, in the Terman sample, Neuroticism was *negatively* related to risk of mortality for men (though the relationship was positive for women). Research shows that one factor that can moderate the effects of Neuroticism is Conscientiousness. Specifically, high Neuroticism combined with high Conscientiousness may lead to protective behaviors; whereas when combined with low Conscientiousness, it can lead to greater risk (Kern, Martin, & Friedman, 2010).

Conclusion

It is unusual to think of personality traits when we contemplate our health. Commonly, we would discuss genetic disposition, environmental influences, activities, and lifestyles of people as the most relevant factors. Yet, there are several ways in which personality traits can influence our health—and even how long we live. Although a pure biological model looking at the common biological pathways underlying personality and illness provide us with valuable information, it is clear that personality and health have a more complex relationship. Personality influences the environments we choose, the types of protective versus risky activities we engage in (as well as the extent to which we do so), and the social bonds we make. While we can attribute differences in health to differences in people's lifestyles (e.g., the job they have, the amount of sports they do, etc.), personality exerts itself through influencing the type of lifestyle a person has in the first place. Such a biopsychosocial model of health provides a valuable account for explaining our physical and mental health.

PERSONALITY AND HAPPINESS

Why do people want to earn lots of money, climb Mount Everest, or find the perfect partner (i.e., "the one")? Surely, having money, being at the top of a mountain, or living with a compatible person are not ends in themselves. Rather, these are means to a more fundamental end; and that end is happiness. It is difficult to think of a human goal that is more desirable and more sought after than that of being happy (although one may argue staying alive is one—many people would prefer not living at all to living an unhappy life). All our actions (be it looking for a better job, moving, buying clothes and gadgets, or traveling) can ultimately be linked to this goal; in essence, they are simply means to an end.

Two basic questions ensue anytime we talk about happiness. First, what is happiness? Second, how does one achieve it? The answer to neither of these questions is simple. Indeed, while interest in happiness stretches back to the beginning of time, our understanding of has been slow to develop, and research into happiness only really took off in the last couple of decades. Nevertheless, in more recent years, research led by Ed Diener, in particular, has taken some big steps in terms of furthering our understanding of happiness. Accordingly, to deal with the two questions above, we will review this research below. The first question we need to address, of course, is what is happiness?

Defining Happiness

Although it is easy to *know* when one is happy, it is slightly more difficult to describe in words what happiness actually is. Most people would nevertheless agree that happiness is a subjective thing, usually associated with inner emotions and thoughts. Psychologists have also conceptualized happiness in this way, with the experience of positive effect and life satisfaction as its central focus.

The preferred term in psychology to refer to happiness is subjective well-being (SWB; Diener, 1984, 2000). Although not universally embraced, there is reasonable consensus among researchers that SWB has three components; these are positive affect (PA), negative affect (NA), and life satisfaction. PA and NA reflects a person's ongoing emotions and mood states, whereas life satisfaction is a more holistic and cognitive evaluation of a person's quality of life (Pavot, Diener, Colvin, & Sandvik, 1991). Although one may presume that the two affective components lie at either end of a continuum, research shows that these are independent. Indeed, the three-factor structure seems to better represent the construct of SWB, than either a two- or a one-factor structure (Arthaud-day et al., 2005).

Overall, therefore, one may say that happiness is what emotions, more positive or negative, we feel subjectively and the appraisal we have of the quality of our life.

How to Achieve Happiness

Defining happiness is important, particularly from a research perspective; however, it is not nearly as important as to figuring out what determines it. Clearly, there are individual differences in happiness. Some people are happier than others. So the question is what are the causes of these differences? If you have a moment, consider this quick exercise: Think about three or four (or more) things that have influenced how happy/unhappy you are currently. In other words, what do you think determines, or has determined, how happy you are or aren't at this moment (i.e., today or this week)?

If we were to take a guess, we would say that most of the reasons you thought of involved situational factors or life circumstances. It may involve your current and specific situation, such as having to read this book as homework (which we hope is not near the negative end), or a more general reason, to do with your job, partner, or friends and family. It may also involve a loaded or tragic event such as a move, loss of employment, or a loved one. This view, whereby happiness is primarily determined by life circumstances, is in line with bottom-up theories of happiness. Bottom-up theories suggest that a person's ratings of their own SWB reflect the sum of evaluations made about a number of life domains (e.g., housing, employment, income, relationships, marriage, etc.) and to ongoing life experiences. That is, people simply evaluate how happy they are with each life domain and then aggregate these evaluations to reach an overall SWB judgment (even if subconsciously). Given this, changes in one domain (e.g., job satisfaction) will mean changes in the overall SWB score.

On the other hand, it is unlikely (in our guess) that a variable that popped up in your head as an important determinant of your current level of happiness was your personality. After all, most people do not attribute how happy or unhappy they are to personality traits such as Extraversion or Conscientiousness. However, a salient view in the SWB literature suggests that personality is indeed a strong predictor of happiness. This top-down view suggests that personality traits set an "affective tone" or "filter," by which all subsequent evaluations about one's emotions and life experiences are influenced. That is, although life events and circumstances will influence SWB, any such effects will be relatively weak and transient in nature, compared to a stronger and more stable influence of personality.

The model suggests that this process happens in three ways:

1. Directly through the baseline levels of affect that personality traits are associated with. As we discussed in previous chapters, it is well known that Extraversion is associated with PA and Neuroticism with NA.
2. Directly through differences in information processing. Again, there is a large amount of literature suggesting that personality traits influence the way people interpret events, in particular, whether they regard events as negative or positive (i.e., positive or negative biases occur based on these traits).
3. Indirectly through the influence of personality on life events. As discussed in Chapter 3, though the environment may have an influence on personality, "niche picking" means that personality traits will affect which environments people chose in the first place.

There has been considerable debate regarding the relative validity of the bottom-up versus the top-down models. However, evidence tends to favor the latter more than the former. To be sure, there is evidence to show that environmental forces such as marital status, income level, and government under which a person lives do have a significant influence on SWB (Diener,

Suh, Lucas, & Smith, 1999). Yet, the magnitude of the correlations between these variables is generally modest. In addition, such effects seem to be rather short-lived.

In comparison, personality factors seem to exert a stronger and more stable influence on SWB. In particular, two personality traits—Extraversion and Neuroticism—seem to be particularly predictive of happiness (although significant correlations have also been found with other personality traits). Furthermore, happiness is generally associated with higher levels of self-esteem, which is also a function of high Extraversion and low Neuroticism. A recent meta-analysis conducted by Steel, Schmidt, and Schultz (2008) indicated that personality traits can account for a substantial amount of the variability in SWB (estimates reaching as high as 63% disattenuated).

Further support for the pervasive influence of personality on happiness comes from studies examining the stability and heritability of SWB. Unlike common conceptions of happiness, studies indicate that SWB is surprisingly stable over time. For instance, in a study spanning 3 years, Lucas, Diener, and Suh (1996) found that test–retest correlations of SWB ranged from .56 to .61. These findings have been replicated in several other studies (e.g., Fujita & Diener, 2005; Magnus et al., 1993). Behavioral genetics research also shows a substantial genetic component to happiness. As Pavot and Diener (2011) conclude: "The evidence from studies focused on establishing the heritability of SWB indicates that approximately 40–50 percent of the variance of SWB can be attributed to genetic influences" (p. 709).

Given this line of evidence, one may question the reason *why* environmental forces have such modest impact on our levels of happiness. One theory, known as the "hedonic treadmill" (Brickman & Campbell, 1971), states that people habituate, or *adapt*, to environments and life events fairly quickly, so that any new environmental change (e.g., winning the lottery) will only have a transient effect on levels of SWB, before these levels fall back to a hedonically neutral point. A refined version of this theory, known as the "set point theory" (Heady & Wearing, 1989) suggests that people return, not to a hedonically neutral point, but rather to a "set point," which is largely a function of the traits of Extraversion and Neuroticism. In either case, the long-term effect of any life change (including any interventions) on long-term SWB will be nil.

While evidence does support the role of adaptation, it is now generally accepted that this process is not as universal and inexorable as first thought. Research has shown that at least some life events, such as loss of a loved one or loss of a job (Lucas, Clark, Georgellis, & Diener, 2004), do have a long-term effect on levels of happiness. Furthermore, it is now also clear that there are individual differences in adaptation. That is, some people will adapt to changes in the environment more readily than others. Ironically, this will also depend on person's personality attributes, such as Neuroticism and optimism.

Conclusion

It seems that factors such as health, income, educational background, and marital status account for only a small amount of the variance in well-being measures. Research instead shows that subjective well-being "is fairly stable over time, that it rebounds after major life events, and that it is often strongly correlated with stable personality traits" (Diener, Oishi, & Lucas, 2003, p. 406). People will suffer many losses (e.g., death of relatives, friends, and partners) and experience a number of other adverse life events (e.g., unemployment, divorce, stress, health problems). At the same time, they will experience important positive events, such as graduation, engagement, marriage, promotion, and children. These events may represent objective causes of happiness or upset. Yet, the subjective component of happiness is equally important and, over longer periods of time, personality traits are pervasive indicators of happiness.

Personality and Career Implications

n the previous chapter, we noted that Freud saw mental health as a function of happy relationships and career success. This notion is also in line with Hogan's (1983) socioanalytic theory, which suggests that people need to get along and get ahead. In evolutionary terms, around 50% of our happiness will result from getting along. The other 50% will be a function of getting ahead, that is, career success. In the previous chapter, we discussed the influence of personality on one of these aspects, that of getting along. In this chapter, we will discuss the effects of personality with respect to the other, that of getting ahead. The literature examining the impact of personality on career-related outcomes is vast and stretches back to the beginnings of psychology. Consequently, we have a comprehensive understanding of this relationship and a solid ground on which to make inferences. Below, we will review the most important research and paradigms within this literature, concerning the areas of (a) academic achievement, (b) work performance, (c) leadership, and (d) entrepreneurship.

ACADEMIC ACHIEVEMENT

Good education and skills are crucial for improving economic and social prospects. According to the latest edition of the Organization for Economic Cooperation and Development (OECD; 2011a), people who do not complete high school face far higher unemployment rates than those who do. In addition, the data show that during the global economic crisis, university graduates have suffered far fewer job losses than those who left school without qualifications; the better educated are less likely to need unemployment benefits or welfare assistance, and tend to pay more taxes when they enter the job market. In fact, the gross earnings premium for an individual with a tertiary degree exceeds $300,000 for men and $200,000 for women across the OECD.

Clearly, academic achievement has important implications on an individual level. However, the data suggest that the academic performance (AP) of students is also highly important for economies and societies. In 2008, OECD countries spent 6.1% of their gross domestic product on education. Furthermore, over the past three decades, the number of international students has risen dramatically, from 800,000 worldwide in 1975 to 3.7 million in 2009 (OECD, 2011b). Accordingly, any addition to our understanding of academic achievement will have substantial implications in every sense. Governments and educators have long been interested in knowing who will perform well, and who will perform poorly, in academic programs, both in terms of selecting the best and also in identifying and developing those who are behind.

There is established evidence for the predictive validity of IQ in educational settings (Chamorro-Premuzic & Furnham,

2005a, 2006). Indeed, IQ tests are still the best and most widely used individual difference predictor of AP (Deary, Whiteman, Starr, Whalley, & Fox, 2004; Gottfredson, 2002). On the other hand, psychologists have long hypothesized that performance in both work and academic settings is determined by factors other than cognitive ability, including will and personality. For instance, as early as 1915, Webb conceptualized *persistence of motives* as an important personality trait for the prediction of academic outcomes. A similar concept was later put forward by Alexander (1935) under the label *factor X*. Spearman (1927) also concurred that this "will" factor is independent of g as a contributor to academic achievement.

One reason for such convictions among psychologists was that while cognitive ability reflects what an individual *can do*, personality traits reflect what an individual will *typically do* (Furnham & Chamorro-Premuzic, 2004). Thus, to the extent that performance in academic settings is influenced by, and evaluated through, behavioral tendencies such as perseverance, precision, interpersonal skills, assertiveness, and so on, we would expect long-term AP to be predicted by measures of typical performance, such as personality scales (Goff & Ackerman, 1992).

Interestingly, early research in this field found inconsistent findings between personality and academic success. Indeed, several reviews of the literature in the 20th century examining this link presented equivocal findings and highlighted the scattered nature of the research. Another salient problem in research was that studies (even in more recent research) frequently failed to account for the effects of cognitive ability. This is a problem because cognitive abilities and personality traits have been consistently (albeit modestly) associated (e.g., Ackerman & Heggestad, 1997; Judge, Jackson, Shaw, Scott, & Rich, 2007; Poropat, 2009). Given that cognitive ability is a strong predictor of AP, any significant association between personality and academic achievement that did not take into account this factor may have been confounded. Hence, early reviewers concluded that the data showed no clear trends (e.g., De Raad & Schouwenburg, 1996; Harris, 1940; Margrain, 1978; Stein, 1963).

Despite this, the past 10 to 15 years has seen an upsurge in the number of studies and reviews on the personality correlates of AP (see reviews by Chamorro-Premuzic & Furnham, 2004; O'Connor & Paunonen, 2007). With methodological advances, meta-analytical techniques, and the growing acceptance of broad factorial models of personality (i.e., the Five Factor Model), modern reviews have, by and large, refuted early conclusions. In particular, three recent meta-analyses (O'Connor & Paunonen, 2007; Poropat, 2009; Trapman, Hell, Hirn, & Schuler, 2007) of the relationship between personality and AP have shown that individual differences in AP can be accurately explained by personality traits.

Big Five Predictors of AP

Without doubt, the strongest and most reliable personality correlate of AP has been shown to be the Big Five dimension of Conscientiousness. Numerous empirical studies have identified positive relations between this trait and diverse indicators of AP. Conceptually this finding is logical since conscientious individuals are more organized, motivated, responsible, and proactive than less conscientious individuals. In addition, Conscientiousness is associated with sustained effort and goal-setting (Barrick, Mount, & Strauss, 1993), compliance with and concentration on homework (Trautwein, Lüdtke, Schnyder, & Niggli, 2006), and learning-related time management and effort regulation (Bidjerano & Dai, 2007). These attributes have all been shown to predict AP. Thus several behaviors that may lead to improved AP, such as attending class, doing homework, and revising for exams, may be a natural consequence of higher Conscientiousness. Likewise, less conscientious individuals may be more likely to miss out on, or be late for, class, forget to complete assignments, and be more careless about revision and preparation for exams (Chamorro-Premuzic & Furnham, 2003a, 2003b, 2005a).

A particularly noteworthy finding from the most recent meta-analysis, conducted by Poropat (2009), is that the correlation between Conscientiousness and AP appears to be largely independent of intelligence. Indeed, the results of the meta-analysis showed that Conscientiousness is *as strong* a predictor of AP as intelligence, and this is true both in the secondary and in the tertiary levels of education. Poropat revealed that students low on Conscientiousness would be nearly twice as likely to fail as those high on Conscientiousness. Such findings have led researchers to call this personality dimension the "g-factor of personality."

A second factor that has been identified as relevant to educational outcomes is Openness to experience. It has been suggested that open-minded individuals use a wider set of strategies and learning techniques, including critical evaluation, in-depth analysis, and flexibility (Chamorro-Premuzic, 2011). Such strategies may all contribute to academic achievement. Furthermore meta-analytic studies (notably Ackerman & Heggestad, 1992) have shown that Openness to experience is moderately correlated with IQ, which, as mentioned, is a strong predictor of AP. Accordingly, it would seem reasonable to presume a link between Openness and AP. Despite this, however, results from studies examining this link have generally been mixed. For instance, in their review of the literature, Chamorro-Premuzic and Furnham (2005a) noted that several studies had reported no association between Openness and exam grades. Correspondingly, O'Connor and Paunonen (2007) in their meta-analysis found the average correlation between Openness to experience and achievement to be a mere $r = .06$. In addition, many studies have failed to control for the effect of cognitive ability, which casts doubts even over significant associations that do exist. On the other hand, O'Connor and Paunonen (2007) found that there is substantial variation across research studies in the magnitude of the effect sizes (with correlations ranging from $r = .10$ to $r = .22$). The authors suggest that this relationship may therefore be more complex and depend on other factors (or moderator variables).

In a more recent meta-analysis, however, Poropat (2009) found larger overall effect sizes in the relationship between Openness and academic achievement (even if these still were of modest magnitude—i.e., $r = .12$). Unlike previous research, Poropat (2009) was also able to control for the effect of intelligence. Interestingly, the results showed that the correlation between Openness and academic achievement was significant even when controlling for intelligence, with only a minor mediation (effect size reduced from .12 to .09). Thus, Poropat's analysis only partially supports the hypothesis that the relationship between Openness and AP can be explained in terms of links between this personality trait and cognitive ability.

A final point on Openness relates to the recent discussions about the two related, but distinct, aspects of this trait. That is, Openness is thought to comprise two components: one reflecting intellectual engagement and ideas, and the other reflecting artistic qualities related to esthetics and fantasy (DeYoung et al., 2009). The former aspect of Openness is thought to be more closely related to intelligence—and AP—than the latter. Thus, von Stumm, Chamorro-Premuzic, and Ackerman (2011) argue that "the lack of evidence for an effect of Openness on intellectual accomplishments at the phenotypic level is likely to be due to studying such associations on the higher order factor, rather than at facet level" (p. 226).

Neuroticism is another trait hypothesized to impact AP. In particular, it is thought that this trait is detrimental for success in these settings. This notion is based on the fact that many forms of assessment (e.g., exams, deadlines, presentations) in educational settings may be anxiety-inducing. Given that the tendency to worry is an inherent characteristic of high Neuroticism, pupils higher on this trait are more likely to react more anxiously and worriedly during such assessments. Thus, they would be disadvantaged because such internal states would interfere with attention to relevant tasks, reducing their ability to cope effectively in these situations (Lazarus & Folkman, 1984; Matthews, Davies, Westerman, & Stammers, 2000). For example, it has been documented that Neuroticism is a strong predictor of test anxiety (e.g., Chamorro-Premuzic, Ahmetoglu, & Furnham, 2008). Test anxiety during exams can divert an individual's attention from the actual task at hand (the test), which may lead to difficulties in, for instance, understanding test instructions or concentration, which, in turn, would hamper exam performance (Halamandaris & Power, 1999).

These hypotheses, however, have not been confirmed by research. Despite some specific studies indicating that Neuroticism is detrimental for AP, particularly when assessed via exams (e.g., Chamorro-Premuzic & Furnham, 2003a), research on the relationship between Neuroticism and AP has generally yielded trivial results. Indeed, O'Connor and Paunonen (2007) and Poropat (2009) meta-analyses found effect sizes of .03 and .12 respectively, which can be considered relatively inconsequential. Nevertheless, while Neuroticism may not be a strong determinant of overall scholastic achievement, in some specific assessment settings, such as school or university exams, anxious tendencies and worries are likely to have significant effects on performance.

Evidence for the link between AP and Extraversion has been variable. It has been suggested that the relationship may be moderated by the type of assessment (Furnham & Chamorro-Premuzic, 2005). For example, tasks that highlight social interaction, such as oral or viva-voce exams, as well as participation in class, may be easier for extraverts. On the other hand, tasks requiring long-term intellectual investment, such as revising for long hours, may be advantageous to introverts. In addition, extraverts may perform better academically because they have naturally higher energy levels and positive outlooks on life, which may lead to a desire to learn and understand. However, it is also possible that such dispositions may lead students to pursue activities that are more stimulating than reading and listening to lectures, which, in turn, may lead to lower levels of performance.

Given such arguments, it is unsurprising to find that the literature on Extraversion and academic achievement has yielded mixed results. For instance, while some studies have found Extraversion to be negatively correlated with various academic outcomes such as grade point average (GPA; Furnham et al., 2005), grades in introductory psychology exams (Hair & Hampson, 2006) and grades in statistics exams (Furnham & Chamorro-Premuzic, 2004), numerous other studies have failed to find any association between this personality trait and educational outcomes, and some research has even identified a positive association (see O'Connor & Paunonen, 2007). The two recent meta-analyses (O'Connor & Paunonen, 2007; Poropat, 2009) examining the association between Extraversion and AP have reported small effect sizes (i.e., $r = -.05$ and $-.02$, respectively). Thus, currently there is little evidence of an overall relation between Extraversion and AP in the literature, although it is likely that this relationship is influenced by contextual variables (mentioned previously).

Finally, although Agreeableness has traditionally not been seen as an obvious predictive factor in academic settings, several authors (e.g., De Raad & Schouwenburg, 1996) have argued that this trait may positively impact AP by facilitating cooperation with learning processes. For instance, more agreeable individuals may comply with teacher instructions and make an effort to stay focused on learning tasks (Vermetten, Lodewijks, & Vermunt, 2001). Indeed, Poropat's (2009) meta-analysis showed that Agreeableness is a small but significant predictor of AP, confirming such propositions.

Conclusion

Success and achievement in educational settings have important social and economic implications, both for individuals and for the society as a whole. It is no surprise therefore that interest in the predictors of AP has been evident in psychological research for over a century. AP is a function of many things, including teaching style and quality, educator resources, and home factors. The literature, however, converges on the central influence of scholastic individual differences. While cognitive ability has traditionally been seen as the biggest contributor to academic outcomes, it is clear that dimensions of personality can contribute significantly to these outcomes.

Conscientiousness has been shown to be a highly powerful personality predictor of AP. Thus, there is clear empirical support for the notion that persistence, self-discipline, and an orientation toward achievement really do pay off (Chamorro-Premuzic & Furnham, 2004). Although other personality traits (e.g., Openness to experience, Neuroticism, and Agreeableness) may have a smaller impact, evidence suggests that they also may contribute significantly to students' academic success, particularly when contextual variables are considered.

Although some have argued that relationships between personality and AP may be due to their mutual relationships with intelligence, studies clearly show that controlling for intelligence has only minor effects on the validity of the Five Factor Model (FFM) dimensions. Indeed, the strongest personality correlate of AP, Conscientiousness, has been inversely related to intelligence. Thus, personality may be considered a complementary, rather than an indirect, predictor of scholastic achievement.

It is worth noting that unlike intelligence measures, personality tests were not designed to predict AP. So, it is particularly striking that Conscientiousness predicts AP as well as intelligence. Furthermore, there is evidence to show that the validity of intelligence to predict educational outcomes decreases the higher up one goes on the educational ladder (because of increased homogeneity among students in their cognitive abilities). However, the validity of Conscientiousness does not show any such declines. Finally, unlike intelligence, personality factors may not have adverse impact on certain social groups. Combined, these facts highlight the importance of including personality, in addition to ability factors, when predicting AP. Researchers and practitioners must consider not only what students are able to do, but also what they will typically do. Such considerations will no doubt lead to more accurate predictions of individual differences in AP and may have important implications for educational institutions.

PERSONALITY AND WORK OUTCOMES

Work performance is perhaps one of the most important outcomes in today's society, economically, for businesses and for individuals. In line with Freud, individuals' well-being depends on their capacity to love and work. People with fulfilling careers are happy and achieve important goals for themselves and the organization; people who are dissatisfied at work suffer and desperately look for career and even life changes. Given that stable individual differences exist in work performance (i.e., some employees consistently perform better than others), it is important to businesses to understand the causes of these differences. One major source of performance differences is stable psychological characteristics such as intelligence, motivation, values and interests, and, notably, personality. This is why we rarely see random selection of job applicants—with employers commonly using curriculum vitae (CVs) and interviews to better understand an applicant's personal makeup, and thus predict how he or she will act within the job role.

While the predictive power of CVs and interviews is relatively low (because of unreliability in measurement in both), there are some psychometric tests that have a track record in predicting performance, namely, IQ tests. There is a large body of literature spanning World War II showing that IQ tests are the best predictors of performance across jobs and other work-related outcomes. Yet, common sense tells us that IQ, or general cognitive ability, is probably not the only psychological trait one requires, in order to be successful at one's job. We probably all know of a friend or colleague that has a high intellectual capacity but simply does not know how to effectively interact with others, or "fit in."

Indeed, few of us would deny that a person's personality, whether they are sociable, anxious, organized, and so on, will have an impact on how well they perform in their job. Thus, most of us believe that personality is an important factor in predicting job performance, just as IQ. The one difference between personality and IQ, however, is measurement. Unlike IQ tests, which are *objective* in nature, personality tests primarily come in a self-report form. As mentioned before, this is mainly because alternatives usually are unreliable (or invalid). While this may not be a problem in general research settings (e.g., assessing romantic compatibility or AP), in selection an important issue is raised. This issue, which we have already touched upon in previous chapters, is that of faking.

Unlike other psychological research, the validity of personality questionnaires in selection is assessed with participants who have something (often important) to lose (e.g., a job opportunity, promotion, salary increase, etc.). In these so-called high-stakes settings, there is a substantial incentive to self-enhance (fake) responses. Thus, the most common argument against the use of self-report personality measures in selection is that if one can fake a test, and one's career depends on it, one will.

The controversies surrounding the issue of faking will be discussed in detail in Chapter 7; however, suffice it to say here that high-stakes settings provide the ultimate test for self-report inventories. The issue, in essence, is that even if we believe that personality predicts job performance, it is possible that personality *tests* do not. This is because scores on personality tests may not be true representations of applicants' "real" personalities. In essence, honest and capable applicants may be selected out, while dishonest but incompetent applicants are hired.

As a consequence, one would not expect test scores to predict performance very well.

Validity of Personality (Self-Report) Inventories

There has been a great debate around the issue of the validity of personality questionnaires in selection settings. To some extent, this debate remains even today (a useful exchange is that between Morgesen et al., 2007, and Ones, Dilchert, Viswesvaran, & Judge, 2007). Early reviews of the relationship between personality and job performance seemed to suggest that personality was a trivial or insignificant predictor of job performance. One of the first quantitative reviews of different inventories across different jobs reported uncorrected correlations ranging from .14 to .36 (Ghiselli & Barthol, 1953). Subsequent reviews during the 1950s and 1960s found that, in most studies (80%–90%), personality traits did not significantly predict work-related criteria.

The lack of support for the usefulness of self-report inventories was to a large extent due to methodological problems in research. Until the 1990s, there had been little consensus as to the structure of personality, which meant that almost every other researcher had his or her own "language" for describing major dispositions. Furthermore, most reviews in the field were descriptive rather than quantitative. However, there were also issues of interpretation. Criticisms directed at personality inventories in selection were often based on the modest associations found between personality traits and the predicted criteria (Morgeson et al., 2007). For example, when the first quantitative reviews on the subject appeared in the 1960s, researchers recommended against the use of personality inventories for work selection (Guion & Gottier, 1965). Yet, while validities in early reviews were low, they were nevertheless significant. The irony is that, in more recent reviews, opposite conclusions are often drawn from exactly the same data. Furthermore, following Ghiselli and Barthol's (1953) review, several more recent meta-analyses have pointed to substantially higher validities in the personality–job performance link. A simple reason for this is that recent reviews have had the benefit of using more advanced statistical techniques such as meta-analysis and also the advantage of a classification system such as the FFM.

Accordingly, the first meta-analytic review of the validity of the "Big Five" in predicting performance provided by Hough and colleagues (Hough, Eaton, Dunnette, Kamp, & McCloy, 1990) showed that personality scales were consistently related to individual differences in performance, including physical fitness and military bearing, effort and leadership, and personal discipline. Although these correlations did not exceed .3 (notably because the authors did not estimate the "true validities" at the construct level), this meta-analysis provided initial support for the idea that personality traits are valid predictors of job performance.

Hough et al.'s (1990) review was soon followed by several similar meta-analyses, each of which supported the validity of personality in the prediction of job performance and other work-related outcomes. The most significant of these was Barrick and Mount's (1991) seminal paper, in which results from 117 investigations (including 23,994 participants) were meta-analyzed (although, in the same year, Tett, Jackson, & Rothstein, 1991, conducted a similar meta-analysis with comparable results). The authors who organized personality according to the Big Five provided compelling evidence for the predictive power of Conscientiousness scales across different settings (predicting job and training performance) and the validity of other traits in specific contexts (for instance, Extraversion was a predictor of managerial and sales jobs, and Openness was a good predictor of training success). The review was also the first to show that personality significantly predicted performance across many occupations, from professionals, the police force, managers, and semiskilled job roles.

A few years later, Salgado (1997) conducted a meta-analysis focusing on the European community to investigate the generalizability of previous reviews that were based on U.S. data. The researcher was able to replicate U.S. findings, showing that not only Conscientiousness, but also emotional stability (low Neuroticism), had generalizable validities predicting job outcomes (Salgado, 1997).

Despite such reviews, there have been criticisms about the magnitude of the effects of personality on job performance. Critics have pointed out that the validity of personality traits (adjusting and correcting for all possible drawbacks and combining all relevant traits) would hardly account for 15% of the variance in job performance (Murphy, in Morgeson et al., 2007), recommending against their use. The counter-argument to this criticism is that even small increases in prediction can be useful in practice. For instance, utility analyses suggest that the correlations between personality and job performance found in the literature are of acceptable magnitude for inclusion in selection settings (Schmidt, Hunter, McKenzie, & Muldrow, 1979). In addition, meta-analyses, particularly in the 1990s (after the consolidation of the Big Five taxonomy), reported validities in the region of .40, though mainly for higher order or "compound" traits (Hogan, 2005; Ones, Viswesvaran, & Dilchert, 2005). Quantitative reviews have thus clearly supported the validity of personality tests in the prediction of job performance and their use in selection settings.

In terms of the specific personality correlates, it appears that, unlike intelligence, the validity of personality traits is moderated by the job in question (Salgado, 2003). That is, some personality traits are more important in some jobs and others in other jobs. For instance, Extraversion seems to be related more to sales and management jobs, while Openness seems to be related to training performance but not job performance (Barrick & Mount, 1991). Agreeableness is essential for jobs where interpersonal interaction is high, for example, customer service-based roles (Hogan, Rybicki, Motowildo, & Borman, 1998), whereby the customer is always right. This is likely to be due to the individual's ability to connect with their customer and make them feel appreciated. Neuroticism, on the other hand, is only beneficial when the individual is low scoring and the job demands a "level-head." This is supported by research, which found that soldiers who are low in Neuroticism are more effective in combat, likely due to low levels of anxiety and depression (Hough et al., 1990).

One personality factor, however, seems to consistently predict performance in all types of jobs; and that factor is Conscientiousness. Across each meta-analysis, Conscientiousness has been found to be the most consistent and strongest personality correlate of performance, paralleling the findings in academic settings. The logic for this is not difficult to understand; performance in pretty much every job would be enhanced if a person is organized, achievement-oriented, disciplined, persistent, and hardworking—all facets of Conscientiousness. The magnitudes of the correlations have generally been in the range of .2 to .3 (Barrick & Mount, 1991). Thus, clearly this factor, as with intelligence, is an important one to assess in job applicants, as it will, despite the high-stakes setting of test administration, predict performance across jobs and occupations.

Although researchers in the field have tended to organize personality into five major factors, a sometimes even more powerful prediction is obtained by so-called compound traits. Compound traits are simply combinations of multiple dimensions of personality. One such example is integrity tests, which have found strong support in the literature with regard to their prediction of job performance. Integrity tests are usually found to assess Conscientiousness, Agreeableness, and emotional stability. However, research shows that integrity tests can add incremental validity over these Big Five traits (Ones, Viswesvaran, & Schmidt, 1993). Furthermore, Schmidt and Hunter's meta-analysis (1998) revealed that integrity had a validity magnitude of .4, placing it in between general mental ability and Conscientiousness. Levels of integrity have unsurprisingly also been found to correlate with levels of deviant work practices (e.g., theft within the workplace) and counterproductive behaviors (e.g., gossip and rumor-spreading; Ones et al., 1993). Other compound scales such as Core Self-Evaluations (Bono & Judge, 2003), which assesses a combination of emotional stability, generalized self-efficacy, locus of control, and self-confidence, have also been shown to predict job performance beyond the Big Five (Ones, Visveswaran, Hough, & Dilchert, 2005). Finally, emotional intelligence (EI), the ability to identify and manage one's own or others' emotions, has recently re-emerged as a valuable predictor of job performance. EI has been found to interact with existing personality constructs, in particular, Extraversion and emotional stability. Although critics have long argued that EI does not have any incremental validity once IQ and personality are taken into account (e.g., Joseph & Newman, 2010), more recent evidence has indicated that these conclusions may have been premature. In particular, a meta-analysis conducted by O'Boyle, Humphrey, Pollack, Hawver, and Story (2010) has shown that EI predicts unique (incremental) variance in job performance, beyond both IQ and the Big Five. The authors conclude that a model of job performance needs to take an integrative view including all three sets of constructs in order to reach maximum prediction.

Overall, the evidence with regard to the causes of differences in job performance show that while predictors such as cognitive ability are important, personality, and specifically Conscientiousness, have a pivotal role in predicting success, despite the self-report nature of the tests. Such results should carry a lot of weight for individuals, organizations, economies, and even societies. Having a healthy grasp of why certain individuals perform better than others, and why they are more satisfied, productive, and loyal, requires information regarding the ability of a person, his or her general tendencies, as well as the person's fit with the specific job and organization. Although there have been (and still are) doubts about whether self-report inventories can do the job in facilitating this understanding, the wealth of literature, which includes thousands of studies, clearly shows that personality test scores do predict all important work-related outcomes, including performance.

PERSONALITY AND LEADERSHIP

Most of us will probably have, at one time or another, wondered whether we "have what it takes" to become a good leader. Leadership is a central aspect of society and has been so since the beginnings of group formation. Indeed, a key reason that we are interested in leadership is that it is universal; it exists across all human cultures and across species. Whenever there is a social activity, a social structure forms, and the key feature of this structure is the leader. Furthermore, there is a common struggle among members of a group for gaining the leadership position, often referred to as the "alpha" status. The alpha status gives easier access to resources and is thus highly consequential for anyone who achieves it.

Crucially, *who* occupies this position will have consequences not only for the individual in that position but also for the group as a whole. Leaders are in charge of what people do and where people go. By definition, followers follow leaders. This is particularly the case for human societies. Leadership (good or bad), therefore, has consequences for the group's survival. This is as much the case today as it was in hunter–gatherer societies. In the 20th century, 167,000,000 people were killed for political reasons. Of that number, invading armies killed 30,000,000 people, and 137,000,000 people were killed by their own government (Rummel, 1994).

Thus, in addition to the struggle for the leadership status, people (who do not occupy that status) want to ensure that the person at the top really does have "what it takes." Here is where individual differences come in. As with job performance or AP, there are individual differences in leadership effectiveness.

Some people are better leaders than others. Given this fact, two basic questions ensue:

1. Why do some people gain the leadership (or alpha) status?
2. What makes a good (effective) leader?

We will assume that you have some (perhaps strong) views about this. Indeed, research shows that people have clear implicit theories about leadership, but what the literature also shows is that the answers to these questions are not always straightforward and implicit theories are not always right. There are some complex issues. The first is the definition of leadership. Leadership can be defined as a status or a process (or behavior). The majority of studies on leadership define the term in relation to the persons who are in charge (Kaiser, Hogan, & Craig, 2008). Yet, Hogan, Hogan, and Kaiser (2010) note that about two thirds of people in charge are regarded as incompetent. This indicates that factors that lead to the achievement of a leadership position are not the same as those that lead to effectiveness in that role. The second issue concerns specificity of leadership. Are good leaders good in all situations? Or, do we need different "types" of leaders in different situations? This also relates to the fundamental question of whether leaders are born or made. Thus, the third issue concerns whether one simply "has it, or doesn't," or whether people can become good leaders (e.g., through experience or formal training).

The "Great Man" Theory

Initial theorizing in the leadership literature placed great emphasis on what leaders "had." Psychological theories focusing on leaders' personality or *traits* were influenced by Carlyle's (1907) "Great Man" theory of leadership, which posited that "the history of the world [was] the biography of great men" (Carlyle, 1907, p. 18). Carlyle's view implied that a limited number of core individual attributes could be used to distinguish between leaders and followers. For example, physical features, such as height and energy; demographic background variables, such as educa-tion and socioeconomic status; and personality characteristics, such as assertiveness, self-confidence, and the capacity to tolerate stress, were crucial to discern between leaders and followers.

The search for the "leadership personality" began in the early 20th century and a colossal amount of traits were inves-tigated as predictors of leadership. In 1948, Stogdill reviewed three decades of research and concluded that, while some traits did seem to set leaders apart from followers, none were univer-sal predictors of leadership; their validity was always moderated by situational factors. Consequently, the following two decades were characterized by pessimistic remarks by psychologists in the field, expressing a great deal of skepticism in regard to the trait approach to leadership. For example, Ghiselli and Brown (1955, p. 47) noted that "[U]nder one set of circumstances an individual will be a good leader and under others he will be a poor one" and Baron and Byrne (1987, p. 405) observed that "[T]he conclusion... that leaders do not differ from followers in clear and easily recognized ways remains valid."

These statements were very much in parallel with the behaviorist and situationist movements of the 50s to 70s, where leadership (and indeed personality) were seen as determined by situational rather than internal forces such as traits. With the widely endorsed view that situational factors undermine the importance of interindividual differences in leadership, interest in person-centered research on leadership decreased substantially.

The literature on personality and leadership laid buried for decades. As with the literature on academic and job per-formance, research had suffered from the lack of a universal personality framework to classify traits and quantitative meth-ods for analyzing large amount of data. However, following theoretical and statistical developments in the 80s and 90s, the trait approach to leadership began to re-emerge. Two impor-tant publications in the mid-1980s anticipated this revival. The first was a highly influential book on the topic of presidential leadership by Simonton (1986), who combined psychometric and biographical analyses to identify the attributes of successful American presidents. The second was a meta-analysis on cognitive ability and leadership by Lord, De Vader, and Alliger (1986), who reported a correlation of $r = .50$ between these variables (although more recently, Judge, Colbert, & Illies, 2004, reported a "true validity" of $r = .27$).

The seminal article on the link between *personality* and leadership was published by Locke in 1997. Like many before him, Locke identified various personality traits as being necessary for leadership. Unlike previous reviewers, however, he suggested that these were timeless and universal. Importantly, Locke contested that the plethora of traits that had been studied in the literature could be organized into some more basic (or higher order) traits. For instance, he conceptualized variables such as active mind, intelligence, and vision under "cognitive ability and thinking modes"; action commitment, ambition, effort, and tenacity under "motivation, values, and action"; and respect for ability and commitment for justice under "attitudes toward subordinates." Though this represented a step forward in the organization of both ability and nonability attributes associated with leadership, a bigger "boost" for trait approaches was to come from the introduction of the Five Factor model of personality to leadership research.

One of the first authors to specifically refer to the role of the *Big Five* personality traits at work was Adrian Furnham. Furnham (1994) speculated that leaders in modern organizations are more likely to be open, conscientious, stable, agreeable, and extraverts than followers. The same year, Hogan, Curphy, and Hogan (1994) organized Stogdill's list of leadership-related personality characteristics on the basis of the Big Five and echoed Furnham's (1994) speculations, pointing out that effective leaders tend to show higher levels of emotional stability, Extraversion, Openness, Agreeableness, and Conscientiousness. The definitive piece of evidence to put personality at the center stage in the leadership field, however, came from a meta-analysis conducted by Judge and colleagues in 2002.

Judge et al. (2002) reviewed the extensive literature on personality and leadership, performing a large-scale meta-analysis, which included 222 correlations from 73 studies. These studies contained more than 25,000 managers from every level in 5,000 organizations, across every industry sector. As Furnham and Hogan had predicted, their results showed that emotional stability, Extraversion, Openness, and Conscientiousness were all positively correlated with both leadership emergence (perceived leadership) and effectiveness (leadership performance). Furthermore, the multiple correlation between personality and leadership was .53. Judge et al. (2002) concluded that Extraversion is the strongest predictor of both leadership and emergence and effectiveness, no doubt because of the assertiveness, dominance, and sociability of extraverts.

Cross-cultural studies have also supported Locke's notion of the universality of these traits. For instance, Silversthorne (2001) described that effective leaders tended to score significantly higher on Extraversion, Agreeableness, and Conscientiousness, and lower on Neuroticism, than noneffective leaders in United States as well as Chinese samples. However, previous studies indicated that, while Conscientiousness and emotional stability (low Neuroticism) tend to represent sociably desirable traits in almost every culture, Extraversion (with its primary facets of assertiveness and dominance) is less likely to be regarded as a virtue in eastern, than in western, cultures (Redding & Wong, 1986).

Bad Leadership

Over the past 20 years, an increasing amount of attention has also been given to the area of bad leadership. This has particularly been the case in the last few years, where corporate failures and financial scandals have been at the forefront of news and media. This area of research is concerned with the link between leadership and the so-called "dark-side" of personality. According to Hogan and Hogan (2001), certain traits that may promote an individual to the top, such as a great sense of confidence, charisma, and political skill, may actually be detrimental for leadership effectiveness. Furthermore, some leaders who deliver exceptional results may do so while causing harm to their followers, to other groups, or to society at large. Such performance, which may initially appear exceptional, and later catastrophic, may be attributed to the same underlying traits.

One example of this is the notion of "charismatic" or "transformational" leadership (Bass, 2008). Bass (2008) argues that charismatic leaders can influence their followers to perform beyond their expectations—to exceptional performance. However, Hogan and Ahmad (2011) point out that charisma can be a double-edged sword. Evidence suggests that charisma correlates significantly with narcissism and that many charismatic leaders are described in the same way as the narcissistic ones (Hogan & Fico, in press). Yet, research suggests that narcissism is detrimental for leadership. For instance, Judge, LePine, and Rich (2006) found a negative link between narcissism, contextual and task performance, and a positive link between this trait and workplace deviance. Furthermore, research examining the personality of highly effective CEOs suggests that the two most common traits used to describe these exceptional performers are "persistent" and "humble" (or modest). Organizations led by such CEOs seem to consistently outperform the competition. On the other hand, organizations with narcissistic CEOs tend to have more volatility in their annual performance and perform worse on average, relative to the organizations with more humble CEOs.

It is no surprise, therefore, that more recent theories of leadership emphasize traits such as integrity, honesty, and empathy as being fundamental to leadership effectiveness (e.g., Greenleaf & Spears, 2002). This line of research is interesting because it suggests that implicit theories people have about what leaders should or shouldn't "have" may be flawed and counterproductive. For instance, Ciulla (2004) argues that the glorification of charismatic leaders means that people often overlook the fact that they can be wrong and take followers in bad directions. Certainly, it is not difficult to think of examples of charismatic but destructive leaders of large organizations (Enron) and nations (Alan Garcia, in his first presidency of Peru).

Conclusion

Leadership, and who is at the top, do matter. It can be the difference between a corporate success story and a financial scandal (Collins, 2001). Sometimes, it can be a matter of life and death. The literature on personality and leadership suggests that a leader's personality has a substantial influence on how the group performs. In plain terms, personality may determine the fate of individuals, organizations, and nations. However, knowing what makes good leadership is not always a matter of intuition. Common conceptions of great leaders may sometimes be flawed. As Hogan (2007) notes, the fundamental question in human affairs is not "who *shall* rule," but rather "who *should* rule"?

PERSONALITY AND ENTREPRENEURSHIP

While the literature on personality and job performance and career success (and leadership) has primarily focused on activity and performance within organizations (consisting of things such as overall job performance, task performance, unit performance, dysfunctional behavior, promotions, income, etc.), a more recent trend in psychological investigation has been to look at less traditional outcomes, such as that of entrepreneurship. This is unsurprising given that almost one in two adults is self-employed at some point in their life (Shane, 2008).

Entrepreneurship has traditionally been operationalized (and defined) as the creation of organization(s) (Shane, 2008), though this definition has been criticized for narrowing and decontextualizing (McKenzie, Ugbah, & Smothers, 2007). Several authors have suggested that entrepreneurship can occur both outside organizations and within them, and does not necessarily have to involve business activities (e.g., Ahmetoglu, Leutner, & Chamorro-Premuzic, 2011; Kuratko, 2007). Here, entrepreneurship is viewed as a set of activities, comprising the recognition and exploitation of opportunities, innovation/ change, and value creation (Ahmetoglu et al., 2011; Shane & Venkataraman, 2000). These two views are complementary, given that the creation of a new business is a highly effective means of innovating and exploiting recognized opportunities (though a substantial portion of new ventures are not created for such reasons; Shane, 2008).

Research on the link between personality and entrepreneurship has a relatively short history and has generally fallen outside the realm of psychology (Baron & Henry, 2010; Hisrich, Langan-Fox, & Grant, 2007), being investigated primarily by researchers in economics, politics, and management. Even so, the most common denominator in the literature, including economics and management, is the investigation of psychological factors involved in entrepreneurship (Hisrich et al., 2007). Thus, in the last three to four decades, hundreds of studies have examined the relationship between personality and entrepreneurship.

Although initial qualitative reviews of the literature in the 80s and 90s found little evidence for the impact of personality traits in entrepreneurship research (see Aldrich, 1999), more recent research has reached more positive conclusions. Since Aldrich's (1999) qualitative review, several meta-analyses have been conducted in the entrepreneurship field. These studies have found significant effects of personality on entrepreneurial outcomes such as business creation and business success (e.g., Rauch & Frese, 2007; Zhao, Siebert, & Lumpkin, 2010).

Furthermore, promising evidence has also emerged in regard to the role of personality in the wider set of entrepreneurial activity, both within and outside organizations. For instance, Ahmetoglu et al. (2011) found that the compound personality traits of Core Self-Evaluations (Judge & Bono, 2001) and Trait EI (Petrides & Furnham, 2001) both predicted entrepreneurial outcomes (i.e., innovation, exploitation of opportunities, and value creation) across a variety of settings. In addition, they found a moderate to strong effect of a specific measure of entrepreneurial personality (measure of entrepreneurial tendencies and abilities; Ahmetoglu & Chamorro-Premuzic, 2010a, 2010b) on entrepreneurial activity in all settings examined.

These encouraging findings suggest that personality is a highly useful concept for entrepreneurship research. Given that entrepreneurship is a major source of employment, economic growth, and technological progress (Reynolds, Bygrave, & Autio, 2004), such results are likely to have substantial implications. As yet, however, there remain significant knowledge gaps in the psychology literature dealing with individual differences in entrepreneurship (Hisrich et al., 2007). Thus, there is plenty of scope for psychologists to conduct additional research in this field.

In order to understand and facilitate this process, however, some important points need to be noted. First, there is a need to see entrepreneurship as more than the mere creation of organizations. Innovation, exploitation of recognized opportunities, and creation of value are central to entrepreneurship (Shane & Venkataraman, 2000; Shumpeter, 1911). Such activity can occur both within organizations and outside them. Importantly, most business founders do not engage in much innovation or opportunity exploitation; and most fail within the first 5 to 10 years (Shane, 2008). So, in order to understand the forces behind social and economic progress, there must be a clear distinction in research (and practice) between the search for the entrepreneurial personality and the personality of entrepreneurs (i.e., business founders). Entrepreneurial individuals who are more innovative at work (and outside it), who perceive and exploit opportunities more often, and, as a consequence, generate a substantial amount of value are the ones who bring about change and progress in society. As such, those are the individuals that need to be identified and nourished. While some important steps have already been taken in this direction (see Ahmetoglu et al., 2011), future research following this trend will no doubt be highly valuable.

GENERAL CONCLUSION

Personality exerts a pervasive and broadly based influence on many outcomes in our lives. This notion is perhaps more intuitive in certain aspects of life (e.g., in leadership or antisocial behavior) than others. Yet, often people will attribute life circumstances, or events, such as meeting the right one or how happy one is to factors beyond one's control, such as luck, or temporary conditions, such as having an undesirable job. The truth is that the events that shape our lives (e.g., the job we end up taking, the person we end up meeting, or how successful we end up being) are not haphazard; and subjective thoughts and feelings we have are not always the result of these events. In fact, both the events that shape our lives and the corresponding thoughts and feelings are *a function of* who we are already— our character. We end up taking a job because our personality leads us there or restricts us from getting somewhere else; we end up marrying someone because they match our character, or because our character limits our options as to whom we can marry; we have certain political and religious convictions because our personality influences how perceptive or defiant we are, or how curious or traditional we are; we tend to be more or less happy because our personality influences how we interpret events and circumstances in our lives. Yes, our personality even influences how long we will live because of choices we make, or coping strategies we employ.

Some of these proposals will sound commonsensical. Yet, often, without evidence, equally commonsensical but contradictory hypotheses can be developed with regard to each of these scenarios. One could argue that to get a job, who one knows is more important than what one knows; meeting the right person is simply a function of being in the right place at the right time; political and religious attitudes are passed onto us by our parents, and so on. The bottom line is that these hypotheses can only be supported or not through research. We have enough evidence to support that personality affects a wide range of life outcomes. This evidence in parallel supports the utility of personality inventories more generally. Clearly, the study of personality has come a long way through employing such inventories. Thus, we can be confident that personality does affect life outcomes, and that personality inventories are able to capture at least part of what we would think of as our "true" personality.

Controversies and Future Directions

requently, findings concerning individual differences spark heated debates and public outcries. The first chapter of this section (Chapter 7) addresses some of the controversies surrounding the use of personality assessment to profile people in relation to the law (section on Profiling for "Bad" or Problematic Personality Traits), education (section on Using Personality Tests in Educational Selection [School and University]), consumer habits (section on Online Profiling [Psychographic Segmentation]), personnel selection and staffing (section on Personnel Selection), and romantic relationships (section on Personality and "Digital Love"). As you may have gathered from previous chapters, these represent some of the controversial applications and implications of assessing personality. Yet, we find these areas of application exciting because they enable personality researchers to work on useful practical solutions to everyday problems.

In the final chapter (Chapter 8) of this section and this book, we summarize the main themes of the book and discuss the future directions of the field of personality psychology. We will ask and discuss questions such as: What knowledge *do* we have and what gaps remain in our knowledge? What efforts are being made in research, and what new and exciting methods are foreseen for the near future? We conclude the book with a few words of encouragement and points for reflection regarding the nature of personality and its assessment.

Controversies

lthough controversies are plentiful, they can broadly be summarized under the following questions: (1) Is our behavior determined? (issues surrounding personality change and stability— are we free to choose or not?), (2) Is it safe to give other people (especially businesses) information about our personality profile? (issues relating to data confidentiality and anonymity), and finally, (3) Is personality profiling ethical? (Some people believe psychological testing, including personality assessment, legitimizes prejudice and discrimination.) These questions are quite political and philosophical, but we will try to briefly discuss their psychological implications in this chapter. We like to tell our students that the first important lesson they need to learn in their studies is that, in psychology, the answer to any question is "it depends." You may want to remember this too (and that is also the answer to the above questions).

PROFILING FOR "BAD" OR PROBLEMATIC PERSONALITY TRAITS

In this section, we discuss the implications of using personality inventories in the context of identifying "bad" or problematic traits, such as narcissism, Machiavellianism, and psychopathy. Although these traits have been traditionally studied in the context of clinical psychology, the past 10 years have seen an upsurge in research into their nonclinical manifestations. Indeed, many people believe that successful businessmen, CEOs, and entrepreneurs tend to display dysfunctional traits that could present a problem with regard to their interaction with others (such as leadership derailment). So, is personality useful to assess these elements of everyday life psychopathology, and, if it is, should it be used to prevent problematic behaviors?

When people think of psychopaths they tend to think of Hannibal Lecter or Jack the Ripper, but there are many examples in the everyday newspaper, and some that receive global media coverage for weeks: for example, the Columbine school shooting, the Virginia Tech massacre, and the more recent shooting in Norway. These examples are vivid reminders of the threat posed by other humans, even during peaceful times. In America, debate surrounding these issues tends to focus on gun legislation and the role of the media (e.g., violent movies or video games), but as the 2011 shooting in Norway, one of the most peaceful and civilized countries on earth, has shown, nobody is exempt. As personality researchers, our focus is not on the cultural factors that could trigger these events (although we don't deny they exist, we leave that to sociologists and anthropologists), but on the individual or personal characteristics that may drive some people to commit such terrible acts. This is where the moral question kicks in: Assuming that we could predict, with a reasonable degree of accuracy, someone's likelihood of committing the above or comparable atrocities (and kill innocent civilians), would it be justified to take preventive action? Imagine, for instance, that a psychological test had revealed that the perpetrators of the Virginia Tech and Norwegian massacres had psychopathic tendencies: Would you deem it acceptable, in those circumstances, to provide treatment to, and maybe even institutionalize, those individuals? How many lives would you put at risk in exchange for providing preventive treatment to people who are considered potential threats to others (even when they may not have done anything to anyone in the end)?

To even attempt to answer these questions, we must first explain the nature of psychopathy. Psychopathy was first brought to mainstream attention in 1942 by Harvey Cleckley's seminal book *The Mask of Sanity*. While working in a prison, he conducted many clinical interviews with incarcerated psychopaths. He was most taken back by the psychopath's ability to appear "normal." As Cleckley explains, their callousness and twisted thoughts were hidden by a *mask* of normality. This ability to mask abnormality is what enables psychopaths to become such effective predators. A psychologist named Robert Hare, interested by Cleckley's findings, sought to understand what made psychopaths tick and how they differ from others, initially focusing on personality differences. After reviewing previous research and conducting his own, he developed the "Psychopathy Checklist" (PCL). The PCL is now the standard clinical interview technique that aims to identify psychopaths. It does this by assessing four overarching facets of personality: abnormal interpersonal relations, shallow affect, antisocial tendencies, and impulsive and parasitic lifestyles. Hare noted that while clinical psychopathy only affects around 1% of the entire population, the disorder lies on a continuum (Hare & Neumann, 2008). Ordinary individuals like yourself are likely to possess some psychopathic traits, albeit a lot less prevalently. It is also found that psychopathy has two types: primary and secondary. Primary psychopathy primarily relates to the interpersonal and affective facets, whereas secondary psychopathy (commonly referred to as *antisocial personality disorder*) comprises the lifestyle and antisocial facets.

According to Hare's work, psychopaths will seek to form relationships with others only if it enables them to achieve their own goals. They will do this by being superficial and highly Machiavellian—manipulating others. They will invest lots of time and energy in identifying and winning over individuals that are of "use" to them. Once they have got what they want, they will simply abandon their victim. They have absolutely no problem in being abusive to their victims because they do not understand, or feel empathy toward, others. Unlike most humans, who will feel guilty or saddened when they have committed a wrongdoing, the psychopath will blame the victim for being defenseless. They see the world as a competition; a "survival of the fittest" attitude is constantly running through their mind. A serial killer named Jack Abbott once responded to a question asking him about the reasons for committing such heinous crimes: *"There are emotions, a whole spectrum of them, that I only know through words...I can imagine I feel these emotions, but I do not"* (Babiak & Hare, 2007, p. 54). The sheer lack of regard for others and an amazing ability to charm and manipulate are why they are often regarded as "predators" in the literature.

If the personality traits of a psychopath have been identified, the fundamental question is: What causes psychopathy? That is, are psychopaths born or made? Although this question has been debated for centuries, in recent years, some important steps have been taken to address it. Brain-imaging studies have found that there are structural differences in a psychopath's brain. Specifically, abnormalities are found in the orbital–frontal cortex (a region of brain sitting above the eyes that plays a large role in personality formation and expression). As a result, the typical mechanisms that control and regulate behaviors become deficient. Another region of the brain that has been found to be atypical is the paralimbic system. This system houses various brain structures that are essential for producing emotions such as fear, anger, and empathy. The most significantly affected structures are the amygdala and the hippocampus. In psychopaths, these two structures are found to be smaller than in the average individual. This underdevelopment may explain why psychopaths have such shallow affect toward others; their brains simply cannot process the information adequately. Chillingly, the fact that the amygdala is not functioning appropriately inhibits the psychopath from feeling any fear or guilt from the consequences of his or her actions. A seminal study highlighting this "emotional bluntness" was carried out by Hare in the 1980s. Hare found that the psychopath's brain would process an emotional word the same way as any other word. This clearly showed how the psychopathic individual can be completely disconnected from any emotion that is presented before them. In light of this research, neuropsychologist Kent Kiehl suggests that psychopathy could well be a neurodevelopmental disorder (a disorder marked by abnormal brain growth), whereby the underdeveloped regions are miscommunicating via neural pathways and feedback loops, thus producing the abnormal behavior (Kiehl, 2006).

But what about evolution? Evolutionary theory states that behaviors, traits, and genetic materials survive only if they are adaptive to the environment the organism finds itself in. Larsson, Viding, and Plomin (2008) found compelling evidence for the fact that psychopathy is highly genetic, suggesting environmental factors (such as a stable family environment) have little impact in offsetting the antisocial personality. Crucially, genetic research now suggests that one gene, in particular, may have a disproportionate influence on the development of psychopathy. Studies conducted by Jim Fallon have shown consistent links between the MAO-A gene, also known as the *warrior gene* (Fallon, 2006), and psychopathy.

Given these results, Glenn, Kurzban, and Raine (2008) proposed two evolutionary theories to explain why psychopathy is still found in the current human population: First, psychopathy may be an adaptive response to specific, environmental conditions. For example, the fact that psychopaths can freely victimize others means that they can aid their own survival by gaining free access to valuable resources. Second, psychopathy is an accumulation of a variety of mildly maladaptive traits, evidenced by the fact that psychopaths are able to appear normal (unlike individuals with schizophrenia) and function in everyday life. Thus, there are many psychopaths out there who are not serial killers. Instead, these individuals may be businessmen.

A "successful psychopath" is a psychopath who is able to go about his or her manipulation, conning, and victimizing without ever being caught by the authorities. It is extremely difficult to try and identify successful psychopaths, as they have embedded themselves into society so well. Indeed, research suggests that the prevalence of successful psychopaths could possibly be much higher than we think. Psychologist Paul Babiak recently conducted the first large-scale analysis of psychopathy in the corporate sector. While it has long been a hypothesis, largely driven by Gordon Gekko-esque *(Wall Street)* anecdotes, Babiak found that the individuals in the senior positions of an organization are far more likely to score highly on the PCL. Furthermore, the corporate sector as a whole is four times more psychopathic than the average community. Crucially, studies find negative correlations between highly psychopathic business persons' productivity and (positive) peer ratings (Babiak, Neumann, & Hare, 2010). This means that despite doing poor work, a psychopath's "mask" is worn so well that coworkers still talk favorably of him or her. They have been truly fooled by the psychopath's masquerade.

It may be argued that successful psychopaths may be more of a concern to you than the traditional, stereotyped psychopath. But is there anything we can do about psychopaths running our organizations and countries? Well, it is extremely hard. While there are clinical institutions such as Broadmoor Hospital for the criminally insane in the United Kingdom, the best attempt to offset psychopathic tendencies is to foster good family environments and try to identify "at-risk" individuals at an early age (e.g., through community and family programs). As evidence has revealed, conduct disorder in children is a good marker for predicting psychopathy and antisocial outcomes in later years

(Larsson et al., 2008; Viding, Blair, Moffit, & Plomin, 2005). With this in mind, it follows that if people that are at a high risk of carrying out callous and violent acts are left unchecked, they are able to manipulate, deceive, and abuse individuals throughout their lives. As current developments in behavioral genetics and brain imaging constantly yield new findings about the human brain, perhaps it is only a matter of time before the personality disorder can be fully understood. Until then, however, protecting and identifying risky individuals will remain difficult.

So, next time you are on your way to work or going to see your friends, take a look on either side of you and ask yourself this: "Is that person a psychopath?"

USING PERSONALITY TESTS IN EDUCATIONAL SELECTION (SCHOOL AND UNIVERSITY)

Although personality tests are rarely used for the purpose of educational selection, scores on these tests correlate with several educational performance outcomes (see again Chapter 4). That is, people who score low on Conscientiousness, emotional stability, and, to some extent, Openness, tend to do worse at school and university (Chamorro-Premuzic & Furnham, 2005b). Moreover, there is now compelling evidence from many independent empirical studies highlighting the reasons why people with these personality profiles tend to display weaker levels of performance in educational contexts. The evidence is far from surprising: People with lower Conscientiousness levels tend to be quite disorganized, lazy, and impulsive, and find it hard to adhere to orders (including from their teachers or professors). People who are low on emotional stability tend to stress out quite easily and have lower levels of confidence, which interferes with their ability to do well on examinations (at school and university). Finally, people with low Openness scores are generally less interested in studying and have lower levels of intellectual curiosity and creativity—so, one would expect them to do well only if they are extrinsically motivated. In light of this evidence, should universities and other educational institutions (maybe even schools) employ personality tests for their selection decisions? We are pretty sure your answer would be "no," but let us try to persuade you to the contrary.

In most universities around the world, students are already being selected on some basis. If you are studying in a U.S. university, you will know about Scholastic Aptitude Test (SAT) and Graduate Record Examination (GRE) scores; if you are not, then you need to know that these are standardized tests given as part of the selection process to most higher education institutions in the United States. In fact, even if you are a student at a U.S. university, you may not have considered the following: These tests are designed and administered by the Educational Testing Service (ETS), who charge universities a fee for this service, while also charging you—or most applicants in the United States—a fee for taking the test. In effect, then, you are paying someone to sell your test scores to a university and "help" the university decide whether you are a worthy student or not.

Quite clearly, the ETS has a fantastic business model, and although you would probably prefer not to take an exam in order to gain acceptance to a university, the fact that these exams are actually making the university a more competitive place (at least when the cut-off scores are high enough) can only work in your advantage. So, if you are lucky enough to be an Ivy League student, or part of a good university program, that is probably partly due to these standardized tests administered by ETS (who, incidentally, have something of a monopoly in the United States). Thus, the underlying issue to the controversial question of whether students should be selected on the basis of personality tests or any other basis is that there are marked individual differences in academic performance, whether at Harvard or at a third-rate university, and the same is true in schools.

In Chapter 4, we have highlighted some of the studies demonstrating that personality tests are consistent and powerful predictors of individual differences in educational achievement. Yet, most educational institutions rely on different criteria when selecting their students. Indeed, most do not use any form of testing, focusing instead on (a) income (students whose parents can afford a high tuition fee are eligible), (b) past academic performance (in the previous level of formal education), and (c) entry examination (subject-based or knowledge tests for medicine, law, economics, etc.). Of these, (b) and (c) make perfect sense because they are predictive of future performance; however, they can also be predicted by personality traits. Indeed, the reasons why a student does well on (b) and (c) are the same reasons for him/her doing well at the selected university: Conscientiousness, stability, Openness, and so on. As for (a), you may think that it is unfair (and we do, too), but socioeconomic status also predicts subsequent academic performance and educational achievement (as well as career success thereafter). So, can psychological testing provide a better, more efficient, and predictive approach to assess individual differences in academic potential?

Most psychometric tests for predicting academic performance (such as ETS's) are essentially cognitive ability tests. These tests are timed and include questions that have a predetermined, single, objectively correct answer: For example, what is the capital of Norway? What is 7% of 120? What does GDP stand for? These questions are not arbitrary, but they are selected on the basis of their predictive value or power, and what they attempt to predict is educational success. In fact, the very first IQ tests were developed for this purpose over 100 years ago. The French Educational Ministry had commissioned Alfred Binet (1857–1911) with the task of devising a method for discerning between better and worse learners, independently of how well behaved they were (before Binet, students' potential had been rated by their teachers, who were obviously biased against poorly behaved kids and in favor of well-behaved ones).

The goal of cognitive ability tests today still remains the same: to provide a quantitative and relatively objective and generic measure of a person's learning potential, or how fast and well a person will pick up formal knowledge.

Although the ETS does not refer to its tests as IQ tests, there is ample evidence showing that tests like the GRE and the SAT correlate substantially with scores on standardized IQ tests (Chamorro-Premuzic & Furnham, 2010a, 2010b). The reason why these tests are not referred to as "IQ" is sheer political correctness: "Standardized achievement test" or "graduate record examination" sounds more neutral, boring, and better, and avoids referring to some people as smarter than others, or implying that some people are smart while others are stupid. There are good statistical reasons for using these tests, as top scorers tend to outperform average scorers, who in turn do better than low scorers in academic assignments; but the tests are also problematic because there are often more White, educated, and affluent students than ethnic minorities (except Asians) among the top scorers; so, universities that rely too much on these tests may end up with few Hispanics, Blacks, and people with lower levels of socioeconomic status. Yet, these tests are some of the best predictors of an individual's future academic performance, and the only way we can compare applicants from very diverse backgrounds (e.g., an applicant who went to the 25th best school in Bangladesh and achieved an average grade that puts him/her in the top 5% versus an applicant who went to the 17th best school of Argentina and achieved an average grade that puts him/her in the top 20%). Moreover, standardized "achievement" tests like the GRE and the SAT assess maximal performance or what a student can do, but there are many capable students who end up underperforming at school or university because they lack motivation or discipline, or do not "fit" with the academic climate of the institution.

This is where personality tests can help. Scores on validated personality scales assess individual differences in learning potential, but for different reasons than ETS's achievement tests. Indeed, personality scales provide information on what a person usually does or his/her typical performance, so they should complement IQ and other cognitive ability tests in the prediction of students' academic performance. To illustrate this with a simple example, assume that we have a student with a high GRE score but a low score on Conscientiousness. This person would probably be a "fast learner," but also lack the necessary levels of self-discipline and management skills to engage in the learning program outlined by his/her teacher. Conversely, high levels of Conscientiousness may compensate for lower levels of GRE, SAT, and IQ (von Stumm, Hell, & Chamorro-Premuzic, 2011). What this means is that personality moderates (influences) the effects of ability on learning and academic performance; we therefore need to look at the overall profile of a student in order to gain a better understanding of what he or she will usually do, how he or she will do it, and why.

There is also a second reason for including personality tests in educational selection, namely the lack of consequential group differences in average scores on these tests. For instance, Hispanics, Blacks, and Whites show little differences in their Neuroticism, Conscientiousness, and Openness scores (and these three predictors of academic performance are largely unrelated); moreover, whether you are rich or poor, went to a good school or a bad school, your score on these and other personality traits could be high, average, or low (with roughly the same probability). Given the predictive validity of personality scales at school and university (see again Chapter 4), and the fact that individual differences in personality are largely unrelated to IQ (Chamorro-Premuzic & Furnham, 2005b), using personality tests for academic selection will enable us to better predict and understand individual differences in educational attainment and academic performance, as well as promoting ethnic and socioeconomic diversity at school and university.

Of course, you may argue that it is not fair for schools and universities to deny anyone the opportunity to study, but there are unavoidable supply-and-demand differences between institutions wherever there is choice (and even when there isn't). There is, however, an undeniable paradox in any "competitive" educational system, especially those systems that are strongly market-driven (like the United States). On one hand, those systems end up producing the best and most sought-after institutions and learning programs in the world. For instance, 17 out of the top 20 universities in the world are in the United States (ARWU, 2011). On the other hand, a top reputation enables universities (and schools) to select the best students; that is, students who are quick, confident, well-organized, and curious, and with the financial support behind them to devote most of their time to their studies. This creates a vicious circle, whereby the "rich get richer" and the "poor get poorer," as educational choices enhance rather than reduce baseline differences in academic potential between students. Surely, the true sign of a top university or school would be to select less educated students or "slower learners" and turn them into the leaders of tomorrow. Instead, what Ivy League and comparable institutions do is to identify the top leaders of tomorrow, assess them, and give them prestigious degrees and titles in exchange for their hard work and competition against fellow students. How well would those same students fare at third-rate institutions, and how well would average students from poor institutions do if they went to an Ivy League school? If you think of it, selecting the best students is a way of minimizing some of the common challenges to teaching: Dealing with someone who is curious, willing to work hard, and a quick learner is surely easier (and more rewarding) than dealing with someone who is unmotivated, uneducated, and has conduct problems.

ONLINE PROFILING (PSYCHOGRAPHIC SEGMENTATION)

In this section, we examine current trends in online personality profiling in the context of consumer behavior (also known as psychographic segmentation). Big Internet players like Amazon, Google, and Facebook are competing fiercely in the game of "knowing their customers" and combine behavioral, demographic, and (occasionally) psychometric data to predict what individuals will do, what they may like to buy, and even what sort of lifestyles they live. So, how valid and ethical are these initiatives?

Although we cannot estimate the exact probability, we are quite confident that you will have, at least once, done some of these things: used Facebook, Gmail, Google, YouTube, Amazon, or eBay. If not, you probably still live in the 20th century. If you have, and you are observant (as a psychology student or someone interested in psychology, we would expect you to be), you may have noticed that these sites subsist on advertising; that is, "pop-ads" or visual advertisements displayed next to the main functions in these sites. If you are very observant, you will have noticed that those ads are often relevant to your own interests and consumer preferences. This is what advertisers and marketers refer to as "behavioral targeting": the selection of ads, products, and brands that are likely to be relevant to the consumer. Here are a couple of examples. One of us uses a Gmail e-mail account (rather frequently). When he flicks from one e-mail to the next, the narrow text line above the inbox also flicks from one line of ad to another one. Moreover, the ads tend to display material that is clearly connected with the content of the e-mail message. In fact, one of us recently wrote to the other author about "going out for a drink in Greenwich" (a lively and quite trendy suburb of London); the same message also contained information about our university. What did the text ad display? Surprisingly, it was advertising "new courses at the University of Greenwich." If you have an e-mail account with Gmail, you can test this now—in fact, you can write about exotic holidays in Cuba and you will probably be "offered" Cuban cigars (not in the United States of course, because of the embargo) or a time-share in the Caribbean. Although this is exemplified behavioral targeting, the "behavior" is actually just text, and the ads are selected via semantic text scanning or matching of keywords (this is also how Google became the most popular search engine in the world, and why it is now the most profitable advertising company in the world).

Here's another example. If you bought things on Amazon (CDs, DVDs, or clothes), or even if you "watched" items on their catalogue, Amazon will automatically "redecorate" its window display or screen every time you log on. This is a rather simple mechanism: Amazon enables you to browse items for free, but in order to buy something you need to open an account (which is still free, but requires you to provide certain personal details). This enables Amazon to identify every member who browses items, and record their e-shopping "behaviors." Moreover, this also enables the giant online retailer to customize or personalize its recommendations. For instance, if you bought a movie with Robert De Niro, it will recommend you more movies with that actor (even if one movie was *Meet the Parents* and the recommendations included *The Deer Hunter*—two movies that have nothing in common except, well, Robert De Niro). The system is also inaccurate at detecting how satisfied you were with a previous purchase. So, you may have bought some Levi's jeans but disliked them, and Amazon will still recommend to you other jeans or, what is worse, other products by Levi's (worse in the event that you didn't like your jeans).

There are now more refined and probably controversial examples. For instance, Facebook is apparently using the information of tagged photographs (who the people are, where they are, and what they "like") to "cherry-pick" the ads it displays to each account user. So, if you use Facebook and tag your holiday pictures in Disneyland, you will probably be offered trips to Orlando or the latest Disney movie, and so on. What is controversial and unpopular about these growing advertising strategies and trends is that consumers feel intruded upon, spied upon, and violated in their privacy. However, most people probably find that this is a price worth paying, and that the alternative (not using Amazon, eBay, Facebook, Gmail, etc., or paying more for similar services or products) is worse. The perception of a "big brother" society, especially when we are referring to the web, is no doubt alarming to many consumers, who fear that the information they are volunteering online may one day be used to their own detriment.

Where does personality profiling kick in here? Although few online businesses are assessing personality traits, there is clearly a "digital war" for predicting behavior and profiling consumers. We believe that personality will play a key role in both refining online retailers' (including social networking sites) ability to understand consumers and predict their behavior; and also adding transparency and accountability to the process of consumer-centered recommendations. However, two things need to happen first. First, personality researchers need to highlight the degree to which personality traits predict individual differences in consumer preferences (generic and specific). Some of these associations are rather intuitive: Individuals with higher levels of Openness to experience tend to have unconventional, more creative, preferences. Thus, if we know how "creative" a product is—for example, an Apple Mac laptop is probably perceived as more "creative" than a Dell PC (even in today's world where most people prefer the Mac, which does not really imply that most people are creative)—therefore, higher Openness should correlate positively with preferences for Mac products. There is also some work to be done in terms of classifying the entire range of products, brands, and psychological needs that are fulfilled when individuals purchase them and consume them. As you will see in the forthcoming sections, this cataloguing of phenomena and behaviors has been accomplished much more successfully in the world of human resources (staffing) and dating (romantic relationships). One may argue that those areas are ubiquitous to human life as they concern love and work, two of the fundamental areas of mental health, as well as being universal domains of human motivation: career success and relationship satisfaction (both also feed into key evolutionary goals, namely competition and reproduction).

That said, consumerism has become almost as important, or even more. Even when people are single and unemployed, they remain consumers—and many people (you can call them greedy, superficial, and materialistic, but we all surely have a bit of that too) are in relationships or jobs simply to boost their purchasing power, which translates into consuming more and better products.

Yet there are clear individual differences underlying consumer behaviors. For starters, we don't all like the same products. Then there are also big interindividual differences in how much money and time we spend to acquire things (even when income differences are held constant). Last, but not least, there are marked differences in how people react to advertising, and what they feel, think, and do after they purchased the same product. Surely, the personality has something to say about consumer behaviors. Specifically, information about an individual's character or personality profile should enable us to predict what they will try to consume, what they will enjoy consuming, and how they will respond to marketing and advertising campaigns. What is perhaps more extraordinary is that laypeople already use information about a person's consumer habits to profile his or her personality. For example, what would you think of a 50-year-old man wearing a heavy metal t-shirt (other than guessing that he is probably an IT manager)? That t-shirt, although an inanimate object, has a personality: It displays the behavior and preference of its owner, and knowing that someone of that age likes heavy metal music can signal many things other than suggesting that the person is going through a midlife crisis (or has bad taste in music). What could those things be? Counter-conformity, antisocial behavioral tendencies, problems with authority, rebelliousness, introversion, low Agreeableness, Openness to new experience, sensation–seeking, the list goes on. Yes, this may just be us brainstorming, but there are simple ways of testing these hypotheses and some research has already managed just that.

For example, our own work has shown that individual differences in personality explain why certain people like some forms of art, but not others (Chamorro-Premuzic, Reimers, Hsu, & Ahmetoglu, 2008). People high on Openness like most forms of art, but they especially prefer unconventional, novel, or less popular forms of art—like cubism, abstract, and Japanese art. Likewise, open people tend to prefer music that is complex and unusual (Chamorro-Premuzic, Fagan, & Furnham, 2010), and also consume more music than the average person. In a similar vein, personality predicts individual differences in movie preferences: neurotics like nostalgic, dramatic, and emotionally laden films; extraverts like cheerful, superficial, and uplifting movies; open people like arty, factual, and science fiction films, and there are many more associations between people's film preferences and their personalities (Chamorro-Premuzic, Kallias, & Hsu, in press). While it is easy to categorize these and other forms of media—mainly because the job has been done by art historians, film critics, and musicologists—psychologists must be more proactive when it comes to classifying other consumer products and brands. One psychologist who has done a great deal of work in this area is Jacqueline Aaaker.

PERSONNEL SELECTION

This section will aim to critically evaluate the use of various personality instruments and methodologies for identifying key employee features across different organizational settings. Personality traits have been assessed in the context of selection for decades and the best-known personality inventory is the Myers-Briggs "type" indicator (MBTI), which is completed by 2 million people each year. Yet, few academic research psychologists talk about the MBTI, which reflects an all too common discrepancy between what goes on in the world of science, on one hand, and the real world, on the other. One of the reasons for this discrepancy is that academics and businesses have different agendas. For academics, personality research is often about measuring "traits" or validating psychometric tests; for businesses (or, if you prefer, organizations), personality is a useful currency only if it helps them attain their goals: to increase profits (or, if you prefer, organizational effectiveness—note that nonprofit organizations can still be more or less effective). Ironically, this is also where the science and practice of personality assessment should meet. Indeed, applied psychologists, notably industrial/organizational psychologists, are interested in predicting individual and organizational performance. To the degree that personality scores enable them to anticipate what a person is likely to do, they will regard personality scales as powerful instruments and use them to inform their policies and decision-making processes. The typical scenario where this would occur is during the process of personnel selection, which concerns the search for the best available employee to fill a job opening: Can personality tests help us to identify the right person for the job? The short answer is "yes," and the longer answer is as follows.

Scores on well-established personality scales (self-report scales) correlate in the region of .2 to .3 with job performance "scores." We say "scores" because measures of job performance are rarely reliable. Consider the following: Three candidates turn up for a job interview and the best-looking person is offered the job (this is not a joke, there is a well-established literature on lookism or how good-looking people are rated more favorably on a number of psychological traits, including competence— Langlois et al., 2000). Most educated people—even when they are not liberals—would complain about the prejudiced nature of this selection; surely, it is unfair to select against people just because they are less attractive. However, what if the selected candidate is also evaluated positively on his or her job performance (because she/he is attractive or any other reason)? That would demonstrate that the selection has been successful: Picking someone for a job and having that person perform well later on would be evidence for having made the right choice in the first place (even if the "validity" of the selection method would be due to bias during both stages, the selection and the assessment of job performance). Again, that would not be a surreal or unimaginable example. Humans are subject to biases and ultimately both the selection and the evaluation of someone's performance are made by humans.

This leads us to consider the next question. How would you decide whether someone is the right candidate for a job? Well, whatever methods you use to select that person, the answer remains the same: One needs to identify the characteristics of a high-performing individual, and then assess someone's potential to display those attributes later on, on the job. Ultimately, this concerns defining individual differences in job performance, and identifying the predictors or determinants of those individual differences. Let us assume that the job in question is a sales job. What do good salespeople look like? They tend to be confident (to persuade others and cope with rejection if they don't); they tend to be good at reading people's emotions (to understand what others want); they are also sociable and outgoing (as they have to deal with people, even if via e-mail or social networks). Once we have profiled the personality of successful sales people—or any successful job performers—we can consult the literature or scientific evidence on what traits predispose those behaviors. Rather than reviewing the literature on the personality predictors of sales performance, we will discuss the generic findings on how well personality predicts "job performance" across all job families—even though this is a bit like mixing apples and oranges (because some personality characteristics are useful in some jobs rather than in others).

As stated, correlations between personality and job performance can average up to .3 (see Ones & Vishveswaran, 2011, for a recent review). What this means is that a candidate or job applicant with the "right" personality profile will be 65% more likely to do well at the job, compared to just 35% for a candidate with the "wrong" personality profile (and 50% for a candidate with average profile). The question, of course, is what personality traits most candidates need to display to do well in most jobs. The answer is far from counterintuitive: People who are emotionally stable (low Neuroticism), responsible, disciplined, organized (high Conscientiousness), confident, sociable, and likeable (high Extraversion) tend to show higher levels of job performance in general, whether performance is assessed objectively or subjectively. Objective indicators of performance are quantitative estimates of an employee's output: In low-level jobs, they may include the number of calls taken per hour in a call center; in highly qualified jobs, they may include millions of dollars made in stock share investment or sales. Subjective indicators of performance tend to refer to supervisory ratings of their employee's contribution to the organization's goals. Inevitably, these will be more biased, and may just boil down to whether your boss likes you or not. So, putting all this together, well-adjusted or emotionally stable, sociable, and diligent employees tend to be appreciated more by their bosses and also show higher outputs of objective performance.

Given that the above personality traits are relatively independent of each other, a person who displays all of them (high Extraversion, low Neuroticism, and high Conscientiousness) will be more than 15% more likely than the average person to do well. Indeed, if we assume that individual differences in those three traits are totally independent, then we would add 15% + 15% + 15%, which would mean 45% more likely than the average person to do well. Unfortunately, the three traits are not really independent, as modest to moderate associations have been found between them (Rushton & Irwing, 2011; but see also Ferguson, Chamorro-Premuzic, Pickering, & Weiss, 2011, for a rebuttal to their postulate). But these are all generalizations that do show that personality traits are useful predictors of performance— they are generalizations based on data, namely meta-analysis of thousands of studies in many different organizations, countries, and cultures, and where many different instruments have been employed. It is likely that these studies underestimate the real impact of personality at work. How so? Well, because defining the specific attributes that contribute to high performance in a given job, and taking into account how performance is assessed, will enable us to identify (a) better predictors and (b) the most effective methods for predicting performance. It is the second point that requires further consideration.

Personality tests are still not used very widely for selection purposes. Indeed, other than in the United States and the United Kingdom, few big economies base their staffing decisions on the results of personality tests. If you have ever applied for a job somewhere, the chances are that you did not complete a personality test as part of your selection process. More likely, you would have completed an application form, sent your curriculum vitae (CV), requested letters of recommendation from people with whom you have worked or studied, and, almost certainly, attended an interview. Although most of these methods tend to be preferred by candidates, and despite being more frequently employed than personality tests, they are all less reliable and far less valid predictors of performance than good personality tests (Chamorro-Premuzic & Furnham, 2010a, 2010b). You do not need to consult the scientific evidence on this, it is almost a matter of common sense. Application forms tend to assess the very demographic factors that we ought to ignore to avoid discrimination, except when they ask people to report on previous accomplishments. To be sure, past behavior is the best predictor of future behavior (this is one of the main premises of personality theory—Chamorro-Premuzic, 2011). However, what if candidates are young and have no previous experience for the job? Surely, it would be unfair to discriminate against them on that basis, and prefer more experienced candidates, unless you decide that you wanted to hire the oldest applicant in the pool. With regard to CVs, people lie on their vitas and are even trained to "customize" their CVs for every job application. In fact, we always advise our students to exaggerate their achievements and skills in their CVs, because if they don't, employers will still expect them to do so and "discount" 20% or 30% of their accomplishments. For instance, saying that you are "fluent" in French is usually interpreted by recruiters as "speaking some French" or having studied it for a couple of years in high school; so if you say that you have "basic" knowledge of French, they will assume that you can barely say "oui." References are an even weaker candidate to predict performance, as even the laziest and most problematic employee can find one or two people to comment positively on some aspects of his or her personality (in fact, in many countries, it is almost illegal to provide a negative reference for someone—certainly in the United States you may be sued if you do). We already highlighted the problems with the interviews: People ask irrelevant questions, focus on irrelevant behaviors, and are biased against unattractive and uncharismatic candidates. Psychopaths and narcissists tend to interview very well because they can charm anybody and display exuberant signs of social potency, at least during a couple of hours (when they are hired, employers are often shocked by their "dark side" and end up paying the price for their destructive conduct; Hogan, 2007). Thus, personality scales may not be the perfect selection devices, but they are better than most alternatives. The only single alternative that seems to predict performance more accurately, across an even wider range of jobs, is cognitive ability (IQ tests). However, these are even less popular than personality tests, and they "discriminate" against ethnic minorities and (sometimes) women. By "discriminate," we don't mean that they are biased, but that certain groups of people tend to score lower on average than others—and those people also tend to perform lower on average than others. The reason why IQ tests predict performance is that they are great predictors of learning speed and ability, and many jobs require individuals to learn things while on the job (in fact, most jobs do to some extent).

Finally, studies have also shown that all the methods we considered (interviews, CVs, references, and application forms) tend to predict performance, albeit poorly, when they are correlated with personality test scores. Thus, they do not provide additional information on a candidate but are used as different ways of obtaining information about their personality. Needless to say, those methods are more time-consuming, hard to interpret, and unreliable than valid personality scales. Even if they don't replace personality tests, it seems quite foolish to ignore the contribution—and value added—of personality scales when it comes to identifying and predicting performance differences or potential between different job candidates.

PERSONALITY AND "DIGITAL LOVE"

The market for online dating is huge and growing and an increasing number of single individuals subscribe to these services in order to find their "ideal" partners. In 2005, Americans spent $500 million on online dating (forecast for 2011 is $1 billion). Online dating is now the largest segment of paid content on the web, other than pornography. Increasingly, too, online dating sites, such as Match.com and eHarmony, are employing psychological tests to profile individuals in terms of their romantic compatibility and help them identify their "perfect matches." Our own research has looked at some of the associations between personality trait and romantic preferences (Ahmetoglu, Swami, & Chamorro-Premuzic, 2009). In this section, we review this somewhat polemic application of personality assessment; we refer to this as "digital love," but we may as well have used "personalized" love to label the concept.

What is love? Psychologists have rarely tried to answer this question. One exception is the famous U.S. psychologist Robert Sternberg, who conceptualized a three-way theory (all his theories come in "threes") of love (Sternberg, 1986). In his view, there are three major types of romantic relationships, namely romantic, companionate, and fatuous. Romantic love is how most people—at least in western cultures or when they are teenagers—think of love. It's being almost infatuated with another person and getting butterflies in your stomach; it also involves high levels of intimacy with the other person. This is the main reason why most people today are reluctant to accept the idea that you can customize your romantic partner online. Then again, meeting him on a drunken night out is hardly more romantic. The second type of love, companionate, is like a great friendship: It involves sharing or wanting to share every moment with the other person, and being committed to that relationship for a long time because it is so much fun to hang out with them. Finally, fatuous love is based on sexual attractiveness and passion but lacks commitment (this could include affairs or one-night stands). Although these three major love types describe most relationships, there are also relationships that may have it all: That is, they have commitment, passion, and intimacy; these relationships are what Sternberg refers to as consummate love, and perhaps best reflect what most people mean in terms of "a perfect match."

The relationship between personality and romantic relationships is not just of theoretical interest. In fact, there are hundreds of websites and phone applications dedicated to dating, and, increasingly, they incorporate some psychology of personality in them. Although people are still shocked by the idea that you can simply "shop around" for your partner by browsing on the web, it should come as no surprise to anybody. The Internet has become ubiquitous in most parts of the world, with people spending hours online. Unlike the physical world, the virtual world enables you to connect with many people at the same time, wherever they are. The Internet also enables us to meet new people on a much bigger scale than the physical world does. Why do you think Facebook has over 700 million users (at the time this book was written; by the time you read it, it will probably have well over 1 billion)? Well, it all started as a university website to rate and meet fellow students; then it expanded to students from other universities, cities, countries...the rest is history. What few people think of is that Facebook functions as a hidden dating site. The most common way to meet your romantic partner (even today) is via "word of mouth" or a friend's recommendation. So, we are more likely to be open to meeting other people if we have friends in common. This is really quite ancestral and if you think back to medieval times or go far enough from big industrialized cities, you will find that parents will try to hook up their son or daughter with their neighbors' son or daughter. Scale that and add a bit of technology and you have the online dating revolution.

There is an urban legend about how Facebook grew exponentially after they included "relationship status" as one of their main profile fields. Indeed, just as people are less interested in befriending or "liking" someone if they don't have a profile picture, they are less interested in someone if their relationship status is "engaged" or "married." Given that most of the people in the world are probably unhappy with their love life (some because they are single, others because they are with the wrong person), and as people spend so much time online, it is only normal that the Internet has become a popular pick-up place. Indeed, in many places, it is now the second most popular way of meeting your partner (after friends in common). So, how can personality profiling be used to improve people's online dating experience?

Most online dating sites require members to browse through hundreds or thousands of profiles. These profiles tend to include a picture (and we will not discuss the psychology of physical attractiveness here, but as you probably imagine these pictures tend to portray users in a very favorable way). Online profiles also tend to include a biographic blurb, written by the date-seeker or an acquaintance (the latter is like a reference or recommendation letter). For example: "Love a good night out and pepperoni pizza, good dancer, politics is not my thing, prefer beach to mountains, and would like a gym partner as I find exercise boring." Even if you are not a psychologist, when you read this profile you will build a sketch of that person's character. Now that you have read something about personality, you should be able to translate this profile into Big Five language (as well as other taxonomies). This is how we would do it (but there are many interpretations, not least because behaviors and preferences have different meanings in different cultures):

- "Love a good night out": extraverted, outgoing, sensation-seeker, party animal (probably not studious and quite street-wise; may also be quite unhealthy if a "good night out" implies drinking and smoking, as it does in the United Kingdom)
- "Good dancer": ditto…and maybe overconfident, as few males (assuming, as we did, that this is a male) feel competent dancing and even fewer would brag about it; then again males tend to brag about things more than females do
- "Politics is not my thing": unintellectual, low Openness, no hungry mind, possibly anarchic or resentful about public affairs, low Conscientiousness (feels no civic responsibilities, etc.)
- "Prefer beach to mountains": possibly vain and somewhat superficial, back to sociability and Extraversion, more conventional, unintellectual
- "Would like a partner for the gym as I find exercise boring": lazy, no self-control, low Conscientiousness, high sociability

Oh, and we almost forgot the "pepperoni pizza" comment: clearly unsophisticated, but also warm and down-to-earth and grounded; comfortable person, hedonistic, honest (many people on online dating sites will pretend to like Bach when they really just like Lady Gaga—pepperoni pizza is to fine dining what Lady Gaga is to Bach).

Admittedly, there is not much science to our method but there still is some science, namely translating self-descriptive adjectives into personality traits. Many studies (and these are serious empirical studies and experiments) have shown that independent raters tend to agree in their perceptions of strangers' personalities. In fact, even 30-second video clips of random people yield reliable and rather accurate personality ratings by viewers who are told to profile the targets using Big Five or comparable personality language (Graham, Sandy, & Gosling, 2011). This is because we cannot communicate our personality; that is, in everything we do and everything we say, there is personality information that others will decipher and decode, whether they are trained psychologists or distracted laypeople. If you pay attention to, and have some knowledge of, the clues people project, you will be able to build rather accurate profiles of people, and online dating blurbs contain important information about a person's character. Therefore, if you are "shopping around" for a partner, you will need to have a trained eye and sophisticated radar to predict what that person will be like. The good thing about online dating is that you can "meet" many people in a few minutes time, from the comfort of your home and in your pajamas. This also presents a challenge in terms of requiring date-seekers to discriminate between available candidates. Although the search is both time-efficient and cost-effective (compared to, say, spending a lot of money in a bar or club), there are hundreds of profiles to filter and once you have a short list, you still need to invest time in exchanging a few e-mails and then, after all, you still need to meet up and see if there is "chemistry."

Personality can make the process much more efficient if: (a) daters are aware of what their suitable matches are and (b) daters are able to read other daters' personality from their available profiles. In that sense, online daters are no different from "analogue" daters: Every person should be aware of what other people are like and then, consequently, decide whether they are a good match for them or not. Although our notion of love is still very romantic—most people intuitively believe that they have just one "perfect match" or love of their life—that is just unfeasible. There are over 6 billion people in the world and even an extremely popular person may just meet around 10,000 people in their adult life (try to work out how many you have met so far, even briefly). So, the probability of having just one perfect match and meeting him/her is, well, very slim. We don't want to bore you with math, but 10,000 out of 6,000,000,000 is less than 0.0002% (even if you are Mr. Popularity or have 5,000 "friends" on Facebook). This raises the question of just how many people we are compatible with: Is it 10, 100, 1,000, or 1 million? Although 1 million seems excessive, that would represent just under 0.02% of the world's population, which would mean two suitable matches in every 1,000 people. Most people would surely settle for that.

Personality psychology can teach us three important lessons about online dating, and dating in general: (1) Personality (including values) partly explains why some couples are more successful than others. In broad terms, people who are compatible in their values and personalities (though they can often complement each other by having contrasting personality styles) are more satisfied with their relationships and are together for a longer time. (2) People's personalities determine the degree to which they prefer certain values and personality traits in other people; this is because romantic partners help us validate our self-concept and identity, and loving someone who is similar to us enables us to maintain high levels of self-esteem (Freud saw this as a normal manifestation of narcissism, and he was right). Finally, (3) there is no such thing as a perfect match; rather, it is naturally easier to get along with some people than others, and that is also determined by our and their personality profiles. It follows that online dating sites that incorporate valid and reliable measures of personality should make it easier for people to predict how compatible they will be with a person (even if the prediction won't be perfect, it will be significantly better than chance).

That said, we do understand that readers will be somewhat skeptical about the need to inject some science into the process of dating. They believe that chance is something we should embrace rather than something we should replace by probability and psychological generalizations. In an article published 10 years ago in the technology magazine *Wired*, we found the following quote (which we believe addresses this point): "Twenty years from now, the idea that someone will look for love without looking for it online will be silly, akin to skipping the library card catalog to instead wander the stacks because 'the right books are found only by accident.' Serendipity is the hallmark of inefficient markets, and the marketplace of love, like it or not, is becoming more efficient" (*Wired*, 2002).

FAKING

As mentioned earlier (see Chapter 3), a big criticism of personality assessments is that it is extremely easy for participants to fake their responses, which does question their validity and practical uses regarding personnel selection. This is an important criticism as many organizations will ask new applicants to undergo a personality assessment. This is because the literature abounds with examples of certain personality traits being good predictors for specific work outcomes (Li, Liang, & Grant, 2010; Seibert & Lumpkin, 2009). It would therefore make sense to screen possible employees if your aim is to easily identify worthwhile applicants. It also allows the possibility to focus attention only on applicants who demonstrate certain traits that would provide a catalyst to foster a specific type of work environment (for example, a creative-based organization, such as an advertising company, may want to foster a sociable and highly interactive environment between employees so that there is a healthy flow of ideas, leading to a preference to employ more extraverted individuals).

However, sometimes this screening can backfire. For example, earlier in this chapter, it was discussed how certain types of individuals (e.g., those with high levels of psychopathy) are drawn to corporate environments. If organizations use personality inventories to screen possible employees, a psychopath would be wise enough to respond "correctly" to socially desirable questions. If they are then hired, they would have the resources and a platform to form a network of manipulation, which is undoubtedly costly to an organization's stability and levels of productivity (Babiak & Hare, 2007). It can also be costly to the applicant. Michael Campion (in Morgeson et al.,

2007) cites an applied situation, whereby 5% of job applicants achieved a perfect score: an achievement that is so virtuous that it is extremely unlikely that the applicants were answering truthfully. Campion found that these fakers were overshadowing the genuine applicants and distorting the results of the assessments, causing the genuine and good applicants to have a decreased chance of being employed. This demonstrates that faking does affect people's personal lives and is a real ethical dilemma within the field of occupational psychology.

Research investigating faking is somewhat mixed, leaving the findings to a matter of personal interpretation. Meuller-Hanson, Heggstad, and Thorton (2003) suggested that job applicants are only likely to fake good responses, not bad. Therefore the validity of personality inventories only comes into question at the high end of the score distribution. This hypothesis was supported when the researchers compared two groups (an incentive group compared to a control group) on a performance task. Meuller-Hanson and her colleagues found a significant discrepancy between the high scorer's levels of self-reported motivation between the two groups. They concluded that personality inventories are susceptible to faking and that they should be used only for filtering possible applicants and not as a platform on which to make absolute hiring decisions.

On the other hand, studies have shown that people fake responses even when there is no actual incentive to do so (e.g., McDaniel, Margaret, Perkins, Goggin, & Frankel, 2009), suggesting that people in general simply (and rather innocently) want to be seen in a favorable light. This poses the question of whether the context of selection (and thus assessment in this context) is really an issue. Thus, the real question may, in fact, only relate to whether faking distorts the relationships between personality and job outcomes.

This notion was investigated in a meta-analysis conducted by Ones, Viswesvaran, and Reiss (1996). The reviewers examined whether faking—or "social desirability" as psychologists refer to it—influenced the validity of personality inventories by distorting the personality–performance relationship. Contrary to common belief, their results showed that social desirability scales did not predict any performance criteria, and correlated instead with actual individual differences, namely emotional stability and Conscientiousness. Ones et al. further found that removing the effects of social desirability from the Big Five dimensions of personality does not change the validity of personality constructs for predicting job performance. The authors concluded that faking might, in fact, not be a problem, even in settings where there is a real incentive to fake.

Arguments have also been put forward to suggest that faking may not be a problem, even from a theoretical standpoint. For instance, Hogan (2005) argued that faking is, in fact, a sign of social adjustment (the level of ease with which the individual is able to accommodate his or her own needs and desires to circumstances in the environment). According to Hogan, this should be regarded as a positive personality trait as it generally indicates that the individual has good "social skills." In that connection, if the applicant can identify the socially correct responses within a personality assessment, he or she is likely to be able to do the same when making decisions within the workplace. The ability to monitor one's own behaviors and urges is necessary in social settings, and something that we all do to an extent. These types of "faking" behaviors are desired and effective in many types of business situations. For example, to be able to make more sales, salesmen need to be able to read social cues effectively and engage with their customers appropriately by adjusting their own behavior.

Nevertheless, in a comprehensive review of the literature, Morgeson et al. (2007) revealed that there was evidence to suggest that faking was detected in 50% of the studies conducted in the field. Regardless of how big or small the issue of faking is, inevitably organizations will want to minimize its occurrence. So, can they do it and if so how? There is a good amount of research in this area and several strategies for reducing faking have been suggested. The most basic has been to warn test-takers that faking can be detected. While this is a logical approach, the response to, and therefore the effectiveness of, such warnings will inevitably also be a function of individual differences between test-takers. For example, deviant individuals may choose not to listen to the interviewer, whereas anxious individuals may read into the warning too much and in turn ruminate over each question. Another approach is to implement forced-choice, as opposed to the usual Likert-type scales. For example, a forced item may require you to select between the options "You are sociable, chatty and friendly" or "You are reserved, quiet and introspective." Some argue that using forced-choice scales removes any ambiguity regarding the responder's answers; however, Goffin, Jang, and Skinner (2011) found that outcomes from forced-choice and traditional assessment techniques were highly correlated, suggesting that neither approach has any benefit over the other.

The most commonly employed strategy to overcome faking is the use of social desirability scales—that is, including bogus items in the inventory. This technique adopts the same principle that can be found in the school playground; you ask applicants to answer a question that is totally fictional. If the responder provides a positive answer, then it is clear they are faking. For example, "I am highly proficient in the computer language ULTNIX." This is a completely made-up computer language; however, fakers are likely to answer "yes." As mentioned before, however, even if this technique is effective in detecting socially desirable responding, it does not solve the problem because social desirability does not affect the validity of personality inventories.

Conclusion

Faking is considered to be the most serious problem in personality assessment. This is particularly the case in settings where there is a substantial incentive to fake. Yet, research investigating the issue of faking suggests that socially desirable responding may neither be a practical problem nor a theoretical one. It certainly does not pose a significant enough threat to the validity of personality inventories to warrant the omission of their use. Disputes regarding the use of self-report inventories no doubt remain most salient in selection settings. The bottom line, however, is still that organizations must have a filtering process—be it using CVs, interviews, or personality question-naires. Clearly, the issue of faking is not eliminated by either procedure. Given that one procedure must be chosen, however, the question remains as to which one that should be. Employers will generally trust their gut instinct and therefore prefer to use the interview. Yet, the evidence is unequivocal in showing that self-report inventories have better reliability and validity indi-ces than interviews and other selection methods. In addition, they are far more efficient to administer. In essence, the ques-tion is not really about whether faking is a problem or not but whether there is any better alternative to self-report invento-ries. Given that personality measures do predict performance, they must be considered an option for employees; when other options are put alongside them, they fare no better than self-reports. Accordingly, if the aim is to assess a person's personal-ity, or his or her potential to do a job, self-report inventories are (currently) one's best bet; and this is regardless of whether this person is or isn't responding in a socially desirable way.

GENERAL CONCLUSION

There is still controversy surrounding the use of personality inventories for profiling purposes. The debate can divided into two broad themes. The first concerns whether self-report inven-tories work; and the second whether it is ethical, or "moral," to use them. There is little doubt as to the former question: Self-report inventories are the most accurate tools available for assessing people's personalities and potential. The latter is open to debate and is sometimes more a matter of personal values than scientific truth. You may believe that dysfunctional and dangerous personality attributes should be identified and "dealt with" early on, or that a person is innocent until proven guilty. You may believe that consumer profiling is an efficient means of locating relevant products, or that it is a breach of privacy. You may believe that online dating sites are a perfect way to meet somebody matching, or that they go against the notions of romance and destiny. Clearly, the moral aspect of personality profiling is more difficult to resolve than the empirical one. Discussions about ethics require an interdisciplinary approach and are beyond the scope of this book. As scientists, our primary goal is to provide empirical facts. The interpretation of these facts is often a subjective matter and people may choose to construct reality differently based on the same facts. The facts are that personality inventories are valid and reliable and are fit for the purpose of profiling people. Whether they should or shouldn't be used for that purpose is where the subjective aspect of the issue arises. This issue is one still open for debate among psychologists; it is also one open for academics in other fields, as well as the general population.

Directions and Future Research

We have come to the end of our discussion with regard to the nature of personality. In this final chapter, we will review some of the main themes that were discussed throughout Chapters 1 to 5 and try to give an overall conclusion of what these chapters have told us about the nature of personality. We will then suggest some new directions that personality research is, or should be, taking as well as the future agenda of this research.

WHAT WE KNOW ABOUT PERSONALITY

Any time we talk about *personality*, be it our own or someone else's, three bottom-line questions seem to require clarification.

These are the *how*, the *why*, and the *so what* of personality. That is, we first need to address how people differ from one another. In what way does your colleague, or classmate, differ from you? Is he or she more reserved, less confident, more focused, more carefree, and so on? Once agreed, the question is, why does this person differ from you in the way he or she does? That is, what is the cause of the differences between you and your colleague or classmate? Is it the place you grew up, the way your parents taught you to behave, or is it some inherent genetic differences that you were born with? Finally, and quite crucially, what do these differences between you mean? Do they have any consequences? Will they impact on your life—now, and in the future?

We all have some intuitive answers to many of these questions. As mentioned in Chapter 4, however, a problem with using intuitive answers is that observations often have two conflicting answers that sound equally intuitive. In contrast, personality psychology provides us with a solid evidence base that we can lean on when searching for answers about human nature. Clearly, there are gaps in our knowledge. Yet, more than a century's theory building and research into the human psyche have today provided us with a pretty good understanding of the nature of personality. Thus, we can be reasonably confident in answering some fundamental questions such as "What is personality?" "How do people differ from each other?" "Why do people differ the way they do?" "How much does our personality influence the course of our future?" and, finally, "Can personality change?"

The answers to these questions, from a psychological standpoint, are well established. Personality refers to the stable and consistent patterns we observe in how people behave, feel, and think. Even though there are hundreds or even thousands of different ways people can differ, it seems that many behavioral, cognitive, and emotional patterns go hand in hand to such a degree that they actually form broader patterns; and these broader patterns are much fewer in number. Several decades of research has shown over and again that there are five broad patterns of behaving, feeling, and thinking.

In regard to the question of *why* people differ, the answer is twofold. The first reason is that environment strongly influences behavior, thought, and emotion, impacting both short- and long-term patterns. Given that no two individuals can be exposed to the same environment, differences between individuals are inevitable. The second reason is that humans and other animals differ biologically in terms of basic arousability levels and reactivity to external stimuli. Such biological mechanisms have a genetic basis, which means that genes are directly responsible for some differences between people. Genes also indirectly lead to individual differences by shaping the environment; that is, by determining what people will evoke in, or how they will react to, environments, as well as influencing which environments they will choose in the first place.

In terms of the significance of our personality on the course of our life: While few would deny that personality is consequential in some areas of life, particularly to do with social interaction, its pervasive influence seems to be broader than commonly assumed. Personality influences not only how we will match with others, or the way we will act in social situations, but also the political and religious convictions we will have, how happy we will tend to be, and even how long we will live.

A final question regards change. Given that personality is by definition stable and consistent, the notion of change would seem to contradict the notion of personality. There is no doubt that the vast amount of evidence suggests a considerable stability in personality across time and situations. This is not to say that personality cannot change should one wish to change or even more naturally through exposure to different environments. Indeed, the same evidence that supports the notion of stability also supports the concept of change in personality. Behavior, thought, and emotions do change, both naturally as people age, and also through exposure to various environments and situations (in particular, long-term exposure)—and this change can be lasting. However, drastic changes are not common and when change does occur, it generally occurs to the same degree across all people. Thus, one should neither deny nor expect a lot of change in personality in relation to others.

FUTURE DIRECTIONS

So what does the future hold for personality psychology? First, having a wide knowledge about the nature of personality does not entitle us to sit back and relax and applaud our achievements. There is much to discover and, indeed, much that is still unknown. As with any science, personality psychology needs to continue to explore and attempt to uncover the unknowns of human nature. Several areas of future investigation are worthy of particular attention.

As a most basic step—a lot more ground can, or needs to, be covered with regard to the relevance of personality in diverse life domains. We have conducted an ample amount of research in areas examining the impact of personality on academic performance, job performance, and leadership. There is also a growing amount of research in areas of subjective well-being and romantic relationships. Yet, even within these fields there remain questions that need to be addressed. Most importantly, exploring the conditions under which personality factors exert a strong, versus weak, versus no, influence needs ongoing and persistent efforts, so that the accuracy as well as specificity of our predictions become truly satisfactory.

There is also a need to broaden the scope of our prediction. There remain domains of psychology that have received insufficient attention from personality psychologists. One such example is consumer psychology—the prediction of consumer preferences and behaviors. While there is a vast amount of research examining universal psychological mechanisms underlying all consumers (e.g., cognitive biases and heuristics; Ahmetoglu et al., 2010), very little research has examined *individual differences* in consumer behavior, affect, and cognition. Yet, informing consumers about best practices, or basing government policy and interventions solely on general psychological principles, no doubt neglects a wide spectrum of influences in the consumer buying process. Given recent increases in government interventions and regulations aimed at protecting consumer welfare (e.g., Ahmetoglu et al., 2010), knowledge of differences among consumers in cognition, affect, and behavior in informing such interventions would probably be necessary.

Other questions, which are at the forefront of contemporary personality psychology, concern the actual data obtained in research and their interpretations. One domain that has recently drawn attention in this respect is neurobiological and genetic characteristics underlying personality differences (Canli, 2006). For instance, while there is great enthusiasm within the realm of fMRI research and personality, there has recently been increased skepticism raised about the feasibility of fMRI-generated research results. Some have argued, for instance, that correlations found in studies that examine the link between brain activity and personality measures are higher than should be expected given the (evidently limited) reliability of both fMRI and personality measures (Vul et al., 2009). Thus, it seems some serious thought should be given as to whether current findings using fMRI inflate relationships between brain and personality processes.

Similarly, despite the initial excitement about genome-wide association studies (GWAS)—which are concerned with the examination of common gene variation associated with traits—there are increasing doubts in the field about the usefulness of this research (Kraft & Hunter, 2009). GWAS are high cost, and despite some great discoveries in the past (Amos, 2007), the infrequency with which such discoveries occur, and the generally trivial, and thus disappointing, results have been troubling. This is not to say that one should abandon such research altogether. Yet, we certainly need to ask questions about new directions and developments before fully embracing this research.

More general directions relate to establishing integrative models of individual differences and the part personality and other psychological domains play in these models. Often domains of functioning (e.g., personality, intelligence, creativity, motivation, and interests) are studied in isolation from each other. This is inevitably a function of the fact that each level and domain deserve careful attention. However, failure to look at an integrated picture may leave us with gaps or even misconceptions in theories (Revelle et al., 2011). Having empirically established theoretical models within each domain, it seems the time has come for researchers to "come out of their shells" and start reflecting, in a collective way, on the bigger picture—how each domain interacts with the other and the environment to determine behavior.

One area where this is happening fast is within the study of personality and intelligence interface. Associations between personality and intelligence have been found on the measurement level (Chamorro-Premuzic & Furnham, 2006; Furhan, Monsen, & Ahmetoglu, 2009), and hypothesized at a conceptual level. Researchers are now close to establishing models that integrate these domains in a meaningful way. Several conceptual mechanisms have been put forward, three of which have been particularly prominent, namely, investment, compensation, and differentiation (von Stumm, Chamorro-Premuzic, & Ackerman, 2011). For instance, investment has been used to refer to the notion that intelligence is partially determined by personality and interests in that the latter domains influence how much a person invests (or engages) in activities that are conductive to learning (e.g., reading, traveling, trying new technologies; Ackerman, 1996). Compensation represents tendencies or habits (i.e., personality manifestations) employed by a person that enable him or her to compensate for or complement his or her ability (e.g., studying harder, being more persistent, more agreeable in class, etc.; Chamorro-Premuzic & Furnham, 2005b). Finally, differentiation refers to the finding that personality may influence whether intelligence is more "general" or specific, that is, the correlations between different intellectual tasks, or tests (e.g., Austin et al., 2002, found that correlations between a battery of ability tests were stronger among people scoring higher, versus lower, in Neuroticism).

There is still a lot of work to be done in this area. What this research clearly demonstrates, however, is that such integration of domains is probably necessary in order to obtain the ultimate goal of predicting behavior. A lack of integration thus is bound to continue to give incomplete prediction. The good news is that such efforts are increasing among researchers (e.g., von Stumm et al., 2011) and this valuable information is likely to result in more comprehensive models of human nature.

We want to conclude this book by making a final note in regard to personality measurement—a notorious issue, which is likely to endure as a point for debate in the years to come. One cannot help but wonder whether personality measurement will ever fully be embraced, until reliable and valid objective measures of personality are developed. It is supposedly human nature not to trust humankind to provide the unselfish responses in questionnaires, or to possess an adequate level of self-awareness. Admittedly, this trend has been changing. An increasing number of organizations are using self-report personality measures (in fact, one may argue that they are, today, commonplace), and even laypeople seem to accept the notion of questionnaires more kindly than before. This is no doubt due to the increased exposure to, and awareness of, psychometric testing among the general public—or the so-called "informed consumer effect"—where people are increasingly leaning toward the "data tell" rather than the "stories sell" attitude. Nevertheless, reliable and valid objective personality measurement would certainly eliminate any doubts of the usefulness of such measurement. Such research efforts are continuing, and new steps toward achieving the "holy grail" of personality assessment are taken every day. It is our view that such research, in essence, *must* continue, and this goal must remain the gold standard of personality psychology. Yet, until we have reached this standard, we are encouraged to know that we have reliable and valid measures of personality that enable us to understand the structures of personality and its causes, and allow us to predict a universal range of behavior. Through such assessment we have been able to understand much of the nature of human nature.

References

Ackerman, P. L. (2006). A theory of adult intellectual development: Process, personality, interests and knowledge. *Intelligence, 22*(2), 227–257.

Ackerman, P. L., & Heggestad, E. D. (1997). Intelligence, personality and interests: Evidence for overlapping traits. *Psychological Bulletin, 121*, 219–245.

Adorno, T. W., Frenkel-Brunswik, E., Levinson, D. J., & Sanford, R. N. (1950). *The authoritarian personality.* New York, NY: Harper & Row.

Ahmetoglu, G., & Chamorro-Premuzic, T. (2010). *Measure of entrepreneurial tendencies and abilities.* Unpublished Measure (available on request).

Ahmetoglu, G., Fried, S., Dawes, J., & Furnham, A. (2010). *Pricing practices: Their effects on consumer behaviour and welfare.* Prepared for the Office of Fair Trading. London, UK: Mountainview Learning.

Ahmetoglu, G., Leutner, F., & Chamorro-Premuzic, T. (2011). Eq-nomics: Understanding the relationship between individual differences in trait emotional intelligence and entrepreneurship. *Personality and Individual Differences, 51*(8), 1028–1033.

Ahmetoglu, G., & Swami, V. (2012). Do women prefer "nice guys?" The effect of male dominance behavior on women's ratings of sexual attractiveness. *Social Behavior and Personality, 40*(4), 667–672.

Ahmetoglu, G., Swami, V., & Chamorro-Premuzic, T. (2009). The relationship between dimensions of love, personality and relationship length. *Archives of Sexual Behaviour, 39*, 1181–1190.

Alden, L. (1989). Short-term structured treatment for avoidant personality disorder. *Journal of Consulting and Clinical Psychology, 57*, 756–764.

Aldrich, H. (1999). *Organizations evolving.* London, UK: Sage.

Alexander, F. (1939). Emotional factors in essential hypertension. *Psychosomatic Medicine, 1,* 175–179.

Alexander, W. P. (1935). Intelligence, concrete and abstract. *British Journal of Psychology Monograph Supplement, 29,* 177.

Allport, G. W., & Odbert, H. S. (1936). Trait-names: A psycho-lexical study. *Psychological Monographs, 47*(1, Whole No. 211).

American Psychiatric Association. (1994). *Diagnostic and statistical manual of mental disorders* (4th ed.). Washington, DC: Author.

Amos, C. I. (2007). Successful design and conduct of genome-wide association studies. *Human Molecular Genetics, 16*(2), R220–R225.

Anokhin, A. P., Golosheykin, S., & Heath, A. C. (2007). Genetic and environmental influences on emotion-modulated startle reflex: A twin study. *Psychophysiology, 44*(1), 106–112.

Arthaud-day, M. L., Rode, J. C., Mooner, C. H., & Near, J. P. (2005). The subjective well-being construct: A test of its convergent, discriminant, and factorial validity. *Social Indicators Research, 74,* 445–476.

ARWU. (2011). *Academic rankings of world universities–2011.* Shanghai Ranking Consultancy. Retrieved October 26, 2011, from www.shanghairanking.com/ARWU2011.html

Asendorpf, J. B. (2008). Shyness. In M. M. Haith & J. B. Benson (Eds.), *Encyclopedia of infant and childhood development* (pp. 146–153). San Diego, CA: Elsevier.

Asendorpf, J. B., Banse, R., & Mücke, D. (2002). Double dissociation between implicit and explicit personality self-concept: The case of shy behaviour. *Journal of Personality and Social Psychology, 83,* 380–393.

Atkinson, J. W. (1958). *Motives in fantasy, action, and society.* Princeton, NJ: Van Nostrand.

Austin, E. J., Manning, J. T., McInroy, K., & Matthews, E. (2002). A preliminary investigation of the associations between personality, cognitive ability, and digit ratio. *Personality and Individual Differences, 33*(7), 1115–1124.

Babiak, P., & Hare, R. (2007). *Snakes in suits: When psychopaths go to work.* New York, NY: HarperCollins.

Babiak, P., Neumann, C. S., & Hare, R. D. (2010, April). Corporate psychopathy: Talking the walk. *Behavioral Sciences and the Law, 28,* 174–193.

Bandura, A. (1977). Self-efficacy: Toward a unifying theory of behavioral change. *Psychological Review, 84*(2), 191–215.

Bandura, A. (1986). *Social foundations of thought and action: A social cognitive theory.* Englewood Cliffs, NJ: Prentice-Hall.

Bandura, A., Ross, D., & Ross, S. (1961). Transmission of aggression through imitation of aggressive models. *Journal of Abnormal and Social Psychology, 63*, 575–582.

Bannatyne, D. (2007). *Anyone can do it: My story.* London, UK: Orion Books.

Barelds, D. P. H. (2005). Self and partner personality in intimate relationships. *European Journal of Personality, 19*, 501–518.

Baron, R. A., & Byrne, D. (1987). *Social psychology: Understanding human interaction* (5th ed.). Boston, MA: Allyn & Bacon.

Baron, R. A., & Henry, R. A. (2010). Entrepreneurship: The genesis of organizations. In S. Zedeck (Ed.), *APA handbook of industrial and organizational psychology, Vol 1: Building and developing the organization* (pp. 241–273). Washington, DC: APA.

Baron, R. M., & Kenny, D. A. (1986). The moderator-mediator variable distinction in social psychological research: Conceptual, strategic, and statistical considerations. *Journal of Personality and Social Psychology, 51*, 1173–1182.

Barrick, M. R., & Mount, M. K. (1991). The Big Five personality dimensions and job performance: A meta-analysis. *Personnel Psychology, 44*, 1–26.

Barrick, M. R., Mount, M. K., & Strauss, J. P. (1993). Conscientiousness and performance of sales representatives: Test of the mediating effects of goal setting. *Journal of Applied Psychology, 78*, 715–722.

Bass, B. M. (2008). *The Bass handbook of leadership: Theory, research, and managerial applications* (4th ed.). New York, NY: The Free Press.

Bates, G. P. (2005). The molecular genetics of Huntington disease—A history. *Nature Reviews Genetics, 6*, 766–773.

Beloff, H. (1957). The structure and origin of the anal character. *Genetic Psychology Monographs, 55*, 141–172.

Bergen, S. E., Gardner, C. O., & Kendler, K. S. (2007). Age-related changes in heritability of behavioral phenotypes over adolescence and young adulthood: A meta-analysis. *Twin Research and Human Genetics, 10*, 423–433.

Berscheid, E. (1999). The greening of relationship science. *American Psychologist, 54*, 260–266.

Bidjerano, T., & Dai, D. Y. (2007). The relationship between the Big-Five model of personality and self-regulated learning strategies. *Learning and Individual Differences, 17,* 69–81.

Binet, A. (1904). Les frontières anthropométriques des anormaux. *Bulletin de la Société libre de l'étude psychologique de l'enfant, 16,* 430–438.

Bleidorn, W., Kandler, C., Riemann, R., Angleitner, A., & Spinath, F. (2009). Patterns and sources of adult personality development: Growth curve analyses of the NEO-PI-R scales in a longitudinal twin study. *Journal of Personality and Social Psychology, 97,* 142–155.

Blumenthal, T. D. (2001). Extraversion, attention, and startle response reactivity. *Personality and Individual Differences, 4,* 495–503.

Bogaert, A. F., & Fisher, W. A. (1995). Predictors of university men's number of sexual partners. *Journal of Sex Research, 32,* 119–130.

Bono, J. E., & Judge, T. A. (2003). Core self-evaluations: A review of the trait and its role in job satisfaction and job performance. *European Journal of Personality, 17,* S5–S18.

Booth, A., & Amato, P. R. (2001). Parental predivorce relations and offspring postdivorce well-being. *Journal of Marriage and Family, 63*(1), 197–212.

Botwin, M. D., Buss, D. M., & Shackelford, T. K. (1997). Personality and mate preferences: Five factors in mate selection and marital satisfaction. *Journal of Personality, 65,* 107–136.

Bouchard, G., Lussier, Y., & Sabourin, S. (1999). Personality and marital adjustment: Utility of the five-factor model of personality. *Journal of Marriage and the Family, 61,* 651–666.

Bowlby, J. (1969). *Attachment and loss (Vol. 1): Attachment.* New York, NY: Basic Books.

Boyle, G. J. (2008). Critique of the five-factor model of personality. *Humanities & Social Sciences Papers.* Paper 297. Retrieved from http://epublications.bond.edu.au/hss_pubs/297

Boyle, G. J., Matthews, G., & Saklofske, D. H. (2008). Personality theories and models: An overview. In G. J. Boyle, G. Matthews, & D. H. Saklofske (Eds.), *Personality theory and assessment. Personality theories and models* (Vol. 1, pp. 1–29). London, UK: Sage.

Bradbury, T. N., & Fincham, F. D. (1988). Individual difference variables in close relationships: A contextual model of marriage as an integrative framework. *Journal of Personality and Social Psychology, 54,* 713–721.

Brickman, P., & Campbell, D. T. (1971). Hedonic relativism and planning the good society. In M. H. Appley (Ed.), *Adaptation-level theory: A symposium* (pp. 287–305). New York, NY: Academic Press.

Burns, G. N., & Christiansen, N. D. (2011). Methods of measuring faking behavior. *Human Performance, 24*(4), 358–372.

Buss, A. H., & Perry, M. (1992). The Aggression Questionnaire. *Journal of Personality and Social Psychology, 63,* 452–459.

Buss, A. H., & Plomin, R. (1975). *A temperament theory of personality development.* New York, NY: Wiley-Interscience.

Buss, A. H., & Plomin, R. (1984). *Temperament: Early developing personality traits.* Hillsdale, NJ: Erlbaum.

Buss, D. M. (2009). How can evolutionary psychology successfully explain personality and individual differences? *Perspectives on Psychological Science, 4*(4), 359–366.

Cale, E. M. (2006). A quantitative review of the relations between the "Big 3" higher order personality dimensions and antisocial behavior. *Journal of Research in Personality, 40,* 250–284.

Canli, T. (2004). Functional brain mapping of extraversion and neuroticism: Learning from individual differences in emotion processing. *Journal of Personality, 72,* 1105–1132.

Canli, T. (2006). *Biology of personality and individual differences* (pp. xv, 462). New York, NY: Guilford Press.

Canli, T., Zhao, Z., Desmond, J. E., Kang, E., Gross, J., & Gabrieli, J. D. E. (2001). An fMRI study of personality influences on brain reactivity to emotional stimuli. *Behavioral Neuroscience, 115*(1), 33–42.

Carlo, G., Okun, M. A., Knight, G., & de Guzman, M. R. T. (2005). The interplay of traits and motives on volunteering: Agreeableness, extraversion and prosocial value motivation. *Personality and Individual Differences, 38,* 1293–1305.

Carlyle, T. (1907). *On heroes, hero-worship, and the heroic in history.* Boston, MA: Houghton Mifflin.

Caseras, X., Mataix-Cols, D., Giampietro, V., Rimes, K. A., Brammer, M., Zelaya, F.,...Godfrey, E. L. (2006). Probing the working memory system in chronic fatigue syndrome: A functional magnetic resonance imaging study using the n-back task. *Psychosomatic Medicine, 68,* 947–955.

Caspi, A., & Herbener, E. S. (1990). Continuity and change: Assortative marriage and the consistency of personality in adulthood. *Journal of Personality and Social Psychology, 58,* 250–258.

Caspi, A., McClay, J., Moffitt, T. E., Mill, J., Martin, J., Craig, I. W., ... Poulton, R. (2002). Role of genotype in the cycle of violence in maltreated children. *Science, 297,* 851–854.

Caspi, A., Roberts, B. W., & Shiner, R. L. (2005). Personality development: Stability and change. *Annual Review of Psychology, 56,* 453–484.

Cattell, R. B. (1943). The description of personality: Basic traits resolved into clusters. *The Journal of Abnormal and Social Psychology, 8*(4), 476–506.

Cattell, R. B. (1950). The main personality factors in questionnaire, self-estimate material. *Journal of Social Psychology, 31,* 3–38.

Cattell, R. B. (1957). *Personality and motivation structure and measurement.* New York, NY: World Book.

Cattell, R., & Kline, P. (1977). *The scientific analysis of personality and motivation.* New York, NY: Academic Press.

Cattell, R. B., & Schuerger, J. M. (1978). *Personality theory in action: Handbook for the objective-analytic (O-A) test kit.* Champaign, IL: Institute for Personality & Ability Testing.

Cattell, R. B., & Warburton, F. W. (1967). *Objective personality and motivation tests.* Urbana, IL: University of Illinois Press.

Chamorro-Premuzic, T. (2011). *Personality and individual differences.* Oxford, UK: Wiley-Blackwell.

Chamorro-Premuzic, T., Ahmetoglu, G., & Furnham, A. (2008). Little more than personality: Dispositional determinants of test anxiety (the Big Five, core self-evaluations, and self-assessed intelligence). *Learning and Individual Differences, 18*(2), 258–263.

Chamorro-Premuzic, T., Fagan, P., & Furnham, A. (2010). Personality and uses of music as predictors of preferences for music consensually classified as happy, sad, complex, and background. *Psychology of Aesthetics, Creativity and the Arts, 4,* 205–213.

Chamorro-Premuzic, T., & Furnham, A. (2003a). Personality predicts academic performance: Evidence from two longitudinal university samples. *Journal of Research in Personality, 37,* 319–338.

Chamorro-Premuzic, T., & Furnham, A. (2003b). Personality traits and academic exam performance. *European Journal of Personality, 17,* 237–250.

Chamorro-Premuzic, T., & Furnham, A. (2004). A possible model for explaining the personality-intelligence interface. *British Journal of Psychology, 95,* 249–264.

Chamorro-Premuzic, T., & Furnham, A. (2005a). *Personality and intellectual competence.* Mahwah, NJ: Lawrence Erlbaum.

Chamorro-Premuzic, T., & Furnham, A. (2005b). Personality, intelligence, and general knowledge. *Learning and Individual Differences, 16*(1), 79–90.

Chamorro-Premuzic, T., & Furnham, A. (2006). Intellectual competence and the intelligent personality: A third way in differential psychology. *Review of General Psychology, 10,* 251–267.

Chamorro-Premuzic, T., & Furnham, A. (2010a). *The psychology of personnel selection.* New York, NY: Cambridge University Press.

Chamorro-Premuzic, T., & Furnham, A. (2010b). Consensual beliefs about the accuracy and fairness of selection methods at university. *International Journal of Selection and Assessment, 4,* 417–424.

Chamorro-Premuzic, T., Kallias, A., & Hsu, A. (in press). Personality as predictor of movie uses and preferences: A psychographic approach. In J. Kaufman & D. K. Simonton (Eds.), *The social science of cinema.* Oxford, UK: Oxford University Press.

Chamorro-Premuzic, T., Reimers, S., Hsu, A., & Ahmetoglu, G. (2008). Who art thou? Personality predictors of artistic preferences in a large UK sample: The importance of openness. *British Journal of Psychology, 100*(3), 501–516.

Cicchetti, D., & Rogosch, F. A. (1996). Equifinality and multifinality in developmental psychopathology. *Development and Psychopathology, 8,* 597–600.

Ciulla, J. B. (2004). Ethics and leadership effectiveness. In J. Antonakis, A. T. Cianciolo, & R. J. Sternberg (Eds.), *The nature of leadership* (pp. 302–327). Thousand Oaks, CA: Sage Publications.

Clarke, D., Gabriels, T., & Barnes, J. (1996). Astrological sign as determinants of extroversion and emotionality: An empirical study. *The Journal of Psychology, 130,* 131–140.

Cleckley, H. (1942). *The mask of sanity.* St. Louis, MO: Mosby Medical Library.

Coan, R. W. (1974). *The optimal personality.* New York, NY: Columbia University Press.

Cohen, J. (1988). *Statistical power analysis for the behavioral sciences* (2nd ed.). Hillsdale, NJ: Erlbaum.

Collins, J. (2001). Level 5 leadership: The triumph of humility and fierce resolve. *Harvard Business Review, 79*(1), 66–79.

Cohen, J. D. (2005). The vulcanization of the human brain: A neural perspective on interactions between cognition and emotion. *Journal of Economic Perspectives, 19*, 3–24.

Conger, R. D., Cui, M., Bryant, M., & Elder, G. H., Jr. (2000). Competence in early adult romantic relationships: A developmental perspective on family influences. *Journal of Personality and Social Psychology, 79*, 224–237.

Conger, R. D., & Ge, X. (1999). Conflict and cohesion in parent–adolescent relations: Changes in emotional expression from early to mid-adolescence. In M. Cox & J. Brooks-Gunn (Eds.), *Conflict and cohesion in families: Causes and consequences* (pp. 185–206). Mahwah, NJ: Erlbaum.

Contrada, R. J., Cather, C., & O'Leary, A. (1999). Personality and health: Dispositions and processes in disease susceptibility and adaptation to illness. In L. A. Pervin & O. P. John (Eds.), *Handbook of personality: Theory and research* (2nd ed., pp. 576–604). New York, NY: Guilford Press.

Conway, J. M., Jako, R. A., & Goodman, D. F. (1995). A meta-analysis of interrater and internal consistency reliability of selection interviews. *Journal of Applied Psychology, 80*(5), 565–579.

Cook, B. G. (2004). Inclusive teachers' attitudes toward their students with disabilities: A replication and extension. *The Elementary School Journal, 104*, 307–320.

Cook, M. (2004). *Personnel selection*. Chichester, UK: Wiley.

Costa, P. T., & McCrae, R. R. (1985). *The NEO Personality Inventory manual*. Odessa, FL: Psychological Assessment Resources.

Costa, P. T., & McCrae, R. R. (1990). Personality disorders and the five-factor model of personality. *Journal of Personality Disorders, 4*, 362–371.

Costa, P. T., & McCrae, R. R. (1992). *The NEO-PI-R professional manual*. Odessa, FL: Psychological Assessment Resources.

Costa, P. T., & McCrae, R. R. (1994a). "Set like plaster?" Evidence for the stability of adult personality. In T. Heatherton & J. Weinberger (Eds.), *Can personality change?* (pp. 21–40). Washington, DC: American Psychological Association.

Costa, P. T., & McCrae, R. R. (1994b). Stability and change in personality from adolescence through adulthood. In C. F. Halverson, G. A. Kohnstamm, & R. P. Martin (Eds.), *The developing structure of temperament and personality from infancy to adulthood* (pp. 139–150). Hillsdale, NJ: Erlbaum.

Covey, S. (1989).*The seven habits of highly effective people.* New York, NY: Simon & Schuster.

Cronbach, L. J., & Meehl, P. E. (1955). Construct validity in psychological tests. *Psychological Bulletin, 52,* 281–302.

Davison, G. C., & Neale, J. M. (1998). *Abnormal psychology.* New York, NY: John Wiley.

De Raad, B., & Schouwenburg, H. C. (1996). Personality in learning and education: A review. *European Journal of Personality, 10,* 303–336.

Dean, G. (1987). Does astrology need to be true? Part 2. *Skeptical Inquirer, 11*(3), 257–273.

Deary, I. J., Whiteman, M. C., Starr, J. M., Whalley, L. J., & Fox, H. C. (2004). The impact of childhood intelligence on later life: Following up the Scottish Mental Surveys of 1932 and 1947. *Journal of Personality and Social Psychology, 86,* 130–147.

Denissen, J. J. A., Asendorpf, J. B., & van Aken, M. A. G. (2008). Childhood personality predicts long-term trajectories of shyness and aggressiveness in the context of demographic transitions in emerging adulthood. *Journal of Personality, 76,* 67–99.

Denissen, J. J. A., & Penke, L. (2008). Individual reaction norms underlying the Five Factor Model of personality: First steps towards a theory-based conceptual framework. *Journal of Research in Personality, 42,* 1285–1302.

Denissen, J. J. A., van Aken, M. A. G., & Roberts, B. W. (2011). Personality development across the life span. In T. Chamorro-Premuzic, S. von Stumm, & A. Furnham (Eds.), *The Wiley-Blackwell handbook of individual differences* (pp. 512–537). Oxford, UK: Wiley-Blackwell.

DeYoung, C. G., Hirsh, J. B., Shane, M. S., Papademetris, X., Rajeevan, N., & Gray, J. R. (2010). Testing predictions from personality neuroscience: Brain structure and the Big Five. *Psychological Science, 21,* 820–828.

DeYoung, C. G., Shamosh, N. A., Green, E. A., Braver, T. S., & Gray, J. R. (2009). Intellect as distinct from openness: Differences revealed through fMRI of working memory. *Journal of Personality and Social Psychology, 97,* 883–892.

Diener, E. (1984). Subjective well-being. *Psychological Bulletin, 95,* 542–575.

Diener, E. (2000). Subjective well-being: The science of happiness and a proposal for a national index. *American Psychologist, 55*, 34–43.

Diener, E., Oishi, S., & Lucas, R. E. (2003). Personality, culture, and subjective well-being: Emotional and cognitive evaluations of life. *Annual Review of Psychology, 54*, 403–425.

Diener, E., Suh, E. M., Lucas, R. E., & Smith, H. L. (1999). Subjective well-being: Three decades of progress. *Psychological Bulletin, 125*, 276–302.

Digman, J. M. (1990). Personality structure: Emergence of the five-factor model. *Annual Review of Psychology, 41*, 417–440.

Digman, J. M. (1997). Higher-order factors of the Big Five. *Journal of Personality and Social Psychology, 73*(6), 1246–1256.

Digman, J. M., & Inouye, J. (1986). Further specification of the five robust factors of personality. *Journal of Personality and Social Psychology, 50*, 116–123.

Donnellan, M. B, Conger, R. D., & Bryant, C. M. (2004). The Big Five and enduring marriages. *Journal of Research in Personality, 38*, 481–504.

Donnellan, M. B., Larsen-Rife, D., & Conger, R. D. (2005). Personality, family history, and competence in early adult romantic relationships. *Journal of Personality and Social Psychology, 88*, 562–576.

Dunn, J., & Plomin, R. (1990). *Separate lives: Why siblings are so different.* New York, NY: Basic Books.

Egan, V. (2011). Individual differences and antisocial behaviour. In T. Chamorro-Premuzic, A. Furnham, & S. von Stumm (Eds.), *Handbook of individual differences* (pp. 522–548). London, UK: Wiley-Blackwell.

Egan, V., & Hamilton, E. (2008). Personality, mating effort and alcohol-related violence expectancies. *Addiction Research and Theory, 16*, 369–381.

Ekman, P. (2001). *Telling lies: Clues to deceit in the marketplace, politics, and marriage.* New York, NY: W. W. Norton.

Exner, J. E., Jr. (1986). *The Rorschach. A comprehensive system volume I: Basic foundations* (2nd ed.). New York, NY: Wiley.

Eysenck, H. J., & Eysenck, M. (1985). *Personality and individual differences: A natural science approach.* New York, NY: Plenum.

Eysenck, H. J., & Eysenck, S. B. G. (1975). *Manual of the Eysenck Personality Questionnaire.* Sevenoaks, UK: Hodder & Stoughton.

Eysenck, H. J., & Eysenck, S. B. G. (1976). *Psychoticism as a dimension of personality.* London, UK: Hodder & Stoughton.

Fallon, J. H. (2006). Neuroanatomical background to understanding the brain of the young psychopath. *Ohio State Journal of Criminal Law, 3*(34), 341–367.

Farringdon, D. P., Barnes, G. C., & Lambert, S. (1996). The concentration of offending in families. *Legal and Criminological Psychology, 1*, 47–63.

Ferguson, E., Chamorro-Premuzic, T., Pickering, A., & Weiss, A. (2011). Five into one doesn't go: A critique of the general factor of personality. In T. Chamorro-Premuzic, S. von Stumm, & A. Furnham (Eds.), *The Wiley-Blackwell handbook of individual differences* (pp. 162–186). London, UK: Wiley-Blackwell.

Ferraro, K. F., & Nuriddin, T. A. (2006). Psychological distress and mortality: Are women more vulnerable? *Journal of Health and Social Behavior, 47*, 227–241.

Fiedler, F. E., & Garcia, J. E. (1987). *New approach to effective leadership: Cognitive resources and organizational performance.* New York, NY: John Wiley.

Fleeson, W., & Gallagher, P. (2009). The implications of Big Five standing for the distribution of trait manifestation in behavior: Fifteen experience-sampling studies and a meta-analysis. *Journal of Personality and Social Psychology, 97*(6), 1097–1114.

Flynn, F. J. (2005). Having an open mind: The impact of openness to experience on interracial attitudes and impression formation. *Journal of Personality and Social Psychology, 88*(5), 816–826.

Forbes.com. (2011). *The world's billionaires.* Retrieved from October 21, 2011, from www.forbes.com/wealth/billionaires/list

Franz, C. (1994). Reconsituting the self: The role of history, personality and loss in one woman's life. In C. E. Franz & A. J. Stewart (Eds.), *Women creating lives: Identities, resilience, and resistance* (pp. 213–227). Boulder, CO: Westview Press.

Freud, S. (1900). *The interpretation of dreams* (std. ed. 4 & 5). London, UK: Hogarth Press.

Friedman, H. S., & Booth-Kewley, S. (1987). The "disease-prone personality": A meta-analytic view of the construct. *American Psychologist, 42*, 539–555.

Friedman, H. S., Kern, M. L., & Reynolds, C. A. (2010). Personality and health, subjective well-being, and longevity as adults age. *Journal of Personality, 78*, 179–216.

Friedman, H. S., Riggio, R. E., & Casella, D. F. (1988). Nonverbal skill, personal charisma, and initial attraction. *Journal of Personality and Social Psychology, 14*, 203–211.

Friedman, H. S., Tucker, J. S., Tomlinson-Keasey, C., Schwartz, J. E., Wingard, D. L., & Criqui, M. H. (1993). Does childhood personality predict longevity? *Journal of Personality and Social Psychology, 65*, 176–185.

Fujita, F., & Diener, E. (2005). Life satisfaction set point: Stability and change. *Journal of Personality and Social Psychology, 88*, 158–164.

Furedy, J. J. (2008). Psychophysiological window on personality: Pragmatic and philosophical considerations. In G. J. Boyle, G. Matthews, & D. H. Saklofske (Eds.), *The Sage handbook of personality theory and assessment: Vol. 2. Personality measurement and testing* (pp. 295–312). Los Angeles, CA: Sage.

Furnham, A. (1994). *Personality at work: The role of individual differences in the workplace* (2nd ed.; 1st ed., 1992). New York, NY: Routledge.

Furnham, A., & Chamorro-Premuzic, T. (2004). Personality and intelligence as predictors of statistics examination grades. *Personality and Individual Differences, 37*, 943–955.

Furnham, A., Monsen, J., & Ahmetoglu, G. (2009). Typical intellectual engagement, Big Five personality traits, approaches to learning and cognitive ability predictors of academic performance. *British Journal of Educational Psychology, 79*, 769–782.

Furnham, A., Moutafi, J., & Chamorro-Premuzic, T. (2005). Personality and intelligence: Gender, the Big Five, self-estimated and psychometric intelligence. *International Journal of Selection and Assessment, 13*(1), 11–24.

Gale, A. (1973). The psychophysiology of individual differences: Studies of extraversion and the EEG. In P. Kline (Ed.), *New approaches in psychological measurement* (pp. 211–256). New York, NY: Wiley.

Gale, A. (1983). Electroencephalographic studies of extraversion–introversion: A case study in the psychophysiology of individual differences. *Personality and Individual Differences, 4*, 429–435.

Galton, F. (1888). Co-relations and their measurement, chiefly from anthropometric data. *Proceedings of the Royal Society of London, 45*, 135–145.

Gattis, K. S., Berns, S., Simpson, L. E., & Christensen, A. (2004). Birds of a feather or strange birds? Ties among personality dimensions, similarity, and marital quality. *Journal of Family Psychology, 18*, 564–574.

Gauquelin, M., Gauquelin, F., & Eysenck, S. B. G. (1979). Personality and the position of the planets at birth: An empirical study. *British Journal of Social and Clinical Psychology, 18*, 71–75.

Geen, R. G. (1984). Preferred stimulation levels in introverts and extraverts: Effects on arousal and performance. *Journal of Personality and Social Psychology, 46*(6), 1303–1312.

Geen, R. G., McCown, E. J., & Broyles, J. W. (1985). Effects of noise on sensitivity of introverts and extraverts to signals in a vigilance task. *Personality and Individual Differences, 6*, 237–241.

Ghiselli, E. E., & Barthol, R. P. (1953). The validity of personality inventories in the selection of employees. *Journal of Applied Psychology, 37*, 18–20.

Ghiselli, E. E., & Brown, C. W. (1955). *Personnel and industrial psychology*. New York, NY: McGraw-Hill.

Glenn, A. L., Kurzban, R., & Raine, A. (2011). Evolutionary theory and psychopathy. *Aggression and Violent Behavior, 16*(5), 371–380.

Glenn, N. D. (1990). Quantitative research on marital quality in the 1980s: A critical review. *Journal of Marriage and the Family, 52*, 818–831.

Glick, P., Gottesman, D., & Jolton, J. (1989). The fault is not in the stars: Susceptibility of sceptics and believers in astrology to the Barnum effect. *Personality and Social Psychology Bulletin, 15*, 572–583.

Goff, M., & Ackerman, P. L. (1992). Personality–intelligence relations: Assessing typical intellectual engagement. *Journal of Educational Psychology, 84*, 537–552.

Goffin, R. D., Jang, I., & Skinner, E. (2011). Forced-choice and conventional personality assessment: Each may have unique value in pre-employment testing. *Personality and Individual Differences, 51*(7), 840–844.

Goldberg, L. R. (1982). From Ace to Zombie: Some explorations in the language of personality. In C. D. Spielberger & J. N. Butcher (Eds.), *Advances in personality assessment* (Vol. 1, pp. 203–234). Hillsdale, NJ: Erlbaum.

Goldberg, L. R. (1990). An alternative "description of personality": The Big-Five factor structure. *Personality Processes and Individual Differences, 59*(6), 1216–1229.

Goldberg, L. R. (1993). The structure of phenotypic personality traits. *American Psychologist, 48*(1), 26–34.

Gottfredson, L. S. (2002). Highly general and highly practical. In R. J. Steinberg & E. L. Grigorenko (Eds.), *The general factor of intelligence: How general is it?* (pp. 331–380). Mahwah, NJ: Erlbaum.

Gough, H. G. (1957). *Manual for the California Psychological Inventory.* Palo Alto, CA: Consulting Psychologists Press.

Graham, L. T., Sandy, C. J., & Gosling, S. D. (2011). Manifestations of individual differences in physical and virtual environments. In T. Chamorro-Premuzic, S. von Stumm, & A. Furnham (Eds.), *The Wiley-Blackwell handbook of individual differences* (pp. 773–800). London, UK: Wiley-Blackwell.

Gray, J. A. (1981). A critique of Eysenck's theory of personality. In H. J. Eysenck (Ed.), *A model for personality* (pp. 246–276). New York, NY: Springer.

Gray, J. A. (1982). *The neuropsychology of anxiety: An enquiry into the functions of the septo-hippocampal system.* Oxford, UK: Oxford University Press.

Gray, J. A. (1987). Perspectives on anxiety and impulsivity: A commentary. *Journal of Research in Personality, 21,* 493–509.

Gray, J. A. (1991). Neural systems of motivation, emotion and affect. In J. Madden (Ed.), *Neurobiology of learning, emotion and affect* (pp. 273–306). New York, NY: Raven Press.

Graziano, W. G., Jensen-Campbell, L. A., & Hair, E. C. (1996). Perceiving interpersonal conflict and reacting to it: The case for agreeableness. *Journal of Personality and Social Psychology, 70,* 820–835.

Greenberg, J., & Jonas, E. (2003). Psychological motives and political orientation—The left, the right, and the rigid: Comment on Jost et al. (2003). *Psychological Bulletin, 129,* 376–382.

Greenleaf, R. K., & Spears, L. C. (2002). *Servant leadership: A journey into the nature of legitimate power and greatness* (25th Anniversary ed.). Mahwah, NJ: Paulist Press.

Greenwald, A. G., McGhee, D. E., & Schwartz, J. L. K. (1998). Measuring individual differences in implicit cognition: The Implicit Association Test. *Journal of Personality and Social Psychology, 74,* 1464–1480.

Greenwald, A. G., Poehlman, T. A., Uhlmann, E. L., & Banaji, M. R. (2009). Understanding and using the Implicit Association Test: III. Meta-analysis of predictive validity. *Journal of Personality and Social Psychology, 97*(1), 17–41.

Griffiths, M. (2007). The psychology of love. *Psychology Review, 12,* 5–6.

Griscom, R. (2002). Why are online personals so hot? *Wired*, Issue 10.11. Retrieved from www.wired.co.uk/magazine

Gross, A. E., & Crofton, C. (1977). What is good is beautiful. *Sociometry*, *40*, 85–90.

Guion, R. M., & Gottier, R. F. (1965). Validity of personality measures in personnel selection. *Personnel Psychology, 18*, 135–164.

Haggbloom, S., Warnick, R., Warnick, J. E., Jones, V. K., Yarbrough, G. L., Russell, T. M., … Monte, E. (2002). The 100 most eminent psychologists of the 20th century. *Reviews in General Psychology, 6*, 139–152.

Hair, P., & Hampson, S. E. (2006). The role of impulsivity in predicting maladaptive behaviour among female students. *Personality and Individual Differences, 40*, 943–952.

Halamandaris, K. F., & Power, K. G. (1999). Individual differences, social support and coping with examination stress: A study of the psychosocial and academic adjustment of first year home students. *Personality and Individual Differences, 26*, 665–685.

Hamer, D., & Copeland, P. (1998). *Living with our genes.* New York, NY: Doubleday.

Hamilton, M. M. (1995). Incorporation of astrology-based personality information into long-term self-concept. *Journal of Social Behavior and Personality, 10*, 707–718.

Hansemark, O. C. (2000). Predictive validity of TAT and CMPS on the entrepreneurial activity, "start of a new business": A longitudinal study. *Journal of Managerial Psychology, 15*(7), 634–654.

Hare, R. D., & Neumann, C. S. (2008). Psychopathy as a clinical and empirical construct. *Annual Review of Clinical Psychology, 4*, 217–246.

Harris, D. (1940). Factors affecting college grades: A review of the literature, 1930–1937. *Psychological Bulletin, 37*, 125–166.

Harris, M. M. (1989). Reconsidering the employment interview: A review of recent literature and suggestions for future research. *Personnel Psychology, 42*(4), 691–726.

Harter, S. (1993). Causes and consequences of low self-esteem in children and adolescents. In R. F. Baumeister (Ed.), *Self-esteem: The puzzle of low self-regard* (pp. 87–116). New York, NY: Plenum Press.

Hathaway, S. R., & McKinley, J. C. (1940). *The Minnesota Multiphasic Personality Inventory manual.* New York, NY: The Psychological Corporation.

Hathaway, S. R., & McKinley, J. C. (1951). *Manual of the M.M.P.I.* New York, NY: The Psychological Corporation.

Heady, B., & Wearing, A. (1989). Personality, life events, and subjective well-being: Towards a dynamic equilibrium model. *Journal of Personality and Social Psychology, 57,* 731–739.

Heaven, P. C. L. (1996). Personality and self-reported delinquency: Analysis of the 'Big Five' personality dimensions. *Personality and Individual Differences, 20,* 47–54.

Heaven, P. C. L., Smith, L., Prabhakar, S. M., Abraham, J., & Mete, M. E. (2006). Personality and conflict communication patterns in cohabiting couples. *Journal of Research in Personality, 40,* 829–840.

Hempel, C. G. (1966). *Philosophy of natural science.* New York, NY: Prentice-Hall.

Hisrich, R. D., Langan-Fox, J., & Grant, S. (2007). Entrepreneurship research and practice. A call to action for psychology. *American Psychologist, 62,* 575–589.

Hogan, J., Barrett, P., & Hogan, R. (2007). Personality measurement, faking, and employment selection. *The Journal of Applied Psychology, 92*(5), 1270–1285.

Hogan, J., Hogan, R., & Kaiser, R. B. (2010). Management derailment. In S. Zedeck (Ed.), *American Psychological Association handbook of industrial and organizational psychology* (pp. 555–575). Washington, DC: American Psychological Association.

Hogan, J., Rybicki, S. L., Motowildo, S. J., & Borman, W. C. (1998). Relations between contextual performance, personality, and occupational advancement. *Human Performance, 11,* 189–207.

Hogan, R. (2005). In defense of personality measurement. *Human Performance, 18,* 331–334.

Hogan, R. (2007). *Personality and the fate of organizations.* Mahwah, NJ: Lawrence Erlbaum.

Hogan, R., & Ahmad, G. (2011). Leadership. In T. Chamorro-Premuzic, A. Furnham, & S. von Stumm (Eds.), *Handbook of individual differences* (pp. 408–426). London, UK: Wiley-Blackwell.

Hogan, R., & Chamorro-Premuzic, T. (2011). Personality and the laws of history. In T. Chamorro-Premuzic, S. von Stumm, & A. Furnham (Eds.), *The Wiley-Blackwell handbook of individual differences* (pp. 491–511) . Oxford, UK: Wiley-Blackwell.

Hogan, R., Curphy, G. J., & Hogan, J. (1994). What we know about leadership: Effectiveness and personality. *American Psychologist, 49,* 493–504.

Hogan, R., & Fico, J. (in press). Narcissism and leadership. In W. K. Campbell & J. Miller (Eds.), *The handbook of narcissism and narcissistic personality disorder*. New York, NY: Wiley.

Hogan, R., & Hogan, J. (2001). Assessing leadership: A view from the dark side. *International Journal of Selection and Assessment, 9*, 40–51.

Holden, R. R., & Passey, J. (2010). Socially desirable responding in personality assessment: Not necessarily faking and not necessarily substance. *Personality and Individual Differences, 49*(5), 446–450.

Hollander, E., Allen, A., Lopez, R. P., Bienstock, C. A., Grossman, R., Siever, L. J.,...Stein, D. J. (2001). A preliminary double-blind, placebo-controlled trial of divalproex sodium in borderline personality disorder. *Journal of Clinical Psychiatry, 62*, 199–203.

Horne, R., Weinman, J., Barber, N., Elliott, R., & Morgan, M. (2005). Concordance, adherence, and compliance in medicine taking (pp. 1–301). *Report for the NCCSDO*. London, UK.

Hough, L. M., Eaton, N. K., Dunnette, M. D., Kamp, J. D., & McCloy, R. A. (1990). Criterion-related validities of personality constructs and the effect of response distortion on those validities [Monograph]. *Journal of Applied Psychology, 75*, 581–595.

Hundleby, J. D., Pawlik, K., & Cattell, R. B. (1965). *Personality factors in objective test devices: A critical integration of a quarter century's research*. San Diego, CA: Robert R. Knapp.

Hunsley, J., & Bailey, J. M. (1999). The clinical utility of the Rorschach: Unfulfilled promises and an uncertain future. *Psychological Assessment, 11*, 266–277.

Jacobson, K. C., Prescott, C. A., & Kendler, K. S. (2002). Sex differences in the genetic and environmental influences on the development of antisocial behaviour. *Development and Psychopathology, 14*, 395–416.

Jaffee, S. R., Caspi, A., Moffitt, T. E., Dodge, K. A., Rutter, M., Taylor, A., & Tully, L. A. (2005). Nature x nurture: Genetic vulnerabilities interact with physical maltreatment to promote conduct problems. *Development and Psychopathology, 17*, 67–84.

James, W. (1950/1890). *The principles of psychology*. New York, NY: Dover.

Jensen-Campbell, L. A., & Graziano, W. G. (2001). Agreeableness as a moderator of interpersonal conflict. *Journal of Personality, 69*(2), 323–362.

John, O. P., Robins, R. W., & Pervin, L. A. (2008). *Handbook of personality: Theory and research*. New York, NY: The Guilford Press.

Johnson, D. L., Wiebe, J. S., Gold, S. M., Andreasen, N. C., Hichwa, R. D., Watkins, G. L., & Boles Ponto, L. L. (1999). Cerebral blood flow and personality: A positron emission tomography study. *American Journal of Psychiatry, 156,* 252–257.

Johnson, W., McGue, M., Krueger, R. F., & Bouchard, T. J., Jr. (2004). Marriage and personality: A genetic analysis. *Journal of Personality and Social Psychology, 86*(2), 285–294.

Jorgensen, R. S., Blair, T. J., Kolodziej, M. E., & Schreer, G. E. (1996). Elevated blood pressure and personality: A meta-analytic review. *Psychological Bulletin, 2,* 293–320.

Joseph, D. L., & Newman, D. A. (2010). Emotional intelligence: An integrative meta-analysis and cascading model. *Journal of Applied Psychology, 95,* 54–78.

Judge, T. A., & Bono, J. E. (2001). Relationship of core self-evaluation traits—Self-esteem, generalized self-efficacy, locus of control, and emotional stability—with job satisfaction and job performance: A meta-analysis. *Journal of Applied Psychology, 86,* 80–92.

Judge, T. A., Bono, J. E., Ilies, R., & Gerhardt, M. W. (2002). Personality and leadership: A qualitative and quantitative review. *Journal of Applied Psychology, 87*(4), 765–780.

Judge, T. A., Colbert, A. E., & Ilies, R. (2004). Intelligence and leadership: A quantitative review and test of theoretical propositions. *Journal of Applied Psychology, 83*(3), 542–552.

Judge, T. A., Jackson, C. L., Shaw, J. C., Scott, B. A., & Rich, B. A. (2007). Self-efficacy and work-related performance: The integral role of individual differences. *Journal of Applied Psychology, 92,* 107–127.

Judge, T. A., LePine, J. A., & Rich, B. L. (2006). The narcissistic personality: Relationship with inflated self-ratings of leadership and with task and contextual performance. *Journal of Applied Psychology, 91,* 762–776.

Kagan, J. (1994). *Galen's prophecy.* New York, NY: Basic Books.

Kagan, J., & Snidman, N. (1999). Early childhood predictors of adult anxiety disorders. *Biological Psychiatry, 46*(11), 1536–1541.

Kaiser, R. B., Hogan, R., & Craig, S. B. (2008). Leadership and the fate of organizations. *American Psychologist, 63*(2), 96–110.

Kelly, E. L., & Conley, J. J. (1987). Personality and compatibility: A prospective analysis of marital stability and marital satisfaction. *Journal of Personality and Social Psychology, 52,* 27–40.

Kelly, I. (1997). Modern astrology: A critique. *Psychological Reports, 81,* 1035–1066.

Kern, M. L., & Friedman, H. S. (2011). Personality and differences in health and longevity. In T. Chamorro-Premuzic, A. Furnham, & S. von Stumm (Eds.), *Handbook of individual differences* (pp. 461–490). London, UK: Wiley-Blackwell.

Kern, M. L., Martin, L. R., & Friedman, H. S. (2010). *Personality and longevity across seven decades.* Poster presented at the 11th Annual Meeting of the Society of Personality and Social Psychology, Las Vegas, NV.

Kiehl, K. (2006). A cognitive neuroscience perspective on psychopathy: Evidence for paralimbic system dysfunction. *Psychiatry Research, 142*(2–3), 107–128.

Kline, P. (1988). *Psychology exposed, or the emperor's new clothes.* London, UK: Routledge.

Kline, P. (1992). *Psychometric testing in personnel selection and appraisal.* Surrey, UK: Croner Publications.

Kline, P. (1993). *The handbook of psychological testing.* London, UK: Routledge.

Kline, P. (2000). *The handbook of psychological testing.* London, UK: Routledge.

Koenigsberg, H. W., Reynolds, D., Goodman, M., New, A. S., Mitropoulou, V., Trestman, R. L.,…Siever, L. J. (2003). Risperidone in the treatment of schizotypal personality disorder. *Journal of Clinical Psychiatry, 64,* 628–634.

Korn, J., Davis, R., & Davis, S. (1991). Historians' and chairpersons' judgments of eminence among psychologists. *American Psychologist, 46*(7), 789–792.

Kraft, P., & Hunter, D. J. (2009). Genetic risk prediction—Are we there yet? *The New England Journal of Medicine, 360*(17), 1701–1703.

Kring, A., Davison, G., Neale, J., & Johnson, S. (2007). *Abnormal psychology.* Hoboken, NJ: John Wiley.

Krueger, R. F., Hicks, B. M., & McGue, M. (2001). Altruism and antisocial behavior: Independent tendencies, unique personality correlates, distinct etiologies. *Psychological Science, 12,* 397–402.

Kuratko, D. F. (2007). Entrepreneurial leadership in the 21st century: Guest editor's perspective. *Journal of Leadership and Organisational Studies, 13,* 1–11.

Langlois, J. H., Kalakanis, L., Rubenstein, A. J., Larson, A., Hallam, M., & Smoot, M. (2000). Maxims or myths of beauty? A meta-analytic and theoretical review. *Psychological Bulletin, 126,* 390–423.

Larsson, H., Viding, E., & Plomin, R. (2008). Callous unemotional traits and antisocial behavior: Genetic, environmental, and early parenting characteristics. *Criminal Justice and Behavior, 35*(2), 197–211.

Latham, G. P., Ganegoda, D. B., & Locke, E. A. (2011). Goal-setting. In T. Chamorro-Premuzic, S. von Stumm, & A. Furnham (Eds.), *The Wiley-Blackwell handbook of individual differences* (pp. 579–588). Oxford, UK: Wiley-Blackwell.

Lazarus, R. S., & Folkman, S. (1984). *Stress, appraisal, and coping.* New York, NY: Springer.

Lehnart, J., & Neyer, F. J. (2006). Should I stay or should I go? Attachment and personality in stable and instable romantic relationships. *European Journal of Personality, 20,* 475–495.

Lesch, K. P., Bengel, D., Heils, A., Sabol, S. Z., Greenberg, B. D., Petri, S.,...Murphy, D. L. (1996). Association of anxiety-related traits with a polymorphism in the serotonin transporter gene regulatory region. *Science, 274,* 1527–1531.

Lewandowski, G. W., Aron, A., & Gee, J. (2007). Personality goes a long way: The malleability of opposite-sex physical attractiveness. *Personal Relationships, 14,* 571–585.

Li, N., Liang, J., & Crant, J. M. (2010). The role of proactive personality in job satisfaction and organizational citizenship behavior: A relational perspective. *Journal of Applied Psychology, 95*(2), 395–404.

Lilienfeld, S. O., Wood, J. M., & Garb, H. N. (2000). The scientific status of projective techniques. *Psychological Science in the Public Interest, 1,* 27–66.

Linehan, M. M., & Heard, H. (1999). Borderline personality disorder: Costs, course, and treatment outcomes. In N. Miller & K. Magruder (Eds.), *The cost-effectiveness of psychotherapy: A guide for practitioners, researchers, and policy-makers* (pp. 291–305). New York, NY: Oxford University Press.

Little, A. C., Burt, D. M., & Perrett, D. I. (2006). What is beautiful is good: Face preference reflects desired personality. *Personality and Individual Differences, 41,* 1107–1118.

Locke, E. A. (1997). The motivation to work: What we know. *Advances in Motivation and Achievement, 10,* 375–412.

Loehlin, J. C. (1992). *Genes and environment in personality development.* Newbury Park, CA: Sage.

Lord, R. G., De Vader, C. L., & Alliger, G. M. (1986). A meta-analysis of the relation between personality traits and leadership perceptions: An application of validity generalization procedures. *Journal of Applied Psychology, 71*(3), 402–410.

Lucas, R. E. (2007). Long-term disability is associated with lasting changes in subjective well-being: Evidence from two nationally representative longitudinal studies. *Journal of Personality and Social Psychology, 92,* 717–731.

Lucas, R. E., Clark, A. E., Georgellis, Y., & Diener, E. (2004). Unemployment alters the set point for life satisfaction. *Psychological Science, 15,* 8–13.

Lucas, R. E., Diener, E., & Suh, E. (1996). Discriminant validity of well-being measures. *Journal of Personality and Social Psychology, 71,* 616–628.

Lykken, D., Bouchard, T., McGue, M., & Tellegen, A. (1993). Heritability of interests: A twin study. *Journal of Applied Psychology, 78,* 649–661.

Magnus, K., Diener, E., Fujita, F., & Pavot, W. (1993). Personality and events: A longitudinal analysis. *Journal of Personality and Social Psychology, 65,* 1046–1053.

Manuck, S. B., Kaplan, J. R., Adams, M. R., & Clarkson, T. B. (1988). Studies of psychosocial influences on coronary artery atherogenesis in cynomolgus monkeys. *Health Psychology, 7,* 113–124.

Margrain, S. A. (1978). Student characteristics and academic performance in higher education: A review. *Research in Higher Education, 8*(2), 111–123.

Marketdata Enterprises. (2005). *The U.S. market for self-improvement products and services.* Retrieved from www.marketresearch.com/map/prod/1338280.html

Martin, P., Baenziger, J., MacDonald, M., Siegler, I. C., & Poon, L. W. (2009). Engaged lifestyle, personality, and mental status among centenarians. *Journal of Adult Development, 16,* 199–208.

Martin, R. P., Wisenbaker, J., & Huttunen, M. O. (1994). The factor structure of instruments based on the Chess-Thomas model of temperament: Implications for the Big Five. In C. F. Halverson, G. Kohnstamm, & R. Martin (Eds.), *The developing structure of temperament and personality from infancy to adulthood* (pp. 157–172). Hillsdale, NJ: Erlbaum.

Matthews, G., Davies, D. R., Westerman, S. J., & Stammers, R. B. (2000). *Human performance. Cognition, stress, and individual differences.* Hove, UK: Psychology Press.

Matthews, G., & Deary, I. J. (1998). *Personality traits.* Cambridge, UK: Cambridge University Press.

Mayo, J., White, O., & Eysenck, H. J. (1978). An empirical study of the relation between astrological factors and personality. *Journal of Social Psychology, 105,* 179–286.

McClelland, D. C. (1961). *The achieving society.* New York, NY: Van Nostrand.

McCrae, R. R. (1987). Creativity, divergent thinking, and openness to experience. *Journal of Personality and Social Psychology, 52,* 1258–1265.

McCrae, R. R. (1996). Social consequences of experiential openness. *Psychological Bulletin, 120,* 323–337.

McCrae, R. R., & Costa, P. T., Jr. (1997). Conceptions and correlates of openness to experience. In R. Hogan & J. Johnson (Eds.), *Handbook of personality psychology* (pp. 825–847). San Diego, CA: Academic Press.

McCrae, R. R., & Costa, P. T., Jr. (1999). A five-factor theory of personality. In L. Pervin & O. P. John (Eds.), *Handbook of personality* (2nd ed., pp. 139–153). New York, NY: Guilford Press.

McCrae, R. R., & Costa, P. T. (2008). Empirical and theoretical status of the Five-Factor Model of personality traits. In G. J. Boyle, G. Matthews, & D. H. Saklofske (Eds.), *The Sage handbook of personality theory and assessment: Personality theories and models* (Vol. 1, pp. 273–295). London, UK: Sage.

McCrae, R. R., Costa, P. T., Jr., Ostendorf, F., Angleitner, A., Hrebíčková, M., Avia, M. D., … Smith, P. B. (2000). Nature over nurture: Temperament, personality, and lifespan development. *Journal of Personality and Social Psychology, 78,* 173–186.

McDaniel, M., Margaret, E., Perkins, W., Goggin, S., & Frankel, B. (2009). An assessment of the fakeability of self-report and implicit personality measures. *Journal of Research in Personality, 43*(4), 682–685.

McGregor, I., Nail, P. R., Marigold, D. C., & Kang, S. J. (2005). Defensive pride and consensus: Strength in imaginary numbers. *Journal of Personality and Social Psychology, 89,* 978–996.

McGue, M., Bacon, S., & Lykken, D. T. (1993). Personality stability and change in early adulthood: A behavioral genetic analysis. *Developmental Psychology, 29,* 96–109.

McKenzie, B., Ugbah, S. D., & Smothers, N. (2007). Who is entrepreneur? Is it still the wrong question? *Academy of Entrepreneurship Journal, 13,* 23–43.

Meeus, W., Iedema, J., Helsen, M., & Vollebergh, W. (1999). Patterns of adolescent development: Review of literature and longitudinal analysis. *Developmental Review, 19*, 419–461.

Meyer, G. J., Finn, S. E., Eyde, L. D., Kay, G. G., Moreland, K. L., Dies, R. R.,...Reed, G. M. (2001). Psychological testing and psychological assessment. A review of evidence and issues. *American Journal of Psychology, 56*(2), 128–165.

Miller, J. D., Lynam, D., & Leukefeld, C. (2003). Examining antisocial behavior through the lens of the five factor model of personality. *Aggressive Behavior, 29*(6), 497–514.

Mischel, W. (1968). *Personality and assessment.* New York, NY: Wiley.

Monroe, S. M., & Simons, A. D. (1991). Diathesis—Stress theories in the context of life stress research: Implications for the depressive disorders. *Psychological Bulletin, 110*(3), 406–425.

Morgeson, F. P., Campion, M. A., Dipboye, R. L., Hollenbeck, J. R., Murphy, K., & Schmitt, N. (2007). Reconsidering the use of personality tests in personnel selection contexts. *Personnel Psychology, 60*(3), 683–729.

Moutafi, J., Furnham, A., & Tsaousis, I. (2006). Is the relationship between intelligence and trait neuroticism mediated by test anxiety? *Personality and Individual Differences, 40*(3), 587–597.

Mueller-Hanson, R., Heggestad, E. D., & Thorton, G. C., III. (2003). Faking and selection: The use of personality from select-in and select-out perspectives. *Journal of Applied Psychology, 88*, 348–355.

Murray, H. A. (1938). *Explorations in personality.* New York, NY: Oxford University Press.

Murray, H. A. (1943). *Thematic Apperception Test.* Cambridge, MA: Harvard University Press.

Nanninga, R. (1996). The Astrotest: A tough match for astrologers. *Correlation, Northern Winter, 15*(2), 14–20.

National Center for Health Statistics. (2004). *Almost half of Americans use at least one prescription drug, annual report on nation's health shows.* Retrieved from http://www.cdc.gov/nchs/pressroom/04news/hus04.htm

Newman, D. L., Caspi, A., Moffitt, T. E., & Silva, P. A. (1997). Antecedents of adult interpersonal functioning: Effects of individual differences in age-3 temperament. *Developmental Psychology, 33*, 206–217.

Norman, W. T. (1967). *2800 personality trait descriptors: Normative operating characteristics for a university population.* Ann Arbor, MI: Department of Psychology, University of Michigan.

O'Boyle, E., Humphrey, R. H., Pollack, J. M., Hawver, T. H., & Story, P. (2010). The relation between emotional intelligence and job performance: A meta-analysis. *Journal of Organizational Behavior.* Advance online publication.

O'Connor, M., & Paunonen, S. (2007). Big Five personality predictors of post-secondary academic performance. *Personality and Individual Differences, 43,* 971–990.

O'Gorman, J., & Baxter, E. (2002). Self-control as a personality measure. *Personality and Individual Differences, 32,* 533–359.

Ones, D. S., Dilchert, S., Viswesvaran, C., & Judge, T. A. (2007). In support of personality assessment in organizational settings. *Personnel Psychology, 60,* 995–1027.

Ones, D. S., & Vishveswaran, C. (2011). Individual differences at work. In T. Chamorro-Premuzic, S. von Stumm, & A. Furnham (Eds.), *The Wiley-Blackwell handbook of individual differences* (pp. 379–407). London, UK: Wiley-Blackwell.

Ones, D. S., Viswesvaran, C., & Dilchert, S. (2005). Cognitive ability in personnel selection decisions. In A. Evers, O. Voskuijl, & N. Anderson (Eds.), *Handbook of selection* (pp. 143–173). Oxford, UK: Blackwell.

Ones, D. S., Viswesvaran, C., Hough, L. M., & Dilchert, S. (2005). Managers, leaders, and executives: Successful personality. In J. Deller & D. S. Ones (Eds.), *International symposium on personality at work: Proceedings* (p. 8). Lüneburg, Germany: University of Applied Sciences.

Ones, D. S., Viswesvaran, C., & Reiss, A. D. (1996). Role of social desirability in personality testing for personnel selection: The red herring. *Journal of Applied Psychology, 81*(6), 660–679.

Ones, D. S., Viswesvaran, C., & Schmidt, F. L. (1993). Comprehensive meta-analysis of integrity test validities: Findings and implications for personnel selection and theories of job performance. *Journal of Applied Psychology, 78,* 679–703.

Organisation for Economic Cooperation and Development (OECD). (2011a). *Education at a glance: 2011 indicators; how does educational attainment affect participation in the labour market?* Retrieved March 10, 2012, from www.oecd.org/dataoecd/61/62/48630772.pdf

Organisation for Economic Cooperation and Development (OECD). (2011b). *Education at a glance: 2011 indicators; what proportion of national wealth is spent on education?* Retrieved March 10, 2012, from www.oecd.org/dataoecd/61/17/48630884.pdf

Ozer, D. J., & Benet-Martinez, V. (2006). Personality and the prediction of consequential outcomes. *Annual Review of Psychology, 57,* 201–221.

Ozer, D. J., & Reise, S. P. (1994). Personality assessment. *Annual Review of Psychology, 45,* 357–388.

Pavot, W., & Diener, E. (2011). Personality and happiness: Predicting the experience of subjective well-being. In T. Chamorro-Premuzic, A. Furnham, & S. von Stumm (Eds.), *Handbook of individual differences* (pp. 699–717). London, UK: Wiley-Blackwell.

Pavot, W., Diener, E., Colvin, C. R., & Sandvik, E. (1991). Further validation of the satisfaction with life scale: Evidence for the cross-method convergence of well-being measures. *Journal of Personality Assessment, 57,* 149–161.

Pearson, K. (1896). Mathematical contributions to the theory of evolution. III. Regression, heredity and panmixia. *Philosophical Transactions of the Royal Society of London, Series A, 187,* 253–318.

Penner, L. A. (2002). The causes of sustained volunteerism: An interactionist perspective. *Journal of Social Issues, 58,* 447–467.

Penner, L. A., Fritzsche, B. A., Craiger, J. P., & Freifeld, T. R. (1995). Measuring the prosocial personality. In J. Butcher & C. D. Spielberger (Eds.), *Advances in personality assessment* (Vol. 10, pp. 147–163). Hillsdale, NJ: Erlbaum.

Petrides, K. V., & Furnham, A. (2001). Trait emotional intelligence. Psychometric investigation with reference to established trait taxonomies. *European Journal of Personality, 15,* 425–448.

Plomin, R., & Daniels, D. (1987). Why are children in the same family so different from one another? *Behavioral and Brain Sciences, 10,* 1–60.

Ploubidis, G. B., & Grundy, E. (2009). Personality and all-cause mortality: Evidence for indirect links. *Personality and Individual Differences, 47,* 203–208.

Poropat, A. (2009). A meta-analysis of the five-factor model of personality and academic performance. *Psychological Bulletin, 135,* 322–332.

Raine, A., Brennan, P., Mednick, B., & Mednick, S. A. (1996). High rates of violence, crime, academic and behavioural problems in males with both early neuromotor deficits and unstable family environments. *Archives of General Psychiatry, 53,* 544–549.

Rasul, F., Stansfeld, S. A., Hart, C. L., & Smith, G. D. (2005). Psychological distress, physical illness, and risk of coronary heart disease. *Journal of Epidemiology & Community Health, 59,* 140–145.

Rauch, A., & Frese, M. (2007). Let's put the person back into entrepreneurship research: A meta-analysis on the relationship between business owners' personality traits, business creation, and success. *European Journal of Work and Organizational Psychology, 16,* 353–385.

Redding, S. G., & Wong, G. Y. Y. (1986). The psychology of Chinese organization behaviour. In M. H. Bond (Ed.), *The psychology of Chinese people* (pp. 106–170). Hong Kong: Oxford University Press.

Renninger, L. A., Wade, T. J., & Grammer, K. (2004). Getting that female glance: Patterns and consequences of male nonverbal behavior in courtship contexts. *Evolution and Human Behaviour, 25,* 416–431.

Revelle, W., Wilt, J., & Condon, D. (2011). Individual differences and differential psychology: A brief history and prospect. In T. Chamorro-Premuzic, A. Furnham, & S. von Stumm (Eds.), *Handbook of individual differences* (pp. 3–38). Oxford, UK: Wiley-Blackwell.

Reynolds, P. D., Bygrave, W. D., & Autio, E. (2004). *Global Entrepreneurship Monitor 2003 executive report.* Babson Park, MA: Babson College.

Riemann, R., Grubich, C., Hempel, S., Mergl, S., & Richter, M. (1993). Personality and attitudes towards current political topics. *Personality and Individual Differences, 15,* 313–321.

Riggio, R. E., Friedman, H. S., & DiMatteo, M. R. (1981). Nonverbal greetings: Effects of the situation and personality. *Personality and Social Psychology Bulletin, 7,* 682–689.

Roberts, B. W. (1997). Plaster or plasticity: Are adult work experiences associated with personality change in women? *Journal of Personality, 65,* 205–232.

Roberts, B. W., Caspi, A., & Moffitt, T. (2003). Work experiences and personality development in young adulthood. *Journal of Personality and Social Psychology, 84,* 582–593.

Roberts, B. W., & DelVecchio, W. F. (2000). The rank-order consistency of personality traits from childhood to old age: A quantitative review of longitudinal studies. *Psychological Bulletin, 126,* 3–25.

Roberts, B. W., Kuncel, N. R., Shiner, R., Caspi, A., & Goldberg, L. R. (2007). The power of personality: The comparative validity of personality traits, socioeconomic status, and cognitive ability for predicting important life outcomes. *Perspectives on Psychological Science, 2*, 313–345.

Roberts, B. W., Walton, K. E., & Viechtbauer, W. (2006). Patterns of mean-level change in personality traits across the life course: A meta-analysis of longitudinal studies. *Psychological Bulletin, 132*, 3–27.

Roberts, B. W., Wood, D., & Smith, J. L. (2005). Evaluating five-factor theory and social investment perspectives on personality trait development. *Journal of Research in Personality, 39*, 166–184.

Robins, R. W., Caspi, A., & Moffitt, T. E. (2002). It's not just who you're with, it's who you are: Personality and relationship experiences across multiple relationships. *Journal of Personality, 70*(6), 925–964.

Robinson, D. L. (1996). *Brain, mind, and behavior: A new perspective on human nature.* Westport, CT: Praeger Press.

Rorschach, H. (1921). *Psychodiagnostik: Methodik und Ergebnisse eines wahrnehmungsdiagnostischen Experiments.* Bern, Switzerland: Ernst Bircher.

Rosenthal, R. (1990). How are we doing in soft psychology? *American Psychologist, 45*(6), 775–777.

Rosenthal, R., & Rubin, D. B. (1982). Comparing effect sizes of independent studies. *Psychological Bulletin, 92*, 500–504.

Rossen, L., & Rossen, E. (2011). *Obesity 101.* New York, NY: Springer Publishing Company.

Rucas, S., Kaplan, H., Winking, J., Gurven, M., Gangestad, S., & Crespo, M. (2006). Female intrasexual competition and reputational effects on attractiveness among the Tsimane of Bolivia. *Evolution and Human Behavior, 27*, 40–52.

Rugulies, R. (2002). Depression as a predictor for coronary heart disease: A review and meta-analysis. *American Journal of Preventive Medicine, 23*, 51–61.

Rummel, R. (1994). *Death by government.* New Brunswick, NJ: Transaction.

Rushton, J. P., & Irwing, P. (2011). The general factor of personality. In T. Chamorro-Premuzic, S. von Stumm, & A. Furnham (Eds.), *The Wiley-Blackwell handbook of individual differences* (pp. 132–161). London, UK: Wiley-Blackwell.

Sachs, G. (1999). *Die Akte Astrologie* [The astrology file] (Rev. ed.). München, Germany: Goldmann.

Sackett, P. R. (2011). Integrating and prioritizing theoretical perspectives on applicant faking of personality measures. *Human Performance, 24*(4), 379–385.

Salekin, R. T. (2002). Psychopathy and therapeutic pessimism. Clinical lore or clinical reality? *Clinical Psychology Review, 22*, 79–112.

Salgado, J. F. (1997). The five factor model of personality and job performance in the European community. *Journal of Applied Psychology, 82*, 30–43.

Salgado, J. F. (2003). Predicting job performance using FFM and non-FFM personality measures. *Journal of Occupational and Organizational Psychology, 76*, 323–346.

Samuels, J., Bienvenu, J., Cullen, B., Costa, P. T., Eaton, W. W., & Nestadt, G. (2004). Personality dimensions and criminal arrest. *Comprehensive Psychiatry, 45*, 275–280.

Saroglou, V. (2002). Religion and the five factors of personality: A meta-analytic review. *Personality and Individual Differences, 32*(1), 15–25.

Saulsman, L. M., & Page, A. C. (2004). The Five-Factor Model and personality disorder empirical literature: A meta-analytic review. *Clinical Psychology Review, 23*(8), 1055–1085.

Schmidt, F. L., & Hunter, J. E. (1998). The validity and utility of selection methods in personnel psychology: Practical and theoretical implications of 85 years of research findings. *Psychological Bulletin, 124*, 262–274.

Schmidt, F. L., Hunter, J. E., McKenzie, R., & Muldrow, T. (1979). The impact of valid selection procedures on workforce productivity. *Journal of Applied Psychology, 64*, 609–626.

Schnabel, K., Asendorpf, J. B., & Greenwald, A. G. (2008). Using Implicit Association Tests for the assessment of implicit personality self-concept. In G. J. Boyle, G. Matthews, & D. H. Saklofske (Eds.), *The Sage handbook of personality theory and assessment: Vol. 2. Personality measurement and testing* (pp. 508–528). Los Angeles, CA: Sage.

Schnabel, K., Banse, R., & Asendorpf, J. B. (2006). Assessment of implicit personality self-concept using the Implicit Association Test (IAT): Concurrent assessment of anxiousness and angriness. *British Journal of Social Psychology, 45*, 373–396.

Schuerger, J. M. (2008). The Objective-Analytic Test Battery. In G. J. Boyle, G. Matthews, & D. H. Saklofske (Eds.), *The Sage handbook of personality theory and assessment: Vol. 2. Personality measurement and testing* (pp. 295–312). Los Angeles, CA: Sage.

Seibert, S. E., & Lumpkin, G. T. (2009). The relationship of personality to entrepreneurial intentions and performance: A meta-analytic review. *Journal of Management, 36*(2), 381–404.

Sen, S., Burmeister, M., & Ghosh, D. (2004). Meta-analysis of the association between a serotonin transporter promoter polymorphism (5-HTTLPR) and anxiety-related personality traits. *American Journal of Medical Genetics B, 127*, 85–89.

Shane, S. (2008). *The illusions of entrepreneurship: The costly myths that entrepreneurs, investors, and policy makers live by.* New London, CT: Yale University Press.

Shane, S., & Venkataraman, S. (2000). The promise of entrepreneurship as a field of research. *Academy of Management Journal, 25*, 217–226.

Shiner, R. L. (1998). How shall we speak of children's personality traits in middle childhood? A preliminary taxonomy. *Psychological Bulletin, 124*, 308–332.

Shontz, F. C. (1975). *The psychological aspects of physical illness and disability.* New York, NY: Macmillan.

Shumpeter, J. (1911). *The theory of economic development.* Cambridge, MA: Harvard University Press.

Silversthorne, C. (2001). Leadership effectiveness and personality: A cross-cultural evaluation. *Personality and Individual Differences, 30*, 303–309.

Simonton, D. K. (1986). Presidential personality: Biographical use of the Gouch adjective check list. *Journal of Personality and Social Psychology, 51*, 149–160.

Skinner, B. F. (1971). *Beyond freedom and dignity.* Indianapolis, IN: Hackett Publishing.

Smit, D. J., Posthuma, D., Boomsma, D. I., & De Geus, E. J. (2007). The relation between frontal EEG asymmetry and the risk for anxiety and depression. *Biological Psychology, 74*(1), 26–33.

Smith, T. W., & Spiro, A. (2002). Personality, health, and aging: Prolegomenon for the next generation. *Journal of Research in Personality, 36*, 363–394.

Smith, T. W., Uchino, B. N., Berg, C. A., Florsheim, P., Pearce, G., Hawkins, N.,...Yoon, H. C. (2008). Associations of self-reports versus spouse ratings of negative affectivity, dominance, and affiliation with coronary artery disease: Where should we look and who should we ask when studying personality and health? *Health Psychology, 27*, 676–684.

Snyder, M. (1987). *Public appearances, private realities: The psychology of self-monitoring.* New York, NY: W H Freeman.

Spearman, C. (1927). *The abilities of man: Their nature and measurement.* New York, NY: Macmillan.

Spinath, F. M., & Johnson, W. (2011). Behavior genetics. In T. Chamorro-Premuzic, S. von Stumm, & A. Furnham (Eds.), *The Wiley-Blackwell handbook of individual differences* (pp. 271–304). Oxford, UK: Wiley-Blackwell.

Steel, P., Schmidt, J., & Shultz, J. (2008). Refining the relationship between personality and subjective well-being. *Psychological Bulletin, 134*, 138–161.

Steffens, M. C., & Schulze-König, S. (2006). Predicting spontaneous big five behavior with implicit association tests. *European Journal of Psychological Assessment, 22*, 13–20.

Stein, M. I. (1963). *Personality measures in admissions: Antecedent and personality factors as predictors of college success.* New York, NY: College Entrance Examination Board (CEEB).

Sternberg, R. J. (1986). A triangular theory of love. *Psychological Bulletin, 93*, 119–138.

Stogdill, R. M. (1948). Personal factors associated with leadership: A survey of the literature. *Journal of Psychology, 25*, 35–71.

Stone, W. F., & Smith, L. D. (1993). Authoritarianism: Left and right. In W. Stone, G. Lederer, & R. Christie (Eds.), *Strength and weakness: The authoritarian personality today* (pp. 144–156). New York, NY: Springer Verlag.

Strack, F., & Deutsch, R. (2004). Reflective and impulsive determinants of social behavior. *Personality and Social Psychology Review, 8*, 220–247.

Suls, J., & Bunde, J. (2005). Anger, anxiety, and depression as risk factors for cardiovascular disease: The problems and implications of overlapping affective dispositions. *Psychological Bulletin, 131*, 260–300.

Swami, V. (2007). *The missing arms of Vénus de Milo: Reflections on the science of physical attractiveness.* Brighton, UK: Book Guild.

Swami, V., Buchanan, T., Furnham, A., & Tovée, M. J. (2008). Five-factor personality correlates of perceptions of women's body sizes. *Personality and Individual Differences, 45*, 697–699.

Swami, V., & Furnham, A. (2008). *The psychology of physical attraction*. London, UK: Routledge.

Swami, V., Furnham, A., Balakumar, N., Williams, C., Canaway, K., & Stanistreet, D. (2008). Factors influencing preferences for height: A replication and extension. *Personality and Individual Differences*, *45*, 395–400.

Swami, V., Furnham, A., Chamorro-Premuzic, T., Akbar, K., Gordon, N., Harris, T., …Tovée, M. J. (2010). More than skin deep? Personality information influences men's ratings of the attractiveness of women's body sizes. *The Journal of Social Psychology*, *150*, 628–647.

Swami, V., Stieger, S., Haubner, T., Voracek, M., & Furnham, A. (2009). Evaluating the physical attractiveness and oneself and one's romantic partner: Individual and relationship correlates of the love-is-blind bias. *Journal of Individual Differences*, *30*, 35–43.

Tellegen, A. (1982). *Brief manual for the Differential Personality Questionnaire*. Unpublished manuscript, University of Minnesota, Minneapolis, MN.

Terman, L. M., Sears, R. R., Cronbach, L. J., & Sears, P. S. (2002). *The Terman life-cycle study of children with high ability, 1922–1986, Volume 2, 1936–1945*. Ann Arbor, MI: Inter-University Consortium for Political and Social Research.

Tett, R. P., Jackson, D. N., & Rothstein, M. (1991). Personality measures as predictors of job performance: A meta-analytic review. *Personnel Psychology*, *44*, 703–742.

Thomas, A., & Chess, S. (1977). *Temperament and development*. New York, NY: Brunner/Mazel.

Thorndike, R. L. (1959). California Psychological Inventory. In O. K. Euros (Ed.), *The fifth mental measurements yearbook*. Highland Park, NJ: Gryphon.

Tobin, R. M., Graziano, W. G., Vanman, E. J., & Tassinary, L. G. (2000). Personality, emotional experience, and efforts to control emotions. *Journal of Personality and Social Psychology*, *79*, 656–669.

Tolman, E. C. (1938). The determiners of behavior at a choice point. *The Psychological Review*, *45*(1), 1–41.

Tooby, J., & Cosmides, L. (1990). The past explains the present: Emotional adaptations and the structure of ancestral environments. *Ethology and Sociobiology*, *11*, 375–424.

Trapman, S., Hell, B., Hirn, J. O. W., & Schuler, H. (2007). Meta-analysis of the relationship between the Big Five and academic success at university. *Journal of Psychology, 215*(2), 132–151.

Trapnell, P. D. (1994). Openness versus intellect: A lexical left turn. *European Journal of Personality, 8,* 273–290.

Trautwein, U., Lüdtke, O., Schnyder, I., & Niggli, A. (2006). Predicting homework effort: Support for a domain-specific multilevel homework model. *Journal of Educational Psychology, 98,* 438–456.

Tupes, E. C., & Christal, R. E. (1961). *Recurrent personality factors based on trait ratings.* Technical Report. TX: USAF, Lackland Air Force Base.

Tupes, E. C., & Christal, R. E. (1992). Recurrent personality factors based on trait ratings. *Journal of Personality, 60,* 225–251.

Twenge, J. M. (1997). Changes in masculine and feminine traits over time: A meta-analysis. *Sex Roles, 36,* 305–325.

Twenge, J. M. (2000). The age of anxiety? Birth cohort change in anxiety and neuroticism, 1952–1993. *Journal of Personality and Social Psychology, 79,* 1007–1021.

Twenge, J. M. (2001b). Birth cohort changes in extraversion: A cross-temporal meta-analysis, 1966–1993. *Personality and Individual Differences, 30,* 735–748.

Twenge, J. M., & Campbell, W. K. (2001). Age and birth cohort differences in self-esteem: A cross-temporal meta-analysis. *Personality and Social Psychology Review, 5,* 321–344.

Twenge, J. M., Zhang, L., & Im, C. (2004). It's beyond my control: A cross-temporal meta-analysis of increasing externality in locus of control, 1960–2002. *Personality and Social Psychology Review, 8,* 308–319.

Van Hiel, A., & Mervielde, I. (1996). Personality and current political beliefs. *Psychologica Belgica, 36,* 211–216.

Van Rooij, J. J. F. (1994). Introversion-extroversion: Astrology versus psychology. *Personality and Individual Differences, 16*(6), 985–988.

Van Rooij, J. J. F. (1999). Self-concept in terms of astrological Sun-sign traits. *Psychological Reports, 84,* 541–546.

Vermetten, Y., Lodewijks, J., & Vermunt, J. (2001). The role of personality traits and goal orientations in strategy use. *Contemporary Educational Psychology, 26*(2), 149–170.

Verona, E., Patrick, C. J., & Joiner, T. T. (2001). Psychopathy, antisocial personality, and suicide risk. *Journal of Abnormal Psychology, 110,* 462–470.

Viding, E., Blair, R. J. R., Moffitt, T. E., & Plomin, R. (2005). Evidence for substantial genetic risk for psychopathy in 7-year-olds. *Journal of Child Psychology and Psychiatry, and Allied Disciplines, 46*(6), 592–597.

Vollrath, M. (2001). Personality and stress. *Scandinavian Journal of Psychology, 42,* 335–347.

Von Eye, A., Lösel, F., & Mayzer, R. (2003). Is it all written in the stars? A methodological commentary on Sachs' astrology monograph and re-analyses of his data on crime statistics. *Psychology Science, 45*(1), 78–91.

Von Stumm, S., Chamorro-Premuzic, T., & Ackerman, P. L. (2011). Re-visiting intelligence-personality associations; vindicating intellectual investment. In T. Chamorro-Premuzic, A. Furnham, & S. von Stumm (Eds.), *Handbook of individual differences* (pp. 217–241). London, UK: Wiley-Blackwell.

Von Stumm, S., Hell, B., & Chamorro-Premuzic, T. (2011). The "hungry mind": Intellectual curiosity as third pillar of academic performance. *Perspectives on Psychological Science, 6*(6), 574–588.

Vul, E., Harris, C., Winkielman, P., & Pashler, H. (2009). Puzzlingly high correlations in fMRI studies of emotion, personality, and social cognition. *Perspectives on Psychological Science, 4*(3), 274–290.

Wacker, J., Chavanon, M. L., & Stemmler, G. (2006). Investigating the dopaminergic basis of extraversion in humans: A multilevel approach. *Journal of Personality and Social Psychology, 91,* 171–187.

Walton, K. E., & Roberts, B. W. (2004). On the relationship between substance use and personality traits: Abstainers are not maladjusted. *Journal of Research in Personality, 38,* 515–535.

Watson, D., Hubbard, B., & Wiese, D. (2000). Self-other agreement in personality and affectivity: Effects of acquaintanceship, trait visibility, and assumed similarity. *Journal of Personality and Social Psychology, 78,* 546–558.

Webb, E. (1915). *Character and intelligence: An attempt at an exact study of character.* Cambridge, UK: Cambridge University Press.

Wiebe, R. P. (2004). Delinquent behavior and the Five Factor model: Hiding in the adaptive landscape? *Individual Difference Research, 2,* 38–62.

Wilde, O. (2003). *The picture of Dorian Gray.* London, UK: Penguin Classics.

Wilson, G. D. (1973). *The psychology of conservatism.* London, UK: Academic Press.

Wilson, G. D. (1994). *Psychology for performing artists: Butterflies and bouquets.* London, UK: Jessica Kingsley.

Winston, A., Laikin, M., Pollack, J., Samstag, L. W., McCullough, L., & Muran, J. C. (1994). Short-term psychotherapy of personality disorders. *American Journal of Psychiatry, 151,* 190–194.

Wood, D., & Brumbaugh, C. C. (2009). Using revealed mate preferences to evaluate market force and differential preference explanations for mate selection. *Journal of Personality and Social Psychology, 96,* 1226–1244.

Woodworth, R. S. (1919). Examination of emotional fitness for warfare. *Psychological Bulletin, 16,* 59–60.

Yerkes, R. M., & Dodson, J. D. (1908). The relation of strength of stimulus to rapidity of habit-formation. *Journal of Comparative Neurology and Psychology, 18,* 459–482.

Zeidner, M., & Matthews, G. (2010). *Anxiety 101.* New York, NY: Springer Publishing Company.

Zhao, H., Siebert, S. E., & Lumpkin, G. T. (2010). The relationship of personality to entrepreneurial intentions and performance: A meta-analytic review. *Journal of Management, 36,* 381–404.

Zimmerman, M., & Coryell, W. (1989). DSM-III personality disorder diagnoses in a nonpatient sample: Demographic correlates and comorbidity. *Archives of General Psychiatry, 46*(8), 682–689.

Zuckerman, M. (1991). *Psychobiology of personality.* Cambridge, UK: Cambridge University Press.

Zuckerman, M. (1996). Psychobiology of sensation seeking. *Neuropsychobiology, 34,* 125–129.

Index